SICILY: ISLAND OF BEAUTY AND CONFLICT

Reflections on its History and Culture

Jeremy Dummett

To Theo and Maya

TAURIS PARKE
Bloomsbury Publishing Plc
50 Bedford Square, London, WC1B 3DP, UK
1385 Broadway, 5th Floor, New York, NY

BLOOMSBURY, TAURIS PARKE and the TAURIS PARKE logo are trademarks
of Bloomsbury Publishing Plc

First published in Great Britain by Bloomsbury Publishing Plc 2020
This edition published 2020

Jeremy Dummett has asserted his right under the Copyright, Designs and
Patents Act, 1988, to be identified as Author of this work

A catalogue record for this book is available from the British Library

Library of Congress Cataloguing-in-Publication data has been applied for

ISBN: HB: 978-1-8386-0216-1; eBook: 978-0-7556-0190-5

2 4 6 8 10 9 7 5 3 1

Typeset by Deanta Global Publishing Services, Chennai, India
Printed and bound in the United Kingdom by CPI Group (UK) Ltd, Croydon, CR0 4YY

To find out more about our authors and books visit www.bloomsbury.com
and sign up for our newsletters

CONTENTS

FOREWORD

This is a book about the history and culture of Sicily, the result of fifteen years of researching and exploring the island. It is presented in the form of wide-ranging articles, in four parts: History, Cities, Ancient Sites and Artists. The reasons for choosing this format are as follows.

In my books on Syracuse and Palermo, I outlined the history of these cities together with a description of their principal monuments. As the leading cities of Sicily, Syracuse from antiquity to the ninth century AD, and Palermo from the ninth century to the present day, they provided a semi-continuous history of large parts of the island. But there remained much of importance that I had not covered.

Apart from Syracuse and Palermo, the island's history is so diverse and fragmented that it does not easily lend itself to narrative treatment. There were so many invasions, so many foreign powers dominating the island, and so much destruction from warfare, that there was little continuity. In eastern Sicily, disruption to normal life was compounded by natural disasters, with earthquakes and volcanic eruptions requiring whole cities to be rebuilt. So much happened across the regions of Sicily that writing a summary is a nearly impossible task. As Churchill once said of the Balkans, 'They produce more history than they can consume.'

Instead, this book focuses upon separate subjects and examines them in detail. Each article puts the spotlight on a specific era, event, place or artist. Piece by piece, the articles build up a bigger picture, touching on both well-known and lesser-known subjects, illustrating historical themes and demonstrating Sicily's rich cultural background.

A similar format was used to good effect by the Sicilian writers Leonardo Sciascia and Vincenzo Consolo in books which brought to life the history and culture of the island. My aim has been to follow their example.

As in my previous books, the history is accompanied by commentary on the monuments and works of art to be seen today, thus linking Sicily's past and present.

JBD, October 2019, London.

PART ONE

HISTORY

INTRODUCTION

Beauty and conflict, civilisation and chaos: these are the opposing forces which define the history of Sicily, first one and then the other holding sway over the fortunes of the island. It is a story of extreme events, representing the peak and the nadir of Western civilisation, played out in one of the most beautiful places on earth.

In ancient times the Mediterranean attracted settlers with its sunny climate, fertile coastal plains and ease of transport along the coast. Conditions for settlements were propitious, as supplies of fresh water and fish were readily available. Many different peoples arrived, establishing rival states which overlapped and competed with one another. It became a region of rapid growth but also one of chronic instability and continuous warfare.

What is the Mediterranean? According to the historian Fernand Braudel, it is many things at once. It is not one sea but many seas. It is not one civilisation, but many civilisations superimposed one upon another. To travel around the Mediterranean is to encounter prehistory in Sardinia, Greek cities in Sicily, the Roman world in the Lebanon, the Arab presence in Spain and Turkish Islam in Yugoslavia. It is a place of almost infinite variety.¹

Despite its climate of violence, the Mediterranean became a vast depository of knowledge and culture. This was the cradle of great civilisations, Egyptian, Greek, Persian, Roman, Arab and Ottoman. This was where Western philosophy, science and art began. In addition, the Mediterranean remains one of the world's most important spiritual centres, the birthplace of three great monotheistic religions, Judaism, Christianity and Islam.

These elements, the attractions of the region, the growth of opposing states, its warfare and instability, the flowering of civilisation and the impact of religion, all played their part in shaping the history of Sicily.

———

To its early settlers Sicily was a mysterious place, the source of myths and legends, famous for its fertile soil enriched by lava from a huge volcano. Waves of different peoples arrived, creating a multi-ethnic population with the potential for inter-racial conflict from the beginning.

The island's earliest recorded name was Trinacria, which was derived from the Greek for the three points of its triangular shape. A symbol appeared, called the *Triskelion* or *Trisceles,* representing the island by a three-legged motif surrounding the winged head of a Gorgon, complete with locks of snakes. The design sometimes included ears of wheat to represent the island's fertility.[2]

Following the arrival of a people called the Sicans, the island became known as Sicania. The Sicels, who arrived after the Sicans, renamed the island Sicelia, from which the modern names of Sicilia and Sicily were derived.

The people who came to Sicily as settlers, invaders and governors included: Sicans, Sicels, Elymians, Phoenicians, Greeks, Carthaginians, Romans, Vandals, Goths, Byzantine Greeks, Arabs, Normans, Germans, French, Spaniards, Austrians, British, Americans and Italians. The result was periods of domination by foreign powers, some long, some short, the best contributing to the island's prosperity, the worst just exploiting it for their own ends.

Religion was important on the island from ancient times, as can be seen from the remains of numerous temples and sanctuaries. Christianity arrived early, establishing a centre at Syracuse. Islam arrived with the Arabs in the ninth century. Having been at the heart of the religious struggles which engulfed the Mediterranean during the Middle Ages, Sicily became a bulwark of Christianity under the Spanish. After the Jews were expelled in 1492, a powerful form of the Catholic faith took hold on the island, promoted by religious orders such as the Jesuits and controlled by the Inquisition. The cult of local patron saints, which became widely diffused across the island, demonstrated the importance of religion to the people.

During periods of foreign rule, Sicily experienced extremes of fortune from the heights of power and prosperity to the depths of oppression and poverty. A change of regime was often swift and total, opening the way to exploitation by foreign armies, unscrupulous barons and criminal gangs (echoed by modern-day examples such as Iraq and Libya of damage caused by foreign interventions). In addition, Sicily was prone to natural disasters such as earthquakes, volcanic eruptions and outbreaks of disease which caused destruction and widespread loss of life on many occasions.

Sicily's rich agricultural produce combined with its strategic position to make it a prize to be fought over by powerful states. This led to the island being drawn into the numerous wider conflicts which inflamed the Mediterranean. These included the Peloponnesian War, the Punic Wars, the civil wars of Rome, the invasions by Vandals and Goths, the rise of the Byzantine Empire, the expansion of the Arabs, the Crusades, the rise of the Spanish Empire, the Napoleonic Wars and the Second World War. The island is currently at the centre of the European refugee crisis, as the route from Libya to Sicily becomes one of the main entry points to the European Union, with large numbers of desperate people being washed up on its shores.

———

The broad sweep of Sicilian history defies rational analysis, for there is little continuity or a common thread to latch onto. The story is confusing and contradictory, with its highs and lows of civilisation, and sudden catastrophic events caused by military intervention or natural disaster. Instead of a single narrative, there are several separate narratives, each one representing domination by a different nation, interspersed with dramatic changes of direction.

Further complicating matters is the fact that these narratives vary by geography, with each region of the island pursuing its own destiny. The population of Sicily has always been fragmented and local in character. Eastern Sicily, for example, was the region of Greek influence through the ancient Greeks and Byzantine Greeks, while western Sicily came under North African influence via the Carthaginians and the Arabs.

Two pinnacles of achievement stand out in the island's history. The first was under the Greeks, during the rule of Hiero II in Syracuse, from 269–216 BC. In Hiero's day, Syracuse was one of the great cities of the Mediterranean, with links to Alexandria as a centre of the arts and sciences, and home to the mathematician and inventor, Archimedes. The second was under the Norman kings, from AD 1130–94, when Sicily became a model state within medieval Europe, with its capital, Palermo, becoming a leading Mediterranean city. At its height under Roger II, the Norman kingdom was a brilliant fusion of Norman, Arab and Byzantine cultures, famous for its racial tolerance. Roger's court, which attracted men of learning from all over Europe, was epitomised by the Arab geographer, al-Edrisi.

Extensive archaeological remains, principally of ancient cities and medieval buildings, have assisted historians in piecing together the island's story. Archaeology provides the material evidence on which to base the narrative, while art and architecture add tangible examples of ancient cultures.

———

Historians of different nationalities have made their contributions. One of the first was Thucydides, a Greek historian who writing towards the end of the fifth century BC described Sicily before the Greeks' arrival. He went on to cover the failed mission by the Athenians to capture Syracuse in 415–413 BC. The Roman, Livy, described the successful siege of Syracuse by the Romans in 214–212 BC. It was a Sicilian Greek, named Diodorus Siculus, who writing between 60 and 30 BC, produced the only semi-continuous history of Greek Sicily. His importance lies not only in the length of his coverage, but also in his sources, which included earlier historians who were close to the events described. Later, Plutarch in his *Lives* provided profiles of six leading figures in ancient Sicily.[3]

The first printed history of Sicily appeared in Palermo in 1558. Dedicated to Charles V, Holy Roman Emperor and King of Spain and Sicily, it was the work of Tommaso Fazello, a Dominican friar. Fazello spent years searching for documents, reading the ancient writers and touring the island to discover its sites. With this work he was the founder of Sicilian historiography, combining archaeology and history and providing a benchmark for future studies.[4]

The nineteenth century saw a renewed interest in Sicilian history. This was the golden age of archaeology when excavations took place all around the Mediterranean. New historical work was published by Sicilians such as Michele Amari on the Arabs, Isidoro La Lumia on medieval and modern Sicily and Francesco Saverio Cavallari on ancient Syracuse.[5]

Edward Freeman, the British historian, published his history of ancient Sicily in the late nineteenth century. In an essay he explained his ideas on the island's past. In Freeman's view, Sicily fitted a pattern set by the other large Mediterranean islands such as Sardinia, Corsica, Cyprus and Crete. All had difficult relationships with their neighbouring countries, all were too big to integrate easily with the mainland and yet were too small to go it alone. All bred fiercely independent populations. He concluded that: 'No parts of the world have ever been the objects of fiercer struggles between creeds and races than the great Mediterranean islands'. Reflecting upon the frequent foreign invasions, Freeman pointed out that

rather than enacting its own history, Sicily provided the stage for
other countries to enact theirs. The island became a meeting place
and a battlefield of nations.[6]

British historians continued their contribution in the second
half of the twentieth century. Three books provided a continuous
history of Sicily which became standard works of reference. Moses
Finley's work on ancient Sicily was a masterpiece of clarity and
compression. Denis Mack Smith's detailed work on medieval
and modern Sicily provided an essential narrative of the island's
development. Important works were published by Steven Runciman
on the Sicilian Vespers, John Julius Norwich on the Normans and
Roger Wilson on Roman Sicily.

The foremost Sicilian historian of recent times was Francesco
Renda, who specialised in modern Sicily, publishing his history of
the island between 1860 and 1970 together with numerous works
on aspects of the Spanish era. In 2003, Renda produced a continuous
account of Sicily, from ancient times to the modern era.

A masterly summary of the island's history to the end of the
Second World War was published by John Julius Norwich in 2015.[7]

Sicilian writers of the twentieth century, steeped in their island's
past, brought a new perspective to the historical debate, examining
issues such as Sicilian identity and what could be learnt from the
island's cultural heritage.

The most influential of these books, and Italy's most widely read
historical novel, is Giuseppe di Lampedusa's, *The Leopard,* published
in 1958. Set at the time of Garibaldi's campaign, it provides a view
of the Risorgimento as seen by the novel's main protagonist, the
Prince Fabrizio di Salina. For the Prince, change was not welcome,
and Garibaldi's revolution came too late. Sicilians were an old
people, exhausted and bearing the weight of different civilisations,
always imposed from outside. Tancredi, the Prince's nephew,

produces the famous line: 'If we want things to stay as they are, things will have to change.' This is interpreted as meaning an ability to make apparent change while maintaining the status quo, thus ensuring the privileges of the elite continue as before. This cynical view of the political process became known in Italy as *gattopardismo*, from the novel's Italian title, *Il Gattopardo*.

Lampedusa pointed out how the island's climate produced extreme conditions which helped to shape its history. He described the summer months, when the temperature could reach 40 degrees Celsius, thus: 'This summer of ours which is as long and as glum as a Russian winter.' He wrote of 'this violence of landscape, this cruelty of climate' which created a 'continual tension in everything'.[8]

A different view of the Risorgimento appeared in Vincenzo Consolo's, *The Smile of the Unknown Mariner*, published nearly two decades later. In this book, Garibaldi's campaign in Sicily was accompanied by an uprising of the common people against their local oppressors in a long-awaited social revolution. For Consolo, far from being an island of exhausted people incapable of change, Sicily was a place of energy, crying out for social justice. It was also a place of ancient culture which should be prized, epitomised by Antonello da Messina's painting which provided the title of the novel.[9]

Leonardo Sciascia was another writer fascinated with Sicily's past. Like Consolo, he loved the culture, while, like Lampedusa, tended towards the pessimistic view of history. He saw Sicily as a world of its own, difficult to understand, difficult to govern and difficult to help. For Sciascia, Sicily was a place of extremes, a metaphor for Italy, representing the best and the worst of its values, culture and society.[10]

While welcoming these writers' contributions, Francesco Renda contested the view of Sicilian history as described by Lampedusa, which he traced back to Fazello. Sicily, seen as a permanent colony downtrodden through 2,500 years of history, was an exaggeration and represented only part of the story. In Renda's view, the reality was more uneven, with high points and low points of civilisation. Domination by foreign powers also brought benefits, so that for many years the island led a flourishing existence. The longer periods of domination under the Greeks, Romans and Spanish, each of which lasted for over 500 years, represented self-contained historical eras. In Renda's view, there was not one history of Sicily, but several.[11]

The articles which follow represent different aspects of the island's history, ranging from ancient times to the nineteenth century. Some have a narrow focus, on subjects such as the castle of Dionysius or the cathedral at Monreale, while others have a broad focus, on eras such as the Roman Republic or the Arab Emirate. All reflect themes mentioned above which run through Sicily's history: a multi-ethnic population, inter-racial warfare, successive invasions and rule by foreign powers, exploitation of the people by a privileged few, revolts against authority, a powerful sense of religion, extreme highs and lows in prosperity, and outstanding cultural achievements. The articles demonstrate the complex nature of Sicily's history, its lack of continuity and the swings between the opposite poles of civilisation and chaos.

THE CASTLE OF DIONYSIUS
IN ANCIENT SYRACUSE

Dionysius I was one of the great tyrants of the ancient world. He ruled Syracuse for thirty-eight years, from 405 to 367 BC, and under his leadership it became one of the most powerful cities in the Mediterranean. He seized power at the age of twenty-five, having been chosen to lead the Syracusan army during a chaotic period of warfare with the Carthaginians, when the Greek cities of Selinus, Himera, Akragas, Gela and Kamarina were all captured and sacked. Manipulating the situation to his own advantage, Dionysius made peace with the Carthaginians, thus buying time to consolidate his position in Syracuse.

His first move was to build a castle on the isthmus that links the island of Ortygia to the mainland. The need for a secure base had been made clear to Dionysius during the fighting with the Carthaginians, when the Syracusan cavalry turned against him, plundered his house by the dockyards, and violated his wife. The castle on the isthmus, next to the harbour where the fleet was moored, provided the power base for his dictatorship, and was both a fortress and a palace. Its construction established a pattern of fortification in Syracuse which was to be copied by later rulers, from the Greeks and Romans to the Arabs and Spanish, and which lasted until the nineteenth century.

Dionysius had lived through the siege of Syracuse by the Athenians and was aware of the city's vulnerabilities, especially from the heights above the city. He went on to build elaborate fortifications around the city including long stretches of wall and a well-defended fortress known as the Euryalus Castle on the Epipoli ridge behind the city. The Euryalus Castle was a military outpost which did not include living quarters for himself. These defences proved impregnable and, unlike other Greek cities, Syracuse never fell to the Carthaginians.

No traces of Dionysius's castle on the isthmus can be seen today. If there are any remains, they lie buried deep below the modern buildings on either side of Corso Umberto that leads up to the main bridge onto Ortygia. The fact that the topography has changed significantly since ancient times, due to raised sea level, makes comparison with the past even more difficult. A good idea of the castle and its fortifications can, however, be gained from the accounts of historians and archaeologists, both ancient and modern.

THE CASTLE AND ITS LOCATION

Visitors to the court of Dionysius would have been impressed by the tyrant's surroundings, for in his day Syracuse was one of the largest and most flourishing cities in the Greek world. Arriving at the *agora* – the marketplace and civic centre – they would have been faced with an array of public buildings and *stoas*, covered walkways which provided meeting places for citizens to carry out their business. Merchandise arrived at the nearby docks from ports all around the Mediterranean. The large square occupied by the *agora* was decorated with statues and a tall sundial.

To the east of the *agora* rose a wall interspersed with towers and pierced by a series of five gates, the *Pentapylon,* which protected the castle beyond. Through the gates on the isthmus, bordered on either side by the harbours, stood the castle. Defensive walls surrounded an interior containing reception halls, courtyards, colonnades and private quarters. Here lived the tyrant and his entourage, protected by personal bodyguards. Contained within the grounds were military barracks, the city's mint for producing and storing coinage, an armoury and reserves of military equipment, stables for the cavalry and well-stocked gardens.

The castle was where Dionysius held his court, entertained guests and conducted his affairs. It was a dangerous place. When the courtier, Damocles, complimented the tyrant on his lifestyle, Dionysius responded with a demonstration of what his life was really like. A gleaming sword was hung above Damocles's neck, suspended by a horse hair, to illustrate the constant danger that he faced. Dionysius trusted no one and punished any sign of insubordination. The poet Philoxenus was sent to the quarries, then used as a prison, for criticising the tyrant's own poems. When Plato visited Syracuse, hoping to find in Dionysius an example of the philosopher-king, he made some remarks in open debate which offended the tyrant. As a result, on his return voyage to Athens, Plato found himself sold into slavery and had to be rescued by his friends.

Beyond the castle lay Ortygia, an island stretching out into the Great Harbour, covered in buildings and surrounded by defensive walls. This was a military zone, occupied by the tyrant's mercenaries, with no access for civilians. A wall defended the side of Ortygia facing the isthmus. The remains of a gate from this period, the Porta Urbica, can be seen today in Via XX Settembre, which may have been part of these fortifications.

Ortygia was connected to the isthmus by a bridge over a canal linking the two harbours. The topography of Syracuse with its two harbours, which followed the Phoenician pattern, was a major strength in the city's defences. It allowed triremes to pass down the canal, one at a time, to the safety of the Little Harbour which was enclosed within the city's walls. The Little Harbour, known as *Lakkios*, meaning basin, could hold sixty triremes.

Referred to by the ancient historians as the *rocca* – the citadel and acropolis – the castle was built not on high ground, as this name implies, but close to sea level. This was the location chosen by Dionysius as it offered control of the city's naval and military resources, as well as providing him with maximum personal protection.

THE ANCIENT HISTORIANS

A key source of this information is Diodorus, a historian whose work was based upon that of earlier writers including Philistus, a wealthy Syracusan and early supporter of Dionysius. Philistus was rewarded for his loyalty by being made Commander of the Citadel. When exiled later by an increasingly paranoid Dionysius, he wrote his history, which concerning events in Syracuse is likely to have been an eye-witness account. [1]

Diodorus tells us that Dionysius built himself a fortified acropolis on the island, enclosing within its walls the dockyards which are connected to the little harbour. Historians have interpreted the reference to the 'island' as meaning Ortygia plus the isthmus, both of which covered a larger area in ancient times due to a lower sea level, and which together formed a peninsular joining the mainland near the *agora*. [2]

Further information on the castle, consistent with that of Diodorus, comes from Plutarch in his lives of Dion and Timoleon. It refers to the years following the death of Dionysius I, when Syracuse was ruled by his son, Dionysius II. In one incident, Dionysius II leads Dion down to the sea below the castle and forces him to board a small boat, confirming that the location was close to the port. We learn that Plato, who returned to Syracuse to educate Dionysius II, stayed in the palace which had its own gardens.

During the rule of Dionysius II, the situation in Syracuse became so unstable that Corinth, the mother-city from where the original colonists had come, sent a general, Timoleon, to restore order. This he succeeded in doing, sending Dionysius to exile in Corinth. So low was the reputation of the Dionysian dynasty by this time that Timoleon determined to destroy the castle. Calling for volunteers from the population, Timoleon had the site levelled and the courts of justice built over it.[3]

Agathocles, who seized power in Syracuse after the death of Timoleon, built new fortifications around the Little Harbour. It is likely that he rebuilt the castle on the isthmus for his own use. In the golden age of Syracuse in the reign of Hiero II, a castle/palace on the isthmus was once again the ruler's headquarters. According to Cicero, it continued as such under the Roman governors.[4]

THE SPANISH FORTIFICATIONS

In the sixteenth century, Sicily was a Spanish colony fortified to repel the forces of the Ottoman Empire, which having taken Constantinople in 1453 was intent upon dominating the Mediterranean. The east coast of Sicily was especially vulnerable to attack and fortifications were built in the port cities, including Syracuse. In this period, two Sicilians noted the remains of ancient buildings being uncovered by excavations on the isthmus to build the new fortifications. An Arab castle, the Castello Marietto or Marieth, which once dominated the isthmus was destroyed by an earthquake in 1542 and the remains demolished by Spanish engineers.

In his history of Sicily published in 1558, Fazello recorded that during excavations on the isthmus, 4,000 huge square blocks of stone were uncovered, the foundations of a massive building. Seven statues were also recovered together with the marble head of a man. Clearly some important structure once stood here – in Fazello's opinion, the *rocca* of Dionysius. 'It was on the island, at the mouth of the two harbours, that the magnificent castle of Dionysius and the other tyrants once stood'. Fazello was also convinced that Hiero II's palace was built on the ruins of Dionysius's castle.[5]

In 1613, a Syracusan nobleman, Vincenzo Mirabella, published his reconstruction of ancient Greek Syracuse. It contained detailed descriptions of its monuments accompanied by maps of the city. Mirabella witnessed excavations on the isthmus which revealed the

ancient mint. Tradition has it that the area became known as *monte
d'oro* (gold mountain) for the quantity of gold coins found when
excavating the area. Mirabella also claimed to have seen documents
showing underground tunnels linking the isthmus to different parts
of the city.[6]

The Spanish went on to build elaborate fortifications across the
isthmus, cutting a new canal towards the mainland, adding two
large bastions and multiple gates. It became known as the *Piazzaforte
Borbonica* (Bourbon Fortress). These fortifications remained in place
until the end of the nineteenth century when the Sicilians, at last in
control of their island, set out to eliminate all signs of Spanish rule.
Prints of the period give an idea of the scale of these fortifications.
Particularly impressive was the Ligne Gate, named after one of the
Spanish viceroys, which led into Ortygia. Similar in concept to
the *Pentapylon,* it provided a succession of narrow entrances for a
defence in-depth.[7]

NINETEENTH-CENTURY HISTORIANS

The late nineteenth century was the golden age of archaeology in
Sicily. After Garibaldi freed the island from the Spanish Bourbons
in 1860, Sicilians began to take a renewed interest in their ancient
monuments. Archaeological museums, displaying the new finds,
were established in Syracuse and Palermo. Ancient Greek Sicily
became the object of international interest, attracting many visitors.

Two works on ancient Syracuse, published in this period, shed
more light on Dionysius's castle. The first was by the Director of
Antiquities, Francesco Saverio Cavallari, together with his colleague,
Adolf Holm, published in 1883. It covered the topography of the
ancient city based upon the evidence of ancient writers and supported
by maps. The location of Dionysius's castle on the isthmus, according
to Cavallari, provided the tyrant with two benefits. It meant that he
lived close to the fleet, the basis of his power, and was reassured to
see the ships from his balcony. In addition, by controlling the isthmus

and Ortygia, he effectively dominated the entire city and put himself in a position to control the population.[8]

The second was by Edward Freeman, a professor from Oxford University, who spent three months in Ortygia researching his history of ancient Sicily, published in 1894. In Freeman's day, the Spanish fortifications on the isthmus were still in place, and he was convinced they were built on the site of the Dionysius castle. In his detailed account of the Greek tyrants of Syracuse, he described the castle as 'a fortress and a capital within a capital' from which Dionysius controlled access to the Little Harbour where he kept his triremes. Freeman was also of the opinion that Dionysius had a second castle, situated on the tip of Ortygia, facing the mouth of the harbour.[9]

THE ISTHMUS TODAY

Standing on the Umbertino bridge, looking up the isthmus towards the Foro Siracusano, site of the ancient marketplace, there are no signs today of these fortifications. The towers, bastions, high walls and defensive gates have all gone, together with the castles of the Greek tyrants, Roman governors, Arab emirs and Spanish viceroys, making way for rows of modern two- and three-storey buildings. Only the harbours remain, together with the backdrop of Ortygia, as a reminder of the city's past glories.

In a small section of the Little Harbour known as the Ribellino Port or the Darsena Montedoro, bordered on one side by Via Moscuzza, can be found a stretch of stone wall from Spanish times. It runs down one side of the little port, with a cornice down the centre, and is all that is left of the *Piazzaforte*. Taking the path that runs along the wall, gaps can be seen opening into the buildings above with footholds carved in the stone for scaling the wall, providing strong links with the past.

3

SICILY UNDER THE ROMAN REPUBLIC

It was under the Roman Republic, in the third century BC, that Sicily became the first Roman province. It was a momentous event on both sides. For Sicily, it saw the beginning of the longest domination by any foreign power, lasting until the fifth century AD. For Rome, Sicily brought security and a supply of grain to feed its troops. The island became a testing ground for administrative procedures and a prototype for future provinces. It was the place which first taught the Romans the advantages of foreign possessions.

The Romans acquired Sicily in 241 BC, at the end of the first Punic War. The term Punic is derived from the Greek word, *phoinix,* which is the origin of the name Phoenician. The Phoenicians, who were the forebears of the Carthaginians, founded the city of Carthage in around 814 BC. Sicily's position, strategically placed between North Africa and the Italian mainland, made the island essential for the protection of Rome.

The Punic Wars, which lasted from 264 to 146 BC, were fought for very high stakes, the prize to the winner being no less than control of the Mediterranean. Carthage was the super-power of the western Mediterranean, a mercantile city in North Africa (in modern Tunisia) with colonies from Spain to Sicily. It was protected by an army of mercenaries and a navy which had enjoyed supremacy for years. The Roman Republic had recently completed the conquest of the Italian peninsula which it ruled through a combination of colonies and alliances. Both sides brought equal determination and ruthlessness to war on a scale not seen before.

In the Second Punic War, Carthage's leading general, Hannibal, took the fight to Rome. After crossing the Alps, he slaughtered the armies sent to stop him, and threatened the city of Rome itself. Hannibal was finally defeated at the Battle of Zama in 202. The Third Punic War ended with the destruction of Carthage in 146.

The Roman conquest introduced a new chapter in the history of the island. Sicily was now subject to rule from Rome, with its economy realigned to serve Rome's interests. The island's Greek cities lost their independence and the brilliance of their cultural life. The Carthaginians, for their part, were finished as a force on the island. In place of the Greco-Carthaginian wars, which had ravaged Sicily for over two centuries, Rome imposed a lasting settlement on the island which provided lengthy periods of peace and prosperity.

THE CONQUEST OF SICILY

The Roman invasion of Sicily was prompted by a request for help from the Mamertines, a group of mercenaries based in Messana (Messina). The Mamertines, whose name means 'children of Mars', were originally from southern Italy and had been brought to Sicily by Agathocles, a tyrant of Syracuse. Initially the Mamertines supported Carthage, but decided to switch their allegiance to Rome, citing their common Italian origins. The Romans saw an increasing threat from Carthage, which already held western Sicily and Sardinia. Messana would be a potential danger in Carthaginian hands, as it offered a bridgehead for attacks on the Italian mainland.

In 264, the Romans invaded Sicily and succeeded in taking Messana. Their arrival marked the beginning of the First Punic War, much of which took place in and around Sicily. Soon after the Roman invasion, Hiero II of Syracuse, who ruled a prosperous kingdom on the east coast, switched sides to become an ally of Rome. Crucially, Hiero provided naval support and food supplies to the Romans.

For twenty-three years the war in Sicily swung to and fro with neither the Romans nor the Carthaginians able to land a knock-out blow. Casualties were huge and the destruction to cities and property was immense. The Sicilian Greeks, who were no strangers to destructive warfare, were appalled at the devastation inflicted upon communities that did not surrender to the Romans, which included selling their populations into slavery.

The Romans' strength lay on the eastern side of the island through their ally, Hiero II in Syracuse, and in the recently captured port of Messana. The Carthaginians' strength lay on the western side, in their port cities of Panormus (Palermo) and Lilybaeum (Marsala) as well as in Agrigentum (Agrigento) on the south coast. From their base in the east, the Romans set out to capture the cities that were in Carthaginian hands. They succeeded in taking Agrigentum in 261 after a six-month siege, while Panormus fell to them in 254. Lilybaeum, the Carthaginians' main base in Sicily, was besieged for ten years but was never taken.

Much of the action took place at sea, forcing the Romans to adapt to naval warfare. For the invasion of Sicily, they borrowed ships from their allies in southern Italy. But as the war dragged on, the need arose for a battle fleet capable of confronting the Carthaginians. The Romans therefore set about building quinqueremes — large war galleys carrying 300 rowers and up to 120 marines — and training their crews. This involved an enormous outlay in resources and equipment. Once in action they introduced new tactics which included closing with enemy ships to board them with the help of grappling irons.

Major battles took place off the Sicilian coast involving hundreds of thousands of men. On one occasion, more than 500 quinqueremes took part in a naval action, on another, more than 700. Most of the early naval battles went in favour of Carthage, due to Rome's inexperience at sea. An attempted invasion of North Africa by the Romans failed. Finally, in 241, with their fleet refitted for greater speed, the Romans won a major naval victory off the Egadi Islands in western Sicily, which ended the war. In the treaty that followed, the Carthaginians agreed to pay a large indemnity, to abandon their city of Lilybaeum and to withdraw their citizens from Sicily. The Carthaginian monopoly of the seas was over.[1]

ROME AND THE KINGDOM OF SYRACUSE

When Rome gained control of central and western Sicily, these regions were left ravaged by war. Large cities like Panormus and Agrigentum had suffered prolonged sieges, with their surviving populations forcibly expelled to be sold into slavery. Lilybaeum had been fought over for a decade with the surrounding territory laid waste. Smaller cities, such as Kamarina and Selinus, were reduced to ruins. Across the island the number of populated urban centres was significantly reduced.

In contrast, Hiero II's separate kingdom in eastern Sicily flourished during the years 241 to 216, thanks to its alliance with Rome. In this period, Syracuse was one of the great cities of the Mediterranean, a prosperous commercial centre with connections to Greece, Asia Minor and Egypt. It was also a city of high intellectual and artistic achievements, the home of Archimedes, the greatest mathematician of the ancient world. The city's cultural centre was the Greek theatre, the remains of which, dating from around 230, can be seen today. It originally held 15,000 people who came to see plays by Euripides, Sophocles and Aeschylus. The kingdom extended into the territory around Syracuse to include Akrai (Palazzolo Acreide), Morgantina, Tauromenion (Taormina), Leontini (Lentini), Neaiton (Noto) and Helorus (Eloro).

This prosperity ended abruptly after Hiero's death in 216. He was succeeded by his young and unstable grandson, Hieronymus, who was persuaded to renege on the Roman alliance and to support Carthage. The Romans could not allow this, and sent one of their best generals, Marcellus, to capture Syracuse. A two-year siege followed, famous for the ingenious machines Archimedes used to defend the city, although it eventually fell in 212. Archimedes was killed in the aftermath of the fighting and the city was sacked by the Romans. The Syracusans lost their property and were suddenly reduced to poverty. Marcellus removed works of art, including statues, paintings, bronze artefacts and silverware, for display in Rome. These stolen treasures gave the Romans their first taste of Greek art. Syracuse, the largest and most prosperous city in Sicily, along with its territory along the east coast, came under the direct control of Rome.

THE FIRST PROVINCE OF ROME

With Sicily providing the security of a buffer state between mainland Italy and North Africa, the Romans turned their attention to grain production. Hiero had supplied Rome with grain during the First Punic War and the Romans had become reliant upon it. To ensure supplies, the Romans encouraged the development of large estates, the *latifundia,* to concentrate upon producing wheat and barley crops. Wealthy investors bought tracts of land, felled the trees, and brought in slaves to work in the fields.

As this was their first province, the Romans had no blueprint for the administration of Sicily and therefore proceeded in stages. At the end of the First Punic War, a *quaestor* was sent to Lilybaeum to organise the collection of taxes, while from 227 a *praetor* – or governor – was appointed, with powers over military action. A garrison of two legions was stationed on the island. Once Syracuse was captured, the city became the seat of the Roman governors, who took over Hiero's royal palace. A second *quaestor* was appointed, based in Syracuse, responsible for tax collection in eastern Sicily.

The Romans left the existing institutions in Sicily intact, adopting the tribute system which had been introduced by Hiero, known as the *Lex Hieronica.* Accordingly, landowners paid 10 per cent of their annual harvest in kind to the state. Additional taxes were levied on the production of wine, olives, fruit and vegetables. In times of emergency, the Romans reserved the right to impose the compulsory purchase of agricultural products at fixed prices.

Sicilian cities were dealt with on an individual basis. Those which had defied the Romans only to be taken by siege were largely destroyed, with property confiscated from their leading citizens. Those cities which had declared themselves on the Roman side early in the conflict were rewarded with special privileges. Thus Messana (Messina), Netum (Noto) and Tauromenium (Taormina) became *civitates foederate*, cities linked by treaty to Rome and granted tax-free status. Another five cities, including Panormus (Palermo) and Segesta, enjoyed tax-free status without being bound by direct treaty.

During the Second Punic War, when Hannibal threatened Rome, the legions stationed in Sicily were withdrawn to defend the homeland. Later in the war, when the conflict swung in Rome's favour, the Roman general Publius Cornelius Scipio raised and trained his army in Sicily, before crossing over to North Africa from Lilybaeum to defeat Hannibal at the Battle of Zama.

To the Romans, Sicily was a foreign country that compared to the rest of the Republic remained overwhelmingly Greek in culture. Latin was spoken only by a small minority of settlers from Italy, including government officials. Sicilians were encouraged to go back to the land, the urban population declined, and the countryside was repopulated. Spread around the island were medium and small-sized farms producing mixed crops. These communities were forced to accept a system of compulsory agricultural production, sometimes without profit, to provide food for export to Rome.

Brutal treatment of the slave gangs on the *latifundia* eventually led to open revolt, creating serious problems for the Romans. Many of the slaves were ex-soldiers, having been captured in the wars in the eastern Mediterranean, and knew how to organise resistance. One revolt, which started near Enna in 139, led to the build-up of a slave army of 60,000 that held out for seven years. A second revolt in 104, which began in Syracuse, produced an army of 40,000. The revolts were eventually put down by the Roman army.

In 75, the young lawyer Marcus Tullius Cicero received his first political appointment as *quaestor*, based in Lilybaeum, responsible for tax collection in western Sicily. Here he became closely involved with the local communities. On his return to Rome, Cicero took

up the case for the Sicilians against Gaius Verres, the corrupt
Roman governor. In successfully winning his case, which resulted
in the banishment of Verres, Cicero made his name and went on to
become the Roman Republic's leading prosecutor.

In Cicero's time, Sicily's population was somewhere between
600,000 and 1,000,000 with only three cities – Panormus, Catania
and Syracuse – containing a population of over 10,000. In the *Verrine
Orations*, Cicero's account of the case, the impact of Verres on Sicily
was exaggerated to emphasise the governor's corrupt practices. The
reality was that the island enjoyed peace and reasonable prosperity,
conditions which were disturbed but not destroyed by Verres.[2]

The civil wars that followed the assassination of Julius Caesar in
44 BC brought more fighting and destruction to Sicily. Sextus, the
son of Pompey the Great, captured Sicily and temporarily blocked
grain supplies from reaching Rome. He was defeated by Octavian
(the future emperor Augustus) and his general, Agrippa.

EPILOGUE

Once established as emperor, Augustus visited Sicily on a tour of
the Empire, and set up a programme of regeneration to repair the
war damage. Major building projects followed. Six cities, including
Syracuse, Palermo and Catania, were granted the status of *colonia*,
which brought the benefits of Roman citizenship.

Under the Empire, Sicily settled down as an agricultural producer
to supply food to Rome. Peace in the region led to the abandonment
of hilltop villages which were no longer needed for security against
raiders. Roman influence spread around the island as more settlers
arrived, veterans from the legions were granted land, and wealthy
Romans built themselves villas. Archaeological evidence suggests a
well-populated countryside with clusters of villages, hamlets and
larger farms covering the island.

One legacy of Rome was the system of *latifundia*, dedicated to
grain production, which survived into the nineteenth century. This

system kept land ownership concentrated in the hands of a few wealthy landlords who employed large numbers of poor labourers. Single crop farming on a large scale condemned most of Sicily's rural population to subsistence living standards for centuries.

Following the systematic looting of Syracuse, Roman interest in Greek culture meant that most original works of art left the island. However, it also encouraged artists to make copies of Greek art, many of which have survived in Sicily, examples of which include the statue known as the Venus Landolina and a marble head of Zeus, both now to be found in the archaeological museum in Syracuse.

The surviving Roman monuments in Sicily come from the period of Empire rather than the Republic. They are fewer in number than those from the Greek era. This is because the Romans took over the Greek cities and adapted them to their needs rather than building anew. While there was significant building under the Romans, for example roads, triumphal arches and amphitheatres, much of their work involved additions and alterations to existing structures.

The outstanding Roman monument is the Villa del Casale, near Piazza Armerina. Built as a luxurious private villa, it is famous for its colourful mosaics which decorate the floors. Well-preserved and beautifully displayed, the mosaics contain a series of lively scenes including a chariot race and a hunt for wild animals. On a much smaller scale, but of comparable quality, more floor mosaics can be seen at the Villa del Tellaro, near Noto.

Other Roman monuments of note in Sicily include the amphitheatres at Syracuse and Catania, a small temple complex in Syracuse and the ancient towns at Soluntum and Morgantina. The archaeological museums in Palermo and Syracuse contain collections of statues and artefacts from the Roman era.

4

THE ARABS IN SICILY

After the death of the Prophet Muhammad in AD 632, his followers erupted out of their homeland in the Arabian Peninsula on a campaign of military conquest. This was made possible by a power vacuum created between the Byzantine and Persian empires, which had fought each other to a standstill. By 709, the Arabs controlled most of North Africa, establishing provinces for themselves together with the local populations. One of these provinces, named Ifriqiya, broadly covered modern Tunisia. From here raids were carried out on the coast of Sicily, only 150 kilometres across the sea. A full-scale invasion of the island was launched in 827.

The Arabs became a diverse people as they advanced out of their homeland. Known as Saracens by the Italians, they absorbed the tribes of North Africa — Berbers, and the descendants of the Carthaginians, Romans and Vandals — into their culture, uniting them in the religion of Islam and the teachings of the Qur'an.

The Arabs revitalised Sicily. They brought immigrants in large numbers, with new skills in irrigation and agriculture. They developed trade with the cities of North Africa. They introduced a sophisticated culture, advanced in the arts and sciences. Like the Greeks before them, Arabs came to Sicily to make a new life for themselves and set out to realise the island's potential.

In Byzantine Sicily, the Arabs found a decadent and run-down province. Conquered in AD 535 by Belisarius, general to the emperor Justinian I, Sicily was consolidated as a Christian possession, with the church playing a major part in society. However, the Byzantines were too preoccupied by their struggle with Persia to have much time for a remote province, and Sicily's role became that of providing Constantinople with grain and tax revenues. Although the Emperor Constans II moved to Syracuse in 663–668 to confront the growing Arab threat, no significant investment was made in the island, and few traces remain of the Byzantine era.

The Arab involvement in Sicily was complex and in total spanned nearly 400 years. It began with the invasion of 827 and ended with the expulsion of the Arabs by Frederick II around 1225. Between these dates the Arabs ruled Sicily for 200 years and then made a major contribution to the Norman Kingdom of Sicily. The history of Arab Sicily can be divided into four phases: conquest, domination, life under Norman rule, and exodus.

THE CONQUEST OF SICILY

The Arab invasion was triggered by the actions of a renegade Byzantine Greek naval commander named Euphemius. He abducted a nun from a convent and married her against her wishes, which led to her family appealing to the emperor for justice. Rather than face arrest, Euphemius launched a revolt against Byzantine rule in Sicily, declaring himself emperor in Syracuse. He also appealed for help to the ruling Arab dynasty in Ifriqiya, the Aghlabids. When opposition to him grew in Syracuse, Euphemius fled to Ifriqiya. Here, largely due to the support of Asad ibn al-Furat, a respected scholar and military commander, it was agreed to invade Sicily.

On 18 June 827, the Arab army landed at Mazara on the south-western coast. It was a mixed force of Arab, Berber and Spanish troops, made up of 700 cavalry and 10,000 infantrymen, transported by seventy warships and 100 supply ships. In addition, there was a small force of mercenaries and foreigners led by Euphemius. The first battle took place on the plain just inland from Mazara, with the defending force greatly outnumbering the Arabs. It began as a cavalry engagement with lances and ended as a resounding victory

for the Arabs. The Byzantine forces withdrew while Asad set out for
Syracuse, the Byzantine capital, on the east coast.

Asad followed the road along the south coast and then headed
inland, on the road through the mountains via ancient Akrai
(Palazzolo Acreide) to Syracuse. Asad knew that Syracuse was the
key to Sicily. Fabulously wealthy, it had been the leading city on the
island since the time of the ancient Greeks. Syracuse had a naturally
strong defensive position and was held by a determined garrison.
The city withstood the initial attack while the Arabs began to
suffer losses from the fever – possibly malaria – that was rife in the
marshland around the harbour. Asad died soon afterwards, either
from the fever or from wounds sustained in fighting. The army badly
missed his leadership and without him the Arab invasion faltered.

So began a long war of attrition to subdue the island, which took
over seventy years to complete. Sicily was dotted with fortress-cities
defended by small Byzantine Greek garrisons who were desperate to
hold on to their territories. These garrisons had little hope of military
support from Constantinople, which was already overstretched.
The fighting was very destructive and cities like Cefalù and Enna,
when finally captured, were burnt out wrecks with their garrisons
massacred. In the battle for one of these cities, Euphemius was killed.

A break-through for the Arabs came in 831 when they captured
Palermo. This became their base and eventually their capital of Sicily.
After several unsuccessful attempts, Syracuse finally fell in 878, after
a bitterly fought siege. The treasure taken from the city was the
greatest from any Christian city in the Arab advance. When Taormina
followed in 902, the Arabs were effectively in control of the island.
Rometta, a stronghold near Messina, was the last to fall in 965.

ARAB DOMINATION
The Arabs brought profound social change to Sicily, becoming
the new elite with Islam the official religion, while the Christian
church lost its lands and its power. Although restrictions were

imposed upon non-Muslims, religious tolerance was observed, with Christians and Jews free to follow their own religions and to live by their own laws. Immigrants poured in from North Africa, fleeing political unrest at home and attracted by the island's fertile conditions. Perhaps 500,000 people arrived in this period, settling mostly in the west and the south-east of the island and bringing the population of the island up to somewhere between a million and a million-and-a-half. Society became a loose federation of peoples, a multi-ethnic mix of Arabs, Berbers, Spaniards, Lombards, Jews and Greeks. After about a generation, ethnic origins became less important and people thought of themselves as Sicilians.

In 909, the Aghlabid dynasty in Ifriqiya was defeated by the Fatimids, who also took control of Sicily. Sixty years later, the Fatimids moved their capital to Egypt, to the newly founded city of Cairo. Sicily fell under the control of the Fatimid emirs, the Kalbids. This brought a large degree of independence to the island.

There followed a period of stability and prosperity. Cities were restored and rebuilt after the fighting. Reasonable taxes were imposed upon the population and commerce flourished. For administrative purposes, Sicily was divided into three districts known as the Val di Mazara, covering the west, the Val di Noto, covering the south-east and the Val Demone, covering the north-east. Mazara, where the Arabs had landed, became their base for the early part of their conquest of the island. Once Palermo became established as their capital, it took over as the administrative centre for the Mazara district. Messina was the centre for the Val Demone and Noto for the Val di Noto. The division into these three districts lasted until the early nineteenth century.

The Arabs brought improvements to agriculture which amounted to a revolution. Well-used to contending with the arid conditions of North Africa and the Middle East, the Arabs had perfected sophisticated irrigation techniques which they introduced to Sicily. Networks of channels, both above and below ground, were built to bring water from the hills into the cities and to the fields of cultivation. Water wheels were used to draw water from the ground and storage tanks were installed. These techniques made the land more productive and extended the growing season. Many of the large estates, established since Roman times to grow wheat, were broken up, with the land redistributed into smaller holdings. This enabled ordinary citizens to benefit from farming and helped to spread income more evenly among the population.

Much Sicilian food can be traced back to the Arabs, who introduced new kinds of fruit and vegetables including oranges and lemons, aubergines and cucumbers, watermelons and spinach. Rice was planted, while crops already grown in Sicily, such as almonds, dates and pistachios, were farmed more intensively. One of the most notable imports was sugar cane, refined by the Arabs to enable the preparation of the sweet desserts typical of the island. The Arabs were the first to make pasta on the island using hard durum wheat to make a product suitable for storage. The Arab geographer, al-Edrisi, described a factory in Trabia on the north coast that produced large quantities of pasta for export to both Muslim and Christian countries.[1]

Along with innovations in agriculture came new fishing methods brought over by Arab fishermen from ports such as Tripoli and Tunis. Since ancient times tuna had been part of Sicily's wealth, circling the island in great schools to be caught near the coast. The Arabs introduced a complex system of nets which channelled the fish into a central pool for killing by harpoon. This became the established Sicilian method of tuna fishing, with the killing known as the *mattanza*. Plants to process the tuna, known as *tonnare*, sprung up around the coast.

Under the Arabs, Palermo became the capital of Sicily, a position it holds to this day. This marked a major change, for ever since the ancient Greek era, Syracuse had been the leading city on the island. Palermo, Bal'harm or al-Madinah (the city) to the Arabs, became one of the great Muslim cities, compared to Baghdad, Cairo and

Cordoba. The seat of the emir (governor) who ruled Sicily, it was a city of some 100,000 inhabitants, filled with palaces, mosques, minarets and markets.

By the year 1000, internal disputes were threatening the stability of Muslim Sicily. Arab society was divided into tribes, each with its own fierce family loyalties. This structure was an advantage in the expansion phase, when rival tribes competed to win new territory. But it was a handicap in the phase of consolidation as disputes arose over the distribution of wealth and property. Cohesion was lacking in the government of the island with the emirs of the different cities going their own ways. This led to open warfare breaking out between Palermo and Kerkent (Agrigento), a Berber stronghold.

In 1038, Constantinople made its last attempt to win back Sicily. George Maniaces, a Byzantine general and governor of the Byzantine territories in southern Italy, collected an army of Greeks, strengthened by Norman mercenaries, and succeeded in recapturing most of eastern Sicily. One of the Normans, William de Hauteville, earned himself the name of 'Strong Arm' for killing the Arab emir of Syracuse in single combat. A year later, Maniaces was recalled to Constantinople, ending Byzantine hopes of reclaiming Sicily. However, the Normans accompanying Maniaces were impressed by the prosperity of the island and, as they established themselves in southern Italy, viewed it with increasing interest.

UNDER NORMAN RULE

The Normans, among the most feared soldiers in Europe, imposed their rule not only upon England but also upon southern Italy and Sicily. Trained as knights from an early age, they fought in squadrons of heavy cavalry, armed with lance and broadsword and supported by archers. Their cavalry charge, which few could withstand, enabled them to defeat much larger forces on many occasions.

Travelling south in small groups, young Norman knights sought
their fortunes in the chaotic conditions of southern Italy where
the rule of the Byzantine Greeks was fading. One family, the de
Hautevilles, dominated the Norman leadership in the south, with
Robert Guiscard (the Cunning) and his younger brother, Roger,
masterminding the campaign for Sicily.

In 1061, the Normans launched their invasion, landing near
Messina with a force of around 2,000, perhaps half of them knights.
They were helped by the emir of Syracuse, who enlisted their
support against his brother-in-law, who ruled the interior of Sicily.
Messina fell quickly, providing a bridgehead for the Norman forces.
There followed battles in the interior of the island from which the
Normans emerged victorious.

The decisive moment for the Normans' campaign came with the
capture of Palermo in January 1072. Robert Guiscard succeeded
in taking the Kalsa, the lower city, while the Arabs were still in
possession of the Cassaro, the citadel upon the higher ground.
Rather than face a lengthy siege, Robert offered the Arabs a
deal. In return for a guarantee of personal safety and freedom to
follow their religion, the Arabs were to accept Norman rule, for
which they would pay tribute. This was the start of an alliance
between Normans and Arabs which became one of the strengths of
Norman Sicily.

After the capture of Palermo, Robert returned to southern Italy
with his knights, leaving Roger in command. While the alliance
with the Arabs held firm in Palermo, elsewhere on the island Arab
communities fought hard to keep their territories. Due to the
lack of Norman forces, the campaign developed into a drawn-out
war of attrition which lasted for twenty years. By 1091, however,
Sicily was under Norman control, with Roger declared Count
of Sicily.

Sicily reached a peak of civilisation, unmatched before or since,
under Roger II, the Count's son, who was crowned King of Sicily
and Southern Italy in 1130. Under Roger II, the kingdom of Sicily

became one of the most powerful states in Europe, recognised by the pope and the crowned heads of Europe.

The Normans were masters at adapting to local cultures and they built upon the Greco-Arab foundations that they inherited. They took readily to the Muslim environment that they found in Palermo. Islamic architecture was well-suited to the hot climate, with its emphasis upon the interior of buildings, with their gardens and fountains. Arab architects and craftsmen were employed on Norman building projects which included summer palaces and Islamic-style churches with red domes.

The Palace of the Normans, built on the high ground in the Cassaro district, employed Arab guards and servants and adopted Muslim culture more broadly. The court, which attracted scholars, artists and scientists from many countries, was distinctly Muslim in character, with King Roger most at his ease discussing scientific subjects with Arab experts. The most significant work to emerge from the court was the study of world geography by the Arab scholar Muhammed al-Edrisi. Under the patronage of Roger II, information was collected from far and wide, being published in 1154 as *The Book of Roger*. It was the outstanding work of geography of its time and became famous across the Muslim world.

The Norman state of Sicily owed much of its success to the Arabs who had already established a prosperous economy. Perhaps the greatest gift of the Arabs was the religious tolerance which illuminated the early years of Norman rule. This tolerance created a state with a unique character based upon the fusion of Latin, Greek and Arab cultures.

EXODUS

The exodus of the Arabs from Sicily took place over many years. The elite already began to leave when Palermo fell to the Normans. Others left as attacks on the Muslim districts escalated. Opposition to the Muslims in Sicily built up as the Christian barons and churchmen increased in number and influence. The paradox of a Christian state hand in glove with a Muslim population, at the time of the crusades, was always likely to end in trouble. A tipping point came early in the reign of William I, when the palace was ransacked by a mob and the Muslim staff massacred. Members of the court, probably including the geographer al-Edrisi, no longer felt safe and left for North Africa. Active opposition to the government became centred on the hilltowns of western Sicily.

After William II died childless in 1189, and despite efforts to maintain it, the Norman kingdom came to an end in 1194. The realm passed to the German emperor, Henry VI, via his wife Constance, the daughter of Roger II. The German occupation was one of the worst episodes in the history of Sicily. The island's riches were shipped off to Germany, while Norman barons were rounded up and killed or imprisoned. The Kingdom of Sicily was then inherited by Frederick II, the son of Henry and Constance, who also became King of Germany and Holy Roman Emperor.

Frederick, although brought up in the Muslim environment of the palace in Palermo and personally at ease with the Muslim community, faced rebellion from different Arab factions. To solve the problem, he had a city especially built for them in southern Italy called Lucera, to which he transferred some 15–20,000 of the Sicilian Arabs. Those who remained were poorer people, who either converted to Christianity or lived like hermits in the mountains. The story of Muslim Sicily ends around 1225 with this transfer. Lucera was then captured by Charles of Anjou in 1269 and the Muslim community dispersed.

For the Arabs, exodus from Sicily was a catastrophe. Ordinary citizens such as farmers, small traders and fishermen lost their livelihoods for an unknown future. Ibn Hamdis, one of their most evocative poets, who was born in Syracuse around 1056, recorded his feelings of grief at having been driven out.

EPILOGUE

Little was known about the Arabs in Sicily until the mid-nineteenth century when Michele Amari, a Sicilian patriot and historian, published his book *Storia dei Musulmani di Sicilia* (History of the Muslims in Sicily). Amari, who came from Palermo, had first published a book on the Sicilian Vespers, telling the story of how Sicilians had risen to throw the French out of the island. He was soon in trouble for this with the Spanish Bourbon government which ruled the island. Amari fled to Paris where he taught himself Arabic and, researching in the libraries of Paris and London, he discovered old manuscripts relating to Sicily. In his book, he told the full story of the Arabs in Sicily, from invasion to final exodus. Well-researched and imaginatively written, it remains the standard work on the subject.[2]

The Arab legacy in Sicily was a strong and lasting one, with Arab culture leaving its imprint upon many aspects of everyday life. In western Sicily, in places like Mazara, Marsala and Trapani, Arab influences endured in the character of the people, in their appearance, their customs, their architecture, their language and literature. The Arab influence continues in the food, in dishes such as *pasta con le sarde* (pasta with sardines), invented by Arab cooks after the landing at Mazara, and in *couscous* (pasta made from semolina), which is celebrated at an annual festival at San Vito lo Capo. Cassata, the name of the sweet ricotta cake and Sicilian speciality, comes from *qashatah*, the Arab word for the bowl used to make it.[3]

In terms of buildings, only traces remain from the period of Arab domination, for example in the irrigation channels cut deep into the rock beneath Palermo to bring water into the city. It is in the monuments of the Norman period that the Arab contribution can be seen. These monuments, representing a blend of Norman, Arab and Byzantine cultures, were built by Arab craftsmen. In the great cathedrals of Monreale, Palermo and Cefalù; in the churches of San

Giovanni degli Eremiti, San Cataldo and the Palatine Chapel; and in the summer palaces of the Zisa and the Cuba, there can be seen outstanding examples of Islamic art and architecture, the work of Sicilian Arabs.

The Arab legacy is also present in Palermo in the winding alleyways of the Capo and Ballarò street markets, with their stalls piled high with fruit and vegetables, and in the squares filled with palm trees. Much of Palermo's street food, to be found in the markets, has Arab origins. The city is filled with echoes of its Arab past.

THE CATHEDRAL AT MONREALE

The small town of Monreale, which stands in the hills above Palermo, contains a cathedral which is one of the wonders of the Middle Ages and a prime example of the cultural achievements of the Normans in Sicily. It is famous for its colourful mosaics, showing scenes from the Old and New Testaments, and for its decorative cloisters. The complex of buildings owes its existence to a power struggle between William II, the Norman king of Sicily, and Walter of the Mill, the English archbishop of Palermo.

WILLIAM AND WALTER

William II was crowned King of Sicily at the age of twelve in the cathedral of Palermo upon the death of his father, William I, in 1166. Blond and handsome, he was welcomed enthusiastically by the population. William was the grandson of Roger II, who had established the Norman kingdom of Sicily in 1130. His father's reign had been plagued by rebellion from the barons which led historians to label the elder William, 'the Bad'. But now the kingdom was more stable with the people tired of rebellion. The young king inherited a well-organised kingdom whose prosperity was based upon a multi-cultural society made up of Normans, Arabs, Greeks and Jews. The wealth of the kingdom, which was legendary, was the envy of the states of Europe.

William, who was mild and tolerant by nature, held strong Christian beliefs, and showed determination when he applied

himself to government. Brought up in the Muslim environment of
the Norman Palace in Palermo, which since his grandfather's day had
been run by Arabs, William was used to luxury. Summer palaces,
country estates and a harem were all part of the royal establishment.
He spoke Norman French at court and Arabic with his servants. In
this semi-oriental atmosphere, watched over by Arab bodyguards,
William was readily distracted from the affairs of state by easy living.

Until William came of age, his mother, Margaret, acted as regent.
Margaret came from Navarre and was a level-headed woman who
handled the regency well. Concessions were made to rebels,
conflicts were avoided, and peace largely maintained. Wary of
her late husband's advisers, Margaret brought her French cousin,
Stephen of Perche, to Sicily to be her chancellor. Stephen also
became Archbishop of Palermo. Along with Stephen came a group
of thirty Frenchmen and a churchman of Anglo-French origins
called Walter of the Mill.

Walter, known in Sicily as Gualtiero Offamilio, came from a
humble background and was probably born in England to a French
mother. On arrival in Sicily his first post was tutor to the royal
children. He was hugely ambitious and rose through the ranks to
become a canon of the Palatine Chapel, the king's private chapel
in the Norman Palace. After Stephen of Perche left Sicily, Walter
became a candidate for Archbishop of Palermo, a position he
eventually won through unscrupulous means including bribery and
use of a mob to deter opposition. Along with the archbishopric
went the position of senior adviser to the king, making Walter the
second most powerful man in the kingdom.

Connections had long existed between the Norman states of
Sicily and England. When William of Normandy was preparing
for his invasion of England, a contingent of Norman knights had
left southern Italy to support him. Their experience of amphibious
warfare, gained during the invasion of Sicily, proved crucial for this
operation. Since then many Englishmen had served in Sicily, several
holding high office under Roger II. During Margaret's regency,

among her senior advisers was one Richard Palmer, Bishop of Syracuse. Walter's brother, Bartholomew, also came to Sicily and became Bishop of Agrigento. In 1177, Walter married William II to Joanna, daughter of King Henry II of England, in the Palatine Chapel in Palermo.

Unlike most of his countrymen, however, Walter did not make a positive contribution to the welfare of the kingdom. He was a man on the make, according to John Julius Norwich, the prototype of those prelates, vain, ambitious and worldly, who were such a feature of medieval Europe. In his quarter of a century as archbishop and chief minister to William II, there is no evidence of his having taken a single constructive step to improve Sicily's position or to advance Sicilian fortunes. Walter's baleful influence with the king ultimately led to the downfall of the kingdom.[1]

When William began his rule, he was faced with a deep division among the ruling elite. On the one hand were the feudalists led by Walter of the Mill, consisting of the leading barons and churchmen who had provided an irresponsible opposition to the crown for decades. On the other hand were the monarchists, loyal supporters of the crown, led by Matthew of Ajello, a lawyer from Salerno in southern Italy, who had served in the government of William I. Matthew had direct experience of the barons' rebellions, having seen his superior, Maio of Bari, assassinated in front of him. Matthew and Walter were bitter rivals.[2]

Recognising the potential threat to the kingdom from the concentration of power in Walter's hands, William made Matthew his vice chancellor, and from early in his reign looked for ways of curbing Walter's power and of reducing his status, short of direct confrontation. Together they hit upon the idea of creating a second archbishopric close to the city to rival that of Palermo. An old Greek church in Monreale was chosen as the site. Monreale, which took its name from Monte Regali (Royal Mountain), had been established as a royal park by Roger II, and stood just seven kilometres away in the hills above the city. In this initiative William and Matthew were supported by the pope, who saw it as a means of acquiring more control over the Sicilian church.[3]

The cathedral of Monreale was thus a royal foundation established for political reasons. The founding legend circulating at the time told a different story. According to this, William was out hunting in the hills when he stopped for a rest and fell asleep. Here he had a dream in which the Madonna appeared to him, telling him of treasure buried by his father and ordering him to use it to build a cathedral in her honour. This story will have helped William justify spending so much money on the project.

BUILDING OF THE CATHEDRAL

In 1174 came the foundation of the immense Benedictine abbey at Monreale, dedicated to the Assumption of the Virgin Mary. William, religious by nature, had grown up surrounded by the sumptuous chapels in Palermo created by his forebears. He was in a hurry to make his mark and the building at Monreale was largely completed by 1183, when the pope gave it an archbishopric. Work on the interior continued until 1189. It was William's greatest act of patronage and the largest monument built by the Normans in Sicily.

Designed in a mix of eastern and western styles, with a combination of Greek, Arab and Norman influences, the abbey is famous for its extensive mosaic decoration showing scenes from the Old and New Testaments in brilliant colours. The effect is one of a gigantic picture gallery. According to an authority on the subject, Otto Demus, the mosaics were created by master craftsmen from Byzantium between 1183 and 1189.[4] There are also some personal touches. One mosaic featuring Thomas Becket, recently martyred for his stand against the English king, Henry II, was included possibly at the request of Joanna, William's English wife and Henry's daughter. Thomas, in his stand against the English king, had several influential supporters in Sicily. Joanna may have wanted it included as penance for her father's crime. In another scene, William is shown dedicating a model of the cathedral to the Madonna. The most powerful image, which dominates the central apse, is that of Christ Pantocrator (the Almighty).

A monastery was built next to the cathedral, with a large set of cloisters that feature a wealth of sculptured columns and capitals. The columns may have come from a Roman villa in southern Italy. The elegant twin columns are decorated with fanciful carvings of human heads, animals and birds, some of which echo images from the mosaics in the abbey. In one corner of the cloisters stands an unusual, Muslim-style fountain. The cloisters still project a strong sense of peace and tranquillity.

The abbot appointed to rule the complex was assigned a hundred monks from Salerno. He was granted sole responsibility, outside the jurisdiction of the Sicilian clergy. To provide revenue for the new cathedral, and to ensure its independence, property was taken from Walter's portfolio and handed over to the abbot. More property and privileges were lavished on the monastery, including the town of Corleone, land in Apulia and fisheries on the coast.

Not to be outdone, as work progressed at Monreale, Walter set about rebuilding the cathedral in Palermo. While he was unable to compete with the resources put to work at Monreale, he nevertheless left an impressive monument. Making use of Arab craftsmen, he created a building the outline of which we see today, complete with Gothic towers and arches and Islamic-style decoration on the facade.

EPILOGUE

William did not long outlive the building of his cathedral, for he died in 1189 at the age of thirty-six. Walter had used his influence at court, against the advice of Matthew, to convince the king to agree to the marriage of his aunt, Constance, to Henry, son of the German emperor, Frederick Barbarossa. So, when William died childless, his kingdom passed to Henry. The Normans attempted to keep their independence, but in 1194 Henry invaded Sicily with his German army, and in a ruthless campaign brought an end to the Norman kingdom.

The invasion by Henry was one of the worst disasters to befall Sicily in its entire history. The three years during which Henry ruled Sicily were characterised by violent reprisals against the Norman elite and the systematic plundering of Sicily's wealth. From being a prosperous, independent kingdom, the island became an outpost on the edge of the German empire, described by a contemporary chronicler as a cauldron of the lost.[5]

By the time of the German invasion, Walter and Matthew had both died, and Joanna had left for France and a second marriage. Bartholomew, Walter's brother, succeeded him as Archbishop of Palermo until the arrival of the Germans who sent him back to Agrigento.

For his gentle character and peaceful reign, historians later dubbed William II, 'the Good', a title he surely did not deserve. Through his poor judgement of foreign affairs, he gave away his kingdom to Germany.

After the death of its founder, the cathedral at Monreale rapidly lost its power and prestige. Its importance declined with its property dispersed, while Palermo's cathedral re-emerged as the seat of the leading archbishopric. After the German invasion, Monreale became the sepulchre not only of its founder but also of the entire Norman kingdom.

The chief protagonists in this story were buried in their cathedrals where their tombs can be seen today, William's, elaborate in white marble at Monreale, Walter's, a stone sarcophagus, in the crypt at Palermo.

FREDERICK II AND THE
SICILIAN POETS

Sicily is well known in modern times for its creative writers, two of whom, the playwright Luigi Pirandello and the poet Salvatore Quasimodo, received Nobel Prizes for literature. Not so well known are the Sicilian poets of the thirteenth century who, building upon the Romance tradition and the legacy of the Arabs, contributed to the development of a national literature.

Sicily has long been a melting pot of different languages and cultural traditions. When Arabic ceased to be used as a literary language on the island, an important development took place. At the court of Frederick II, poets began to write in the local, popular language. These poets, who became known as the *Scuola Siciliana* (the Sicilian School), were pioneers in the use of the vernacular in literature and provided an inspiration for others to follow. Later, similar experiments took place in mainland Italy, especially in Tuscany, where Dante developed the language that became the basis of modern Italian. In the opinion of Michele Amari, historian of Arab Sicily: 'It may be claimed that Sicily owes the Arabs, and mainland Italy owes Sicily, for the birth of our national poetry'.[1]

FREDERICK II'S COURT

For thirty years, from 1220 to 1250, Frederick II was the most powerful monarch in Europe. His titles included Holy Roman Emperor, King of Germany, King of Jerusalem and King of Sicily. His lands stretched from the North Sea to the Mediterranean to include Germany, northern Italy, Burgundy and the Sicilian kingdom. As the grandson of Frederick Barbarossa, the German emperor, and Roger II, King of Sicily and southern Italy, whose territories were combined under his rule, his was an extraordinary inheritance.

Frederick was the son of Henry VI, the German emperor, and Constance, daughter of Roger II, who inherited the Sicilian kingdom after William II died childless. Orphaned as a child, Frederick was brought up by guardians in Palermo, under the protection of the pope. His early years were spent in the Norman Palace, with its Muslim servants, from whom he learnt Arabic. A natural linguist, Frederick also spoke French, German and Greek and acquired a knowledge of Latin. Roaming the streets of Palermo as a boy, he conversed with the local population in the Sicilian dialect.

A man of immense energy and ability, Frederick took a close interest in the government of his diverse empire. In Germany, he ruled through local princes, while in Sicily he established a centralised administration backed by an efficient bureaucracy. Throughout his reign, he pursued a bitter struggle with the papacy. The popes could not accept an empire which united Germany with southern Italy, leaving the Papal States isolated in the middle. Frederick, for his part, scandalised orthodox opinion by his libertine lifestyle and his public statements, which according to the church included that the world had been deceived by three imposters, Moses, Jesus Christ and Muhammad.

Possibly due to his insecure childhood, when he was looked after by untrustworthy guardians, Frederick could be brutal. Two of the people closest to him, his son Henry and his adviser Piero della Vigna, committed suicide rather than continue to face his anger. After his death, an English chronicler referred to Frederick as *stupor mundi* (wonder of the world), an epithet which has stuck to him ever since.

Clever and cultured, Frederick attracted talented people to his court. These included Piero della Vigna, the emperor's long-term adviser and administrator, Hermann von Salza, Grand Master of the Teutonic Knights, Berardo, Archbishop of Palermo and the Scottish philosopher and astrologer, Michael Scot. The court combined different roles which included being a centre of political power, a social centre of elegance and high fashion and a centre for the arts, especially in music and literature, with Frederick playing an enthusiastic part.

Palermo ceased to be the permanent base for the court, as it had been under the Norman kings. Instead, Apulia, in southern Italy, where Frederick built himself several castles, became the emperor's preferred place of residence. Given the disparate nature of the empire, the court was frequently on the move, taking with it a vast caravan of people and equipment. The imperial entourage was designed to impress as it travelled from city to city on government business. First there came an advance guard of Arab cavalry followed by mounted knights and courtiers in colourful costumes. Behind them came the emperor's personal bodyguard, a detachment of black Muslim soldiers, then personal servants, dancing girls, camels, elephants and a display of falcons. In the centre, on a black thoroughbred, rode the emperor himself.

THE RISE OF VERNACULAR LITERATURE

The lasting achievement of Frederick's court was in the field of poetry. Palermo became influenced by the Provençal poets, who were writing lyric love poems at this time. These poems, along with the songs of the troubadours, celebrated the sentiments of the chivalrous knight and his idealised love of a lady. They became popular around the courts of Europe at a time when knights left on long pilgrimages to the Holy Land, taking part in the Crusades and leaving their women behind.

When Frederick was in Palermo during 1233–34, a group of courtiers began experimenting with poems on the theme of courtly love. They were not professional poets, but intellectuals who held other jobs and came from different parts of the kingdom, several from eastern Sicily. The difference was that, using the Arab and Provençal traditions as a starting point, they wrote in the local vernacular, the Sicilian dialect. This was the language of the streets, a synthesis of the varied cultures on the island as spoken in the street markets of Palermo, which Frederick had learnt as a boy.

These poets, who numbered around thirty, were led by Frederick and his adviser, Piero della Vigna, both of whom contributed their own poems. Together they turned the vernacular tongue into a new literary language, which was developed during Frederick's reign and continued by his son Manfred, who followed his father to become King of Sicily.

The emergence of the Sicilian dialect as a literary language reflected social change on the island. Under the Normans, when the Arabs made a major contribution to the island's culture, the language of poetry was Arabic. Frederick was personally at ease with Arab culture, having been brought up in the Muslim environment of the Norman Palace. But he faced serious challenges to his authority by revolts from the Arab community. He decided upon an extreme measure and deported to Lucera, a purpose-built city in Apulia in southern Italy, some 15–20,000 Arabs. Lucera, where Frederick had built himself a castle, became a Muslim ghetto containing the emperor's troops and servants. From around 1225, following the deportation, the Arabs played no more part in the story of Sicily.

THE POETS AND THEIR WORK
The Sicilian School holds a unique place in the island's cultural history. Not only did its poets launch a new literary language, but they invented new forms of poetry which had a major impact upon the literary world. The first of these was the *canzone*, a lyric poem suited to a musical setting, which played a central part in the courtly

entertainments of the time. Even more influential was the invention of the sonnet, a poem of fourteen lines which rhymed to a strict scheme, and which went on to be made famous by Petrarch, Dante, Milton and Shakespeare.

Giacomo da Lentini, a notary from Catania, emerged as the outstanding poet of the group. Admired by Dante, Giacomo is considered to have been the inventor of the sonnet. Some forty poems by Giacomo have survived, including one entitled *A l'aire claro ò vista ploggia dare* ('I have seen a clear sky give rain').[2]

Other poets, such as Rinaldo d'Aquino, Mazzeo di Ricco and Guido delle Colonne, explored similar themes examining romantic love with its highs and lows. They used similes drawn from nature comparing the experience of love to a ship tossed in a stormy sea or a clear, bright morning turning into a cloudy day. Unusually for the times, some of the poems were written from the point of view of a woman. Frederick, himself, tried his hand at this form of poetry, seven examples of which have survived.

Some poignant verses were written by Frederick's illegitimate son, Enzo, who was captured in battle and imprisoned in Bologna, from where he never escaped. While his father was still alive, Enzo kept up his hopes of being ransomed and freed.

The poets of the Sicilian School were at the forefront of the use of vernacular literature. They established a body of work which served as an impetus to mainland Italy where Dante developed the Tuscan dialect that became the basis of modern Italian. When Dante began to write the *Divine Comedy* in 1308, the first book to be written in the vernacular language, he freely admitted the contribution made by the Sicilian poets. In his work *De vulgari eloquentia* ('Concerning vernacular eloquence'), Dante acknowledged that vernacular poetry in Italy had first appeared at the courts of Frederick II and his son Manfred, in Sicily.[3] The origins of the Italian language and Italian poetry can thus be traced back to Palermo and the Sicilian School of the thirteenth century.

EPILOGUE

Frederick's empire did not survive for long after his death in 1250. Charles of Anjou, supported by the pope, invaded southern Italy with his French army in 1265, defeating in battle first Manfred, and then Conradin, Frederick's sons. Charles captured Lucera, dispersing the surviving Arabs to the Muslim territories. He proceeded to rule Sicily until 1282, when the revolt known as the Sicilian Vespers threw his French army off the island. Sicily then fell under the control of the Spanish, who ruled the island in one form or another and with some gaps, until the arrival of Garibaldi in 1860.

While the visual arts flourished in Sicily under the Spanish, promoting the Catholic faith and decorating the palaces of the aristocracy, it was not until the nineteenth and twentieth centuries that Sicilian literature once again held a position of national importance.

7

DOMENICO CARACCIOLO,
THE REFORMING VICEROY

Domenico Caracciolo stands out in the history of Sicily as the viceroy who attempted to reform society in the interests of the common people. This claim can be made for very few rulers of Sicily. Independent minded and filled with liberal ideas absorbed during his time as a diplomat in Paris, Caracciolo applied progressive international standards to the backward conditions of Sicily. Unfortunately, his temperament worked against him and his brash confrontational approach met with implacable hostility from the Sicilian aristocracy, who saw his reforms as a direct challenge to their privileges.

The contradictions in Caracciolo's character were noted by the Sicilian historian, Francesco Renda:

> Domenico Caracciolo, marquis of Villamaina, was the most famous viceroy of Sicily, the most loved and the most celebrated by historians. He was also the most opposed and the most reviled. Such a complex personality is difficult to interpret.[1]

As viceroy of Sicily from 1781 to 1786, appointed by the Spanish Bourbon king, Ferdinand, Caracciolo did achieve some lasting reforms which, however, fell far short of his ambitions.

The viceroyalty of Caracciolo, described by Renda as 'The Great Enterprise', is the story of a liberal reformer meeting the harsh reality of Sicily on the eve of the French Revolution.

BACKGROUND

The attitudes of the aristocracy which Caracciolo came up against in Sicily had been formed over centuries, and had set rock hard, creating a solid barrier to reform. The aristocracy controlled the island's wealth through their large estates, the *latifondi*, which were worked by peasants to produce the grain which had long been Sicily's main export. Families like the Butera, Trabia and Ventimiglia owned great tracts of land and lived like royalty. The peasants worked under conditions little better than slavery and were often forced to travel long distances to get to work. As a class, peasants were too weak and too downtrodden to seek improvement in their conditions. The aristocracy dominated the political and legal systems and, on their estates, had complete control over their workforce. Society was polarised between the wealthy aristocracy, on the one hand, and the peasants and the urban poor, on the other.

This privileged position had been accepted by the Spanish viceroys in order to keep the peace, as the number of Spanish troops assigned to Sicily was not very great. In this way, the barons managed to maintain their feudal privileges while ignoring their obligations to the state. At a time when elsewhere in Europe the power of the barons was being curtailed, in Sicily it was given free rein.

By the mid-eighteenth century, the barons had mostly abandoned their estates in the country to live in the cities, primarily Palermo, where the viceroy had his court. Here they built their palaces, financed by loans against their estates, and lived lives of conspicuous luxury. They became absentee landlords, delegating the management of their estates to a class of manager known as *gabelloti*, who were middlemen out for personal gain. The result was disastrous for agriculture, the backbone of the Sicilian economy. The efficiency and the productivity of the estates declined, and the barons went bankrupt under the burden of their debts.

The Spanish Inquisition was still present in Sicily in the mid-eighteenth century, though it was largely inactive, with the last execution taking place in 1732. First introduced to Sicily in

1487, the Inquisition exerted a malign influence over society for nearly 300 years with the aim of ensuring religious orthodoxy. The prime targets were Jews and Muslims, including those who had converted to Catholicism, as well as Protestants and minorities of all descriptions. Countless atrocities were carried out in the name of the church including executions, torture and long sentences of imprisonment in gaol or in the galleys. Evidence of what prisoners endured can be seen in graffiti, written in several languages in the cells of the Palazzo Chiaramonte, which served as the Inquisition's headquarters in Palermo.

In 1734 the Spanish Bourbons captured the Kingdoms of Naples and Sicily from the Austrians, re-establishing Spanish rule over these territories which they had held for centuries. Sicily, used to the Spanish, welcomed the invasion. The two kingdoms were united under Charles, the son of Philip V of Spain, but were governed as separate entities. When Charles inherited the Spanish crown, he left Naples and Sicily to his youngest son, Ferdinand. Once Ferdinand came of age, he married Maria Carolina, daughter of Maria Theresa, Empress of Austria, and assumed the crowns of the two territories which he ruled, except for a period during the Napoleonic Wars, until 1825. The territories became known as the Two Sicilies, as opposed to the Kingdom of the Two Sicilies, which was founded by Ferdinand in 1816.

Although both ruled by Ferdinand, Naples and Sicily continued to be governed according to their separate laws and traditions. By European standards, they were backward territories with weak economies, dominated by the nobility. Naples, however, was a major European city with a population nearing 400,000, about twice the size of Palermo. While reforms had been introduced in Naples by Charles before he left for Madrid, Sicily had been left behind.

Ferdinand showed little interest in government, preferring to spend his time hunting and fishing. The queen, Maria Carolina, was very influential at court, standing in for her husband. From 1776

to 1786 the government in Naples was run by the prime minister
and Caracciolo's rival, the Marquis of Sambuca, a Sicilian aristocrat,
who held conservative views. Alongside him as Minister for Marine
Affairs was an Englishman, Sir John Acton.

THE MAN

Domenico Caracciolo was born in Spain on 2 October 1715, to
the Marquis of Villamaina, a Neapolitan nobleman, and his Spanish
wife. His education and early career took place in Naples where he
was influenced by the liberal, anti-clerical thinkers fashionable at
the time. As a younger son, he could not inherit the family estate,
so embarked upon a career in the law. At the age of thirty-seven,
he was sent on a diplomatic mission to Turin by the king. Further
missions to London and Paris followed.

Caracciolo was a man of forbidding looks and a massive
presence, with the ability to deal at the highest levels in society.
He was persuasive, energetic and highly literate. His friends noted
his lively, penetrating intelligence, his gaiety and naturalness of
expression. He never married or had children, and little is known
about his private life except that he carried on liaisons with women
of the theatre. He was a great letter writer, whose voluminous
correspondence provides a commentary on his career, quotations
from which appear in Angus Campbell's, *Sicily and the Enlightenment,
the World of Domenico Caracciolo, Thinker and Reformer.*[2]

At home in the salons of Paris, he became friends with some of the
leading figures of his day, including Voltaire, Rousseau and Mirabeau.
He became influenced by the rationalist and scientific approach to
society promoted by the Enlightenment. This encouraged him to
develop progressive ideas on how society should be run, in areas
such as social justice, sound trading practices, equitable taxes, an
effective parliament and freedom of the individual. In the context
of the developed states of northern Europe, his ideas were sound
and practical.

When in May 1780 he was appointed viceroy in Sicily, it came as a shock, as he had hoped to live out his days in Paris where he had spent the last ten years. Caracciolo was an intellectual and an idealist, with no experience of government, convinced of the power of rational thought. He was quite unprepared for what awaited him in Palermo.

THE VICEROY

When the sixty-six-year-old Caracciolo arrived in Palermo in October 1781, having stalled his departure from Paris for over a year, he was immediately thrust into a round of formal meetings, culminating in his installation in the royal palace, former seat of the Norman kings, as viceroy. Palermo's society operated in an environment of rigid formality in public ceremonies, designed to underline the status of the barons and the church. From the beginning, Caracciolo refused to bow to the rules, and ignoring protocol made it clear he did not support the establishment.

The administration that Caracciolo inherited in Palermo was inefficient and corrupt, with a tax burden that fell mostly upon the poor and a food market that was dominated by monopolies and rackets. The price of bread was critical to the poor, leading to riots on many occasions. To underline his authority, Caracciolo rapidly introduced a series of minor reforms. To do so he set up a private office bypassing the usual bureaucratic channels. The reforms included the outlawing of dangerous sports, controlling betting, banning anonymous denouncements of crimes and the cleaning up of urban rubbish. The army was instructed to report directly to himself, while members of the Inquisition were forbidden to carry arms.

Caracciolo faced formidable obstacles. Sicily, as a separate kingdom, had an ancient constitution which had to be respected. Parliament, a semi-feudal institution founded by the Normans, played an essential role in raising the taxes demanded by Naples. Hostility from the barons could only be overcome with the support of the king, who was reluctant to put his tax revenues at risk.

Sambuca, the prime minister in Naples, as a member of the Sicilian aristocracy, was opposed to many of the reforms.

Ignoring the obstacles and displaying a remarkable lack of diplomacy for an ex-diplomat, Caracciolo ploughed ahead. Reforms came thick and fast, unheard of in Palermo. He took initiatives to improve trade, simplifying excise duties, establishing central markets and starting a programme of road building to link Palermo to Messina and Agrigento. Within Palermo, the main streets were paved in marble. A new law freed the peasants to be able to work for themselves as well as for the barons. At the same time, he scandalised society by taking as his companion Marina Balducci, a singer he had known in Paris. The formal society of Palermo, which was used to easy-going viceroys who did not rock the boat, reacted by heaping criticism upon the new viceroy and blocking his initiatives at every turn.

In a letter to a friend written on 21 December 1781, Caracciolo described the difficulties he faced, with Sicilian society's division into rich aristocrats and the mass of the poor leaving little room for compromise.[3] As the environment in Palermo became increasingly hostile, Caracciolo looked for radical ways of re-organising Sicily. He considered moving the government to Messina, the port-city on the far north-east of the island, facing the mainland. An earthquake which damaged the city in February 1783, killing 617 people, put an end to these plans.

To save money, which could be used for reconstructing Messina, he considered reducing the elaborate annual festival in honour of Santa Rosalia, Palermo's patron saint, from five to three days. Caracciolo, who was by nature anti-clerical, did not like religious processions and found the costs excessive. This event, known as the *festino*, was hugely popular at all levels of society and Caracciolo's proposal was met with outrage. So bad did public sentiment become that a sign appeared near the palace displaying the message *o festa o testa,* meaning 'either the festival or your head'. The king was forced to intervene and overrule Caracciolo.

The abolition of the Holy Office of the Inquisition in Sicily was an easier task, as this had the support of the king and his prime minister, Sambuca. In March 1782, the Inquisition's documents were seized, its three remaining prisoners released, and the office closed. In the following year, a selection of books and documents of historical interest having been saved, the whole paraphernalia of the Inquisition, including its archives, vestments and instruments of torture, was burnt outside the Palazzo Chiaramonte in a blaze that lasted for twenty-four hours.

Caracciolo's major battle came over land reform. While the barons and the church owned most of the property, both classes enjoyed historic exemptions from tax. The Austrians, under Maria Theresa, had successfully introduced a land survey in Lombardy which allowed for an updated taxation system to be applied to land ownership. Not only would such a reform reduce the privileges of the elite, but it would also increase the tax revenues for Naples. The implementation of land reform became an obsession for Caracciolo, on which he worked tirelessly. The king, prompted by Sambuca, prevaricated, and fearing a showdown with the barons, failed to give his full support. Caracciolo, after all his efforts, was left worn out, a sick man, and he began to warn Naples that he was ready for retirement.

A crisis over Sicily's grain supply, with the potential for causing riots, was resolved by Caracciolo, proving once again his administrative capabilities. This was followed unexpectedly in January 1786 by an offer from the king to take up the position of prime minister in Naples. The incumbent, Sambuca, who had held the position for ten years, had fallen out of favour with the queen. Caracciolo, who was widely respected, had international standing and proven loyalty to the crown. He accepted the post with alacrity, replacing his long-term rival, Sambuca, who retired from public life. As prime minister in Naples, Caracciolo held the top government post in the Two Sicilies until he died three years later. In Palermo, Caracciolo is remembered by a small piazza in his name in the Vucciria district.

EPILOGUE

Caracciolo's achievements in Sicily were remarkable given the immense opposition he faced from the aristocracy and the lack of support he received from Naples. His determination and ability to get things done in hostile circumstances were extraordinary. Through his leadership, the barons were forced to accept that change was on the agenda, while the poor were helped both in terms of employment conditions and with the price of food. The island's infrastructure was improved through a programme of road building. Culturally, Caracciolo assisted Palermo by supporting the Accademia, which became the nucleus of the city's university, and by diverting funds from the Inquisition into creating the Botanic Gardens and other scientific institutions.

On the other hand, while his policies were sound, reflecting an enlightened view of society, the implementation was flawed. Operating in an unfamiliar territory that was a hotbed of prejudice, he tried to rush through his reforms without preparation or consultation. Caracciolo's impetuous approach alienated practically everyone and limited what he could achieve.

As prime minister in Naples, Caracciolo chose as his successor in Sicily a Neapolitan, the Prince of Caramanico. A convinced reformer with experience in northern Europe, as viceroy Caramanico applied an accommodating approach to the opposition. This enabled him to persuade parliament to introduce a measure of land reform. In this way, Caracciolo's 'Great Enterprise' continued for a few years.

The outbreak of the French Revolution, and the Napoleonic Wars that followed, brought a halt to these developments. Bourbon rule in Sicily was suspended as Britain became involved in the island through the presence of its fleet in the Mediterranean, commanded by Rear-Admiral Horatio Nelson. Reform in Sicily took another step forward when from 1806 to 1815 the island became a British Protectorate.

8

THE BRITISH WINE MERCHANTS

By the eighteenth century, Britain was well-established as an international trading nation. Goods arrived in London from all over the world, while in the far-flung colonies British entrepreneurs developed flourishing trading ventures, among them the East India Company and the Hudson's Bay Company of Canada. Full of confidence, the British went out into the world to seek their fortunes.

Among the sectors in which the British engaged was the wine trade. Wine had long been popular with English aristocrats, who imported favourite clarets and burgundies for their own consumption. The growing middle class developed a taste for fortified wine, which was less expensive and had the advantage of travelling well. The expanding home market led British entrepreneurs to establish businesses in the wine-producing regions of Madeira, Jerez and Oporto. In this way, madeira, sherry and port became widely available in Britain and elsewhere. The wine from Marsala provided another product for these markets.

The British colony, which grew up in Sicily around the Marsala wine trade, lived through turbulent times. Like their counterparts in India, the British in Sicily had to contend with revolution, disease and a forbiddingly hot climate. The colony, which lasted for around 150 years from the 1770s to the 1920s, witnessed the effects of the Napoleonic Wars, Sicily's revolt against the Spanish Bourbons, outbreaks of cholera, Garibaldi's campaign to free Sicily, unification with Italy and the impact of Mussolini's fascist government. A flavour of these times, based on contemporary correspondence, is provided by Raleigh Trevelyan in his book, *Princes under the Volcano*.[1]

JOHN WOODHOUSE, THE PIONEER

The origins of the British wine trade in Marsala can be traced back to the early 1770s when a merchant from Liverpool, John Woodhouse, arrived in the city. It was a chance visit, for Woodhouse had come to Sicily to buy raw materials and was sailing down the west coast of the island when a storm forced his ship into the port of Marsala. At a tavern he was offered some local wine and was impressed by its quality.

Marsala, with its hot, dry climate, had a long tradition in wine making. The local speciality was a wine known as *vino perpetuo*, which was made from white grape varieties stored in barrels and topped up annually with the new vintage. Sometimes the wine was sweetened with cooked grape must. Woodhouse was struck by its similarity to madeira, then popular in England. He set about preparing a consignment of the wine to be sent back to Liverpool.

Woodhouse had a flair for business. His first consignment, which was despatched in 1773, consisted of fifty pipes, a term derived from the Portuguese word, *pipa,* meaning barrel, which contained on average 450 litres. To ensure that the wine travelled well, Woodhouse added two per cent of brandy to the blend, giving it 15–20 per cent alcohol by volume, an innovation that became a hallmark of the product. The wine was well-received in England and sold rapidly.

In 1787 Woodhouse was joined in Sicily by his son, also called John, and together they laid the foundations of their business. Their strategy brought a revolution in wine growing to the Marsala region. Small landowners were encouraged to grow the white grape varieties – Grillo, Inzolia and Catarratto – needed to make the Marsala product. Loans were offered for workers to clear the land to plant vines, while a central market for the wine was established.

The Woodhouses built roads, supplied transport and constructed the jetty in Marsala's port to accommodate merchant ships. It was at this jetty that Garibaldi landed his men in 1860.

In Marsala, they built themselves a walled enclosure, known as a *baglio*, to contain their house as well as storage for the wine. This was necessary as protection from pirates who raided the Sicilian coast from North Africa. Their *baglio* was a large structure with high walls, built facing the port for easy access to the merchant ships.

In 1798 Rear-Admiral Horatio Nelson brought his fleet into the Mediterranean to protect British interests and, at the Battle of the Nile, defeated the French navy. When later in the year the French, aided by Neapolitan rebels, threatened Naples, the Bourbon king and queen, Ferdinand and Maria Carolina, were brought to Palermo in Nelson's flagship. The British ambassador to Naples, Sir William Hamilton and his wife Emma were also on board. It was in Sicily that Nelson and Emma began their love affair.

The Woodhouses met Nelson when the British fleet was recuperating off the Sicilian coast. The men became friends and Nelson was introduced to their Marsala wine. It was a breakthrough for the Woodhouse business, as Nelson followed up by placing an order of 200 pipes for his fleet. Two years later, Nelson placed an even larger order, for 500 pipes. These orders, combined with Nelson's endorsement, meant that the business grew so rapidly that it could hardly keep up with demand.[2]

The Woodhouses were single-minded, choosing to live in western Sicily but showing no interest in Sicilian culture or in expatriate life in Palermo. Together father and son invented Marsala wine for export, first creating the product and then providing the capital and commercial knowhow. Their business model proved so successful that it was copied by the other British merchants who followed them.

When John Woodhouse, Junior died aged fifty-eight in around 1826, his brothers Will and Sam, who had followed him to Sicily, inherited the business. Neither shared their brother's ability and both died within ten years. While the Woodhouse brand lived on, renowned for its quality, the entrepreneurial spirit was no longer there.

BENJAMIN INGHAM, THE TYCOON

In the face of continued French aggression, the British and King Ferdinand came to an agreement for the duration of the Napoleonic Wars. In return for providing a base for their fleet, the British undertook to defend Sicily from the French, and from 1806 to 1815 the island became a British protectorate. An annual subsidy was paid to the king, and a contingent of British troops arrived, which varied in number year by year from 10,000 to 17,000. For Sicily, whose economy was deeply depressed, the presence of the British military contingent, augmented by consular officials, merchants and their families, provided a welcome boost. Sicilians could earn money by supplying the British community with everyday necessities, such as food and drink, while the dockyards were employed to carry out repairs to the British fleet.

Into this environment in 1806 stepped a twenty-two-year-old Yorkshireman, Benjamin Ingham. He came from a family in Leeds, which owned a clothing business, and was looking for new opportunities. He had recently suffered a failed business venture, following which his fiancée had left him. He was impressed with what he found in Sicily, with British interests established on the island and the Marsala wine trade in expansion. His first move was to get his brother, Joshua, to visit Spain and Portugal to study methods of producing fortified wine. He then went to Boston, in America, to appoint agents to handle imports from Sicily.

In Sicily, Ingham built himself a *baglio* in Marsala, close to the Woodhouse establishment, and began his own wine production. This was developed on a large scale, with rough wine bought in bulk from the local landowners and matured in the wooden barrels. The wine was then blended for consistency, sweetened and fortified.

Ingham introduced scientific production methods based upon the
solera system from Spain. This involved using a stack of barrels at
least three high, in which a small amount of wine was drawn out of
the bottom row, then topped up from the barrels above, to create an
aging process of anything from five to twenty years. A flourishing
export business to Britain developed.

As his business grew, Ingham needed reliable assistants. He
appealed to his sister in Britain to send him one of his nephews.
William Whitaker arrived, aged eighteen, only to die four years later,
probably of typhus. Another nephew, Joseph, followed him to Sicily,
who settled down on the island and married Sophia Sanderson, the
daughter of the British consul in Marsala. Joseph Whitaker became
a leading figure in the family business.

In the post-war period, Ingham, who was famous for his fiery
temper, drove his business forward. By 1837 his *baglio* in Marsala
employed sixty men and included a distillery to make brandy for
fortifying the wine, a carpenter's workshop to produce the casks
and a *palmento*, the traditional Sicilian trough in which to tread the
grapes. The *baglio* with its high walls and no windows, dominated
by towers at the corners, looked more like a fortress than a winery.

Gradually, Ingham extended his business interests to include
olive oil, textiles and sulphur, a commodity mined in Sicily which
was in great demand for industrial processes. To support his trading
activities, he became involved in shipping, finance and insurance.
What started as a simple trade in wine, developed into a diversified
business empire.

Ingham, who was a sociable man, preferred Palermo to Marsala
and made it his principal place of residence. Palermo, the capital
of Sicily with a population of 200,000, was dominated by the
aristocratic families. Ingham joined a lively social round of
expatriates and international visitors who were entertained in the
palaces of the aristocracy. Unlike the Woodhouse clan, and most of
the British community, Ingham learnt the local language and joined
Sicilian society, forming a long-term relationship with Alessandra,

the Duchess of Santa Rosalia. His status was recognised by being made a baron.

The period in which Ingham was building his business also saw the rise of a Sicilian entrepreneur, Vincenzo Florio. Florio began in the tuna fish canning business, expanding his interests to include textiles, machinery and sulphur. He also joined Ingham in the Marsala wine trade, building a *baglio* for himself near the port in Marsala.

Benjamin Ingham retired in 1851, leaving his business empire to be run by Joseph Whitaker and his nephew, Ben Ingham. He kept control of the finances, and wary of investing more in Sicily, placed his profits in America, where he bought real estate in New York and Michigan. In central Palermo he built himself a palatial townhouse which later became the Grand Hotel et des Palmes, one of the city's most luxurious hotels. Opposite his house he built an Anglican chapel for use by the British community.

According to a contemporary estimate, in the 1850s the total output of Marsala wine was 30 to 40,000 pipes per year, around half of which was exported to Britain and its colonies, the rest to a variety of destinations including America and Australia. Ingham's wine business accounted for more than half of this output.[3]

Benjamin Ingham died in 1861, aged seventy-six, the richest man in Sicily and possibly in the whole of Italy. A classic nineteenth-century capitalist, Ingham was a man who saw his opportunity and exploited it with determination. He left an international business and a huge fortune to his heirs.

JOSEPH (PIP) WHITAKER, THE ARCHAEOLOGIST

The inheritance was complex, involving the members of a large family and assets spread out in Britain and America, as well as in Sicily. Joseph's second son, William, who was nineteen, emerged as the main beneficiary. Other members of the family received legacies, while the business passed to Joseph Whitaker and Ben Ingham for their lifetimes. After Ben died in 1872, Joseph took control of the business, as William showed no interest in it.

Joseph Whitaker and his wife Sophia had twelve children, nine of whom chose to live in England. Joseph, junior, known to his family and friends as Pip, was born in Sicily in 1850. He grew up fluent in Italian and in the dialect of Palermo. Together with his brothers Joshua (Joss) and Robert (Bob), Pip made his life in Sicily. Educated in England, he was studious and reserved by nature and, unlike his forebears, not a natural businessman. He was in many ways a typical Victorian gentleman, whose interests included wildlife and shooting. He began work at Marsala at the age of seventeen, at a time when the extended family *baglio*, well-defended against bandits, employed 300 men and included 30 warehouses.

In 1883, Pip married Caterina Scalia, known as Tina, a young English woman born in London of Italian parents. Her father, Alfonso, came from a well-established family in Palermo. Tina, though intelligent and a keen observer of the Sicilian political scene, was a difficult woman, snobbish and obsessed with her social position. They had two daughters, Norina and Delia.

When a year later Joseph Whitaker (senior) died, the three Whitaker brothers, Joss, Pip and Bob, inherited the business interests and property in Sicily, making them enormously wealthy. It was decided that Joss, the eldest brother, should run the business with Pip and Bob as partners. Joss was unsuited for the role of managing a complex international business, having neither the dynamism nor the necessary business skills. Fortunately for the family, competent managers had emerged within the business who were able to keep it running.

The brothers established themselves in Palermo in a manner appropriate to their status. Joss and his wife Effie built themselves a palace in Via Cavour in the Venetian-Gothic style. Bob and his wife Maude took over the luxurious Villa Sophia, built by Bob's parents. The grandest property of all, called the Villa Malfitano, was built by

Pip and Tina on a big estate to the north-west of the city. In these
mansions the brothers lived like princes, each with a large retinue
of staff, while their wives organised the social round to entertain
the rich and famous who flocked to Palermo.

This was the period, known as the Belle Époque, when Palermo
became a destination for European royalty and other celebrities.
The city's warm climate and exotic Mediterranean environment
appealed to northern Europeans who made it a fashionable place
to visit. By the early twentieth century, Villa Malfitano was the hub
of English society in Palermo, with Tina a leading hostess. The villa
was set in a large park, tended by fourteen gardeners, and filled
with trees imported from Asia and Africa. It contained reception
rooms in the styles of Louis XV and XVI, a ballroom, a huge dining
room, a billiard room and a conservatory. Elaborate furnishings
came from England and France with tapestries from Brussels.

Vying with the Whitakers, in both social and business terms,
was the Florio family. Ignazio inherited the business in 1891, which
had grown substantially to include merchant shipping. At the age
of twenty-four, handsome and dashing, he married Franca Jacona
di San Giuliano, renowned for her beauty. She was a woman of
character and charm who became Palermo's most famous hostess,
entertaining European high society at the Villino Florio, designed in
the fashionable Liberty style.

Pip, however, was increasingly dissatisfied with life. The main
problem was his marriage to Tina, which was not a happy one,
as their personalities and interests were so different. Nor did he
find the social round and business commitments fulfilling. In this
mid-life crisis, Pip turned to his scholarly interests and became
engrossed in the Punic civilisation, an important site of which
was supposed to exist on the small island of San Pantaleo, near
Marsala. From time to time, artefacts found on the site had been
shown to him and had whetted his appetite. The interest in Punic
culture and the exploration of San Pantaleo became the passion
of his life.

Pip immersed himself in the study of the Phoenicians and Carthaginians, consulting the ancient writers and works by contemporary historians. He visited Tunisia to see the site of Carthage and noted similarities to the geography of San Pantaleo. While in Tunisia, he took the time to follow up another of his interests, ornithology, and to collect specimens as well as to write his book, *Birds of Tunisia*, which was published in 1905.[4]

He became convinced that the island of San Pantaleo, situated in a sheltered lagoon near Marsala, was the site of Motya, an important Carthaginian city destroyed in 397 BC by Dionysius I. While other archaeologists, including the internationally renowned Heinrich Schliemann, had visited the site, no one had found firm evidence of its origins. Pip, with the backing of his family fortune, bought out the farmers who lived on the island and became its sole proprietor.

Excavations, which began in the spring of 1906 under the supervision of Professor Antonio Salinas, director of Palermo's archaeological museum, revealed the ruins of fortifications including defensive walls, towers and bastions. The remains of gateways were unearthed, built on massive, squared blocks of stone. Further work discovered burial grounds with evidence of sacrificial victims, a mosaic pavement and a submerged causeway linking the island to the mainland. These finds proved conclusively that this was indeed the site of a fortified Phoenician city, ancient Motya, as described by the Sicilian Greek historian, Diodorus.

Salinas encouraged Pip to build a museum at the site to house his finds, which in due course amounted to over 4,000 items. They included vases, terracotta ornaments, statuettes, bronze arrow heads and stelae (stone monuments) with Phoenician inscriptions. Pip also built himself a house at Motya, where he spent an increasing amount of time. Tina, who thought too much time and money were being spent on the project, was dismayed. Work on the site continued until interrupted by First World War.

In 1921 Pip's book on Motya was published, entitled *Motya, A Phoenician Colony in Sicily*, a vivid account of the history and archaeology of the site and its Punic background. The book was well-received in London, where he became a celebrity among international scholars interested in the Punic civilisation.[5]

During the 1920s, the British merchants in Sicily faced increasing difficulties. Already harassed by brigands around Marsala and by the growing mafia threat in Palermo, they were the target of Mussolini's nationalist policies. Pip's world collapsed, as excavations on Motya continued to be blocked, and the family business faced deteriorating trading conditions as political pressure from the fascists intensified. When Cinzano, the Piedmontese vermouth producers, made an offer in 1928, the Whitakers sold the business. The Woodhouse and Florio wine companies were sold in the same year.

When Pip died in 1936, aged eighty-six, he was the subject of a long obituary in *The Times,* which praised his work at Motya and as an ornithologist, and which paid tribute to his ability as a host. Before the war, according to the obituary, there was apparently no house in Europe where one met so distinguished and cosmopolitan society as at Malfitano.

Tina lived on in Rome at the family villa in Monte Parioli, an exclusive residential district. She supported fascism and knew Mussolini. She published a diary and, in 1907, a book entitled *Sicily & England*, a shrewdly observed account of political events in Sicily from 1848 to 1870. She died in 1957 at the age of ninety-eight.[6]

EPILOGUE
While the leading British wine merchants made their fortunes, at the same time they helped Sicily by creating an international market for a local product, and in providing the means to exploit it. The wine trade, built by the British, made a major contribution to the Sicilian economy for 150 years, from the 1770s to the 1920s. The trade established a secure market for the wine from the landowners of western Sicily. Generations of Sicilians benefited from employment in the wine trade and in the different services

which grew up to support it such as transport, shipping and finance. For centuries under the Spanish, trade and commerce on the island had been neglected. The British wine merchants, and their Sicilian counterparts like the Florios, revitalised trade and with their diversified businesses and international connections laid the foundations of Sicily's modern commercial sector.

The Whitakers' daughter, Delia, who died in 1971, left the family's remaining assets in Sicily to the Joseph Whitaker Foundation, with the aim of promoting the study of Punic-Phoenician culture in the Mediterranean. The Foundation's headquarters, at Villa Malfitano in Palermo, are responsible for the site of Motya and its museum, all of which are today open to the public. This was Pip's legacy, the discovery and excavation of Motya, one of the most important Punic sites in the Mediterranean.

Benjamin Ingham's townhouse is today the Grand Hotel et des Palmes, to be found in Palermo's Via Roma. The Anglican chapel, which is still in use, stands opposite. In Via Cavour, towards the seafront, Joss Whitaker's Venetian-Gothic palace can be seen behind the trees, now a police headquarters. The remains of the *bagli*, where the British merchants lived and stored their wine, can be seen along the seafront, opposite the port, in Marsala.

9

THE REVOLUTION OF 1848

Eighteen forty-eight was the year of revolutions in Europe. The first took place in Palermo and others followed in mainland Italy, in Naples, Rome, Venice, Florence and Milan, as well as in France, the German states and central Europe. While they were not directly connected, these revolutions were fuelled by a common desire among citizens for more participation in government and an end to authoritarian rule. The liberal spirit of the French Revolution combined with an upsurge in nationalism to send shock waves through society, creating popular uprisings to challenge the old order.

The revolution in Sicily, known as the *quarantotto* (the forty-eight), offered a unique opportunity for Sicilians to take control of their own destiny. For sixteen months, a group of patriotic and liberal-minded Sicilians fought a heroic but doomed battle for the island's independence from Bourbon rule. While the revolution paved the way for Garibaldi's successful campaign in 1860, the consequences of its failure were far-reaching and reverberate on the island to this day.

BACKGROUND

The Congress of Vienna, which imposed a settlement on Europe after the Napoleonic Wars, re-instated the Bourbon king, Ferdinand, in Naples. After Sicily failed to raise the expected taxes, Ferdinand ignored the provisions of the constitution and dissolved parliament. In 1816 he announced the unification of his kingdoms of Sicily and Naples and introduced a central administration along French lines.

The Kingdom of theTwo Sicilies, as it was now called, was subjected to strong authoritarian rule to impose the will of the king.

During the Napoleonic Wars, Sicilians had experienced more enlightened government under the British, who had given them a new, liberal constitution. The return to repressive government was broadly resisted across Sicilian society. The barons wanted autonomy for the island, middle-class activists sought long-awaited reform, while the peasants and urban poor were desperate for food, land and jobs. The plight of Sicily was viewed sympathetically in Britain and France, as well among the Italian states which were beginning to discuss some form of federation.

In the years that followed, Sicily was in ferment, with Palermo in a constant state of subdued rebellion. In 1820 an armed revolt broke out which was brutally repressed. Ferdinand, proud of his authoritarian government, was reported as saying that he ruled through the three 'f's: *forca, farina e festa* (gallows, bread and festivals). Public hangings were followed by the distribution of bread during elaborate street festivals. The massive prisons built in the major cities, such as the Ucciardone in Palermo, are monuments to Bourbon repression.

When Ferdinand died in 1825, his son Francis came to the throne and proved to be even less adequate than his father. After Francis's death five years later, the throne passed to Ferdinand II, who showed no interest in improving conditions for the poor in Sicily. A short revolt in 1837, following an outbreak of cholera, indicated that powerful social forces were ready to erupt on the island.

REVOLUTION

Despite much plotting by liberals, the revolution was not carefully planned. It began casually when a young man, Francesco Bagnasco, acting on his own, posted an anonymous proclamation on the walls of Palermo on 8 January, inciting citizens to rebellion. He named 12 January, the king's birthday, as the day for action. The authorities took notice, and on the morning of the twelfth, the central squares of the city were occupied by troops. Undeterred, people began to assemble and in Piazza Fieravecchia (today's Piazza Rivoluzione), a riot broke out. Suddenly, shots were fired, and the streets were blocked to prevent the passage of horses and carriages.

The events of the revolution are described by Tina Whitaker, an English woman born in London to Italian parents, in her book *Sicily and England* published in 1907. Her husband, Joseph Whitaker, was a member of the British community in Palermo, whose family fortune was made in the Marsala wine trade. Tina's father, Alfonso Scalia, and her uncle, who came from an old Sicilian family, both played prominent parts in the revolution, as she recorded.

> On hearing the first shots fired, they shouldered their guns and went off with my uncle, Luigi Scalia…For three days and three nights my father was absent from his home, and when he returned, he had made three prisoners, one of them a major in the Neapolitan army.[1]

At the time, the population of Palermo numbered around 200,000, controlled by a Neapolitan force of some 7,000 troops. As the news of the uprising reached nearby towns, groups of armed men arrived to support the struggle, including contingents from Monreale and Partinico. While the Sicilians were highly motivated, the Neapolitans showed little appetite for a fight. Lord Mount Edgcumbe, who was staying in Palermo at the time, noted in his diary: 'When anything like a collision occurred, the military ran away. The troops never could be relied upon to make headway against the insurgents in street fighting.'[2]

On 14 January, a meeting was called in Piazza Fieravecchia to set up a general committee to organise the uprising. The barons and middle-class liberals realised that an opportunity was at hand to achieve their aims of reform and freedom from the Bourbons. They called for Ruggero Settimo to be their leader. Settimo, then seventy years of age, had a reputation as a patriot, who as an ex-admiral had served as Minister of War during the British Protectorate. He was a friend of the British envoy, Sir William Bentinck.

Reinforcements arrived by sea for the Neapolitans who remained, however, closed within their palaces and barracks as the people controlled the streets. To break the stalemate, the Neapolitan commander, Marshal De Sauget, ordered a bombardment of the city centre from the cannons of the Castellammare, the fortress next to the old harbour. This had the effect of further enraging the insurgents who stormed the Royal Palace. The fighting continued to favour the Sicilians as the Neapolitans evacuated their barracks one by one and retreated towards the seafront.

While the Neapolitans were hated for their disregard for civilian casualties, even more hated were the Sicilian police known as the *sbirri*. Responsible for working with the Bourbons, and for denouncing insurgents to the authorities, the *sbirri* were considered traitors. They became a special target, to be hunted down and brutally killed. [3]

On 30 January, the last hard fighting took place in Palermo in the attack on the fortress of Castellammare. Here a core of Neapolitan troops held out until overwhelmed by the insurgents, who included Tina Whitaker's father, Major Alfonso Scalia. The prisons were thrown open, releasing 3,000 prisoners to join the fray. While Palermo led the way in the revolution, hatred of the Bourbons and desperation with the social conditions were such that it soon spread across the island. By the end of February, Catania, Messina, Girgenti, (Agrigento) and many smaller towns were all in revolt.

At the end of March, the Sicilian parliament met for the first time for thirty-three years. The Duke of Serradifalco was elected president of the House of Peers and Vincenzo Fardella, Marquis of Torrearsa, president of the House of Commons. A Provisional Government was formed, led by Ruggero Settimo, with Mariano Stabile as Foreign Minister, Michele Amari as Minister of Finance and Giuseppe La Farina as Minister for War. Committees were set up to provide arms and to maintain food supplies. A national guard was established to keep public order in the cities. Financial support came from businessmen such as Ignazio Florio, as well as from a consignment of Bourbon government bullion which was intercepted and claimed by the insurgents. In the general atmosphere of euphoria, the Bourbon flag was pulled down to be replaced by the three-legged symbol of Trinacria, representing ancient Sicily. Optimism for the revolutionary cause was raised by support from the Italian states. A commission was sent from Sicily to Rome, Florence and Turin, which was well-received and blessed by Pope Pius IX.

King Ferdinand, who also faced revolt in Naples, bowed to events and made a concession which offered Sicily a liberal constitution provided Bourbon sovereignty was acknowledged. The Provisional Government, for whom nothing short of total separation from the Bourbons was acceptable, refused this offer. Ruggero Settimo replied to the king that Sicily did not require new institutions but the restoration of her ancient rights.[4]

RETURN OF THE BOURBONS

Up to this point, the revolution appeared remarkably successful. In a moment of rare unity, Sicilians of all social backgrounds had united against the Bourbons, with their untrained men defeating the royal army. A group of liberal-minded leaders had assumed power in Palermo and re-instated the constitution of 1812, introduced by the British. Attempts had begun to win international recognition for a Sicily independent of the Bourbons.

Below the surface, however, all was not well. The leaders lacked experience in both government and diplomacy and were politically immature after years of authoritarian rule. In addition, the revolution had unleashed forces which the Provisional Government was powerless to control. Since 1816, when King Ferdinand re-imposed his rule, resistance had built up across the island. Armed revolt encouraged the growth of criminal gangs, which under the guise of political insurgency followed their own interests, leading to an alarming rise in the crime rate. Once the Bourbon government withdrew, public security came under threat in the big cities and broke down completely in the countryside.

In his novel, *Sicilian Uncles,* Leonardo Sciascia described how the *quarantotto* affected Castro, a small town near Mazara, in western Sicily.[5] His story, based on contemporary accounts, shows how the revolution developed at a grassroots level. Under the Bourbons, the community was run by three figures of authority, the baron, who owned much of the land, the bishop, and the king's judge, who acted as the local magistrate. They had the support of a militia and a police force. Once news of the revolution in Palermo reached Castro, the baron and the judge fled the town fearing mob violence, while the police also vanished. A committee was established to take charge, which left the militia to maintain public order. Criminals became active in the town, maintaining contacts with brigands who operated in the countryside, where they stole animals and extorted protection money from landowners. When brigands raided Castro, gun battles worthy of America's Wild West took place in the town's centre. In the breakdown of law and order, valuable items were stolen from churches and the price of food rocketed. Ordinary citizens began to long for the return of the Bourbons. It became apparent, as recorded by the lawyer, Francesco Crispi, that the moderates feared the victory of the people more than that of the Bourbon troops.[6]

King Ferdinand was determined to maintain his sovereignty over Sicily and, having overcome the revolt in Naples, he set about retaking the island. His troops had retained a foothold in the citadel of Messina and in September 1848 hostilities were resumed under the command of General Carlo Filangeri. They began with a heavy bombardment of Messina's town centre, entire quarters of which were reduced to rubble, earning Ferdinand the nickname of King Bomba. Through the intervention of the British and the French, a six months' armistice was declared.

Early in 1849, Ferdinand repeated his offer to Sicily of a separate parliament and viceroy, which was again refused. As soon as the armistice ended, Filangeri, at the head of a Bourbon army of 16,000, landed in Sicily and recaptured Messina. During the fighting, numerous atrocities were committed against the civilian population by the Neapolitan troops. Catania and Syracuse both capitulated rather than face a similar bombardment to Messina. On 15 May 1849, Palermo fell without a fight. Filangeri was made Duke of Taormina and became governor of Sicily.

A diplomatic mission to London ended in failure, despite sympathy for Sicily's aims from Lord Palmerston, the British Foreign Secretary. Britain, having seen the problems of Sicily during the Napoleonic Wars, was not prepared to intercede further on the island's behalf.

Parliament was abolished and a repressive regime, under the control of tough law-enforcement officers, was put in place by Filangeri. An amnesty was offered to Sicilians who took part in the revolution, except for forty-three named leaders, who went into exile. Aristocrats and business leaders who had supported the revolution made their peace with Filangeri. Despite the promise of amnesty, others with a record of active insurgency were arrested, some of whom were executed or given sentences on the prison island of Favignana. Among the victims was the youth, Francesco Bagnasco, who had pinned up the notice in Palermo naming the day of the revolution. Thinking he was safe to return to Sicily, as his name was not on the list, Bagnasco was arrested in Palermo and died of his torture in prison.

Tina Whitaker described the end of the revolution as follows:

Thus, Palermo fell again, just sixteen months after declaring her independence and thus ended the Sicilian revolution which had begun so brilliantly, and which had called forth the highest patriotism and self-sacrifice amongst her people and had exposed the shameless tyranny of the Bourbon government to the whole of Europe. The revolution died out like a flickering candle, yet it lighted a flame which ultimately devoured every throne in the Peninsula save that of Sardinia.[7]

DESTINY OF THE LEADERS

The leaders of the revolution left Sicily in April 1849. They received no payment for their time in government and were now forced to find refuge abroad. In exile, they lobbied wherever they could for an end to Bourbon rule in their homeland. It was generally accepted that foreign help was now needed. Their actions bore fruit eleven years later, when Sicily was chosen by Garibaldi for his first campaign to free Italy from foreign powers. The leaders were the founding fathers of modern Sicily, and returning with Garibaldi, went on to reach high office in government.

Ruggero Settimo, who settled in Malta, was appointed the first president of the Italian Senate in the newly formed Italian parliament in 1861. Due to ill health, he was unable to take up this position and he remained in Malta, where he died in 1863. Mariano Stabile returned to Sicily in 1860, becoming mayor of Palermo in 1862–63. Vincenzo Fardella, a friend of Cavour, served in the Italian parliament, and became president of the Senate in 1870–74. Michele Amari, the historian, served as minister for public education in Italy's parliament, before retiring to academic life in Florence. Francesco Crispi was Garibaldi's political adviser during the Sicilian campaign. He was then a member of the Italian parliament where he rose to become Italy's first prime minister from the south, serving two terms during the period 1887 to 1896.

Memorials to the leaders of the *quarantotto* are to be found all over Palermo. Ruggero Settimo is remembered by a statue facing the Politeama theatre, in the piazza bearing his name, and in the street that links the piazza to Via Cavour. Several other streets in the district bear the names of leaders including Mariano Stabile, Michele Amari and Francesco Crispi. Their busts are displayed in Piazza Marina and the Giardino Inglese (English Garden). The Risorgimento Museum, with its entrance next to the church of San Domenico, has half its contents of pictures, statues, documents and other memorabilia dedicated to the men of the *quarantotto*.

In 1860, following the campaign of Garibaldi, the place where the revolution started, Piazza Fieravecchia, was renamed Piazza Rivoluzione. The statue of the Genius of Palermo, the mythical founder of the city, was returned to the centre of the piazza, accompanied by a plaque carrying the following statement: *Questo marmo simbolo temuto di libertà sottratto agli occhi del popolo dalla inquieta tirannide il popolo vincitore ripose nel 1860.* ('This feared marble symbol of freedom, removed from the eyes of the people by a troubled tyranny, was replaced by the victorious people in 1860').

EPILOGUE

The revolution of 1848 had a major impact upon the development of modern Sicily. It prepared the ground for Garibaldi's campaign which finally banished the Bourbons from Sicily. But by attracting foreign interventions, first by Garibaldi and then by Cavour, it removed control of government from Sicilians and passed it to others.

The early years of unity with Italy were difficult ones for Sicily with the Piedmontese administration seen as just another foreign domination of the island. Their weak administration was a disaster, for it left public order in disarray. Brigands ruled the countryside and criminal gangs penetrated every aspect of society. It was in this period that the term *mafia* was first coined, with the practices of extortion and political corruption becoming widespread, backed by the threat of assassination.

The *quarantotto*, with its broad support across society and its liberal-minded leaders, was the opportunity for a progressive Sicilian government to take control. This was the moment reformers had been waiting for to start the modernisation of Sicily. Instead, failure of the revolution meant that the underlying social tensions and rising crime rate were left unchecked, with repercussions which are still felt today.

PART TWO

CITIES

INTRODUCTION

Sicily's geography matches its history for infinite variety. The coastline extends for a thousand kilometres over rocky headlands and bays with expanses of sand, while at several points inlets of the sea form large natural harbours. Groups of small islands are dotted around the coast, the Aeolian to the north-east, the Egadian to the west, and to the south the larger islands of Malta, Pantelleria and Lampedusa. Mountain ranges with richly verdant slopes, snow-capped in winter, lie inland from the northern coast. To the east rises the huge shape of an active volcano which occasionally spits fire into the air, threatening nearby territory with molten lava. Down the east coast runs a plain with lava-enriched soil famous for its fertility. Further south, running parallel to the coast, stand rocky tablelands filled with gorges created by fast-flowing streams. Much of the island's interior, formed of a plateau with a succession of hills, is arid and barren.

In antiquity, the forests were filled with wildlife and the coastal waters teemed with fish, including huge tuna and swordfish. Abundant fresh water was supplied by rivers which ran down from the mountains to the sea. For the early settlers, Sicily, the largest island in the Mediterranean, represented a continent in miniature and seemed like paradise.

———

The diversity of the island's geography extends to its cities. The four largest are all located on the coast, all have active ports, and all were founded in the eighth century BC. But here the similarities end, as the following profiles demonstrate.

Palermo is the capital of Sicily, the political centre and the seat of regional government, with a population of 674,000. The compact historic centre is criss-crossed with wide streets interconnected by winding medieval alleyways. It has been described as the most African city in Europe, for there is a strong North African feel to the Arab-style street markets and squares filled with palm trees. The city of Norman kings, it is famous for its Arabo-Norman monuments.

Catania is Sicily's second city and its commercial capital, with the island's busiest airport, and a population of 315,000. Situated below Mount Etna facing the Ionian Sea, the city was laid out on a grid system in the eighteenth century following its destruction by an earthquake. The baroque centre, with its restored Norman cathedral, was built using the local black lava stone.

Messina, the port which maintains communications with mainland Italy and the point of arrival for railway and motor traffic, has a population of 238,000. It faces the narrow strait which divides Sicily from the mainland and the city of Reggio Calabria on the other side. Messina was rebuilt in the early twentieth century following an earthquake.

Syracuse is a commercial and tourist centre with a population of 122,000. Ortygia, the historic centre, is a promontory jutting out into the harbour, filled with medieval streets and baroque buildings. Built in honey-coloured stone, it is the city of Archimedes, famous for its Greek monuments.

Beyond the larger cities lie many smaller towns, for Sicily has always been decentralised. As waves of settlers reached the island, earlier arrivals were pushed inland to the mountainous regions. After the Greeks became established around the coast, they set up outposts inland to protect themselves. A pattern emerged of the main cities located on the coast and satellite communities inland to provide them with security, food and livestock. Racial conflict later led to the establishment of hilltop fortresses. These more isolated communities lived separately in the interior of the island. Until recently, communications between such communities was limited by the lack of passable roads.

Just how decentralised Sicily became is demonstrated by the time it took the Normans to subdue the island, ruled at the time by the Arabs. After their invasion in 1061, it was not for another thirty years that the Normans took full control of the island. The reason was that the Arabs defended their strongholds, strung out across the island, one by one. It is estimated that at this time Sicily contained twenty-four cities and 320 defended hilltowns.[1] In contrast, it took the Normans only a few months to take control of England, a centralised state, after their invasion of 1066.

The decentralised pattern continues today. The four largest cities, described above, account for less than a third of the island's population of five million. Two thirds of Sicilians live in centres of under 70,000 inhabitants, spread among 382 *comuni* (urban centres).[2]

There is no uniformity between cities, with each one having its own character and role to play. Taormina, for example, is Sicily's top international resort; Caltagirone is the production centre for Sicily's traditional ceramics; while Mazara del Vallo is the island's busiest fishing port. As Sciascia wrote, 'Every town in Sicily, whether by the sea or up a mountain, on a desolate plain or a pleasant hillside, is an island within an island'.[3]

For visitors, Sicily is still a paradise but a compromised one, a place where the environment swings from one extreme to the other, from the beauty of the landscape and the historic city centres to gross exploitation by man over the centuries.

Deforestation, which began with the Romans, gathered pace under the Spanish. The forests of fir and pine trees, prized for ship building, were cut down and the wood exported in large quantities, so that by the seventeenth century there was barely enough left for local use. This process continued in the first half of the nineteenth century, further reducing the woodlands. The effect upon the agricultural economy was dramatic. Rivers dried up, marshes appeared, and soil erosion reduced the amount of productive land. Stretches of the island were left bare and abandoned. The climate became hotter and drier, making water shortages more common.

Then in the 1950s and 60s, Sicily was subjected to the unbridled forces of industrial development. After oil was discovered near Ragusa and off the coast at Gela, oil refineries and chemical plants were built along the coast at Milazzo to the north, at Priolo and Augusta to the east, and at Gela to the south. Sicily became the centre of Italy's oil industry, providing the energy that fuelled the growth of the modern nation. The impact on the environment was far reaching. Prime stretches of coastline became dominated by these refineries, which are still operating today, spreading pollution and posing health hazards for nearby residents.

In the same post-Second World War period an uncontrolled building boom took place, putting up cheap apartment blocks which encircled the cities in an unprecedented spate of profiteering. In Palermo, where some of the worst examples were to be found, the building boom became known as the Sack of Palermo. These apartment blocks continue to blight the landscape around the island.

The next threat to the environment will come from mass tourism, which has not yet arrived, but may be just around the corner. More visitors are coming to Sicily, including on cruise ships, putting pressure on the small city centres. In 2017, the official figures showed nearly five million visitors to the island, an increase of thirteen per cent on the previous year.[4] While much of the island remains astonishingly unspoilt, offering a trip back in time compared to northern and central Italy, parts of it show signs of rapid commercialisation. Tension is building between the policies of development and those of conservation, which will need careful handling.

Sicilian cities have fascinated visitors since ancient times. Cicero in his case against Verres, the corrupt Roman governor, praised Syracuse, Messina, Agrigento and Marsala for their reputations as important centres.[5] Under the Norman king, Roger II, an Arab geographer, al-Edrisi, toured Sicily, recording his impressions of the cities. As well as praising the capital, Palermo, Edrisi described Catania: 'This beautiful city, both important and famous, situated by the sea, contains busy markets, splendid palaces, mosques and Christian churches, public baths, hotels and a fine harbour'.[6]

In the late eighteenth century, visitors to Sicily encouraged others to follow them by touring the island and publishing accounts of their travels. Among the most influential were Patrick Brydone and Henry Swinburne from Britain, whose books were widely read in Europe. They were followed by the German, Johann Wolfgang von Goethe. Goethe recognised the importance of Sicily, writing in his journal, 'To me Sicily implies Asia and Africa, and it will mean more than a little to me to stand at that miraculous centre upon which so many radii of world history converge'. This led to his famous statement that 'To have seen Italy without having seen Sicily is not to have seen Italy at all, for Sicily is the clue to everything'.[7]

As Sicily became part of the Grand Tour in the nineteenth century, more travellers added their accounts, notably Douglas Sladen who spent many months in Sicily, and whose descriptions of the monuments in his book, *In Sicily,* have not been bettered. Maupassant, who also toured Sicily, left an imaginative memoir of his visit. Edward Hutton, a prolific travel writer, published his *Cities of Sicily* in 1926.

Since the Second World War, many writers have visited Sicily and
published descriptions of their travels. A format for these books
evolved, based on a tour of the island taking in the main cities and
their monuments, and supported by pieces of historical background
and personal comment. Among the first and most perceptive were
books by Vincent Cronin and Peter Quennell. Others of note
followed by Alfonso Lowe, Lawrence Durrell, Norman Lewis and
John Keahey.

Among the few books on individual cities are two by the current
author, on Syracuse and Palermo. Each one combines a history of
the city with a review of its monuments.

Among the Sicilians, the author that stands out for his travel
writing is Vincenzo Consolo. A compilation of his work, translated
into English, appeared in *Reading and Writing the Mediterranean,*
published in 2006. For him, when travelling around Sicily, history
is never far away. Wherever one goes there are echoes of the past,
which may include a glimpse of an ancient Greek wall, an Arab
watchtower or a Norman castle. It is a world full of signs and
messages from the past that want to be read and interpreted.[8]

The following articles, which contain profiles of eight Sicilian cities
chosen for their historical importance, trace their development
and highlight the monuments to be seen today. They demonstrate
both the originality and the extraordinary diversity of Sicily's urban
centres. Syracuse and Palermo, the subjects of the author's previous
books, are not included here.

CATANIA, SICILY'S COMMERCIAL
CAPITAL, AND MOUNT ETNA

Catania is a large, sprawling city situated at the foot of Mount
Etna facing the Ionian Sea. It is Sicily's commercial capital, and the
second-largest city on the island after Palermo, with a population
of 315,000. Catania's relationship with Palermo is comparable to
that of Milan's with Rome at a national level; one is the commercial
capital, the other the political capital.

Catania is an ancient city with its origins in prehistoric times.
Its strength lies in its position, surrounded by the most productive
agricultural land on the island thanks to the minerals spread by
volcanic ash from Mount Etna. Etna, the largest volcano in Europe,
rises to the north-west, its huge, conical shape forming a backdrop
to the city.

Disaster has overwhelmed Catania on many occasions. Greek
tyrants, Carthaginian generals, German emperors and Bourbon
kings are among those who brought destruction on the city.
In addition, it was destroyed many times, wholly or in part, by
volcanic eruptions and earthquakes. From all these disasters Catania
arose again, phoenix-like, to be rebuilt in the same place. Following
destruction in the earthquake of 1693, the city was redesigned on a
grid plan in an elegant, late-baroque style.

In the second half of the nineteenth century, once freed from war
and natural disaster, the city developed on the back of its agriculture

as the commercial centre of eastern Sicily. After the Second World
War brought more destruction, Catania went from strength to
strength to become the most prosperous city on the island.

FOUNDATION AND EARLY HISTORY

For the early settlers, the site of Catania held many attractions.
The gulf on the Ionian Sea offered a good harbour while fresh
water was provided by two rivers. The volcanic soil at the foot of
Mount Etna and on the coastal plain that extended to the south-east
was highly fertile, giving ideal conditions for agriculture. The risk
of volcanic eruption, which was known from ancient times, was
accepted by the local population as the price to pay for an otherwise
prime location.

Finds made by Paolo Orsi, the pioneering archaeologist, in the
late nineteenth and early twentieth centuries, show that the site was
inhabited before the arrival of the Greeks. Bronze-age implements
and fragments of ceramics, discovered in caves and grottoes, link
the site to the Sicels, people who lived in settlements along the east
coast and inland at Pantàlica. The Sicel name for the settlement was
Katana, meaning grated, referring to the rough soil that was mixed
with pieces of lava.[1]

According to Thucydides, Naxos was the first Greek city to
be founded in Sicily, by men from Chalcis in Euboea, in 734 BC.
Syracuse was founded in the following year by men from Corinth. In
the fifth year after the foundation of Syracuse, the men from Chalcis
drove out the Sicels and founded Leontini (Lentini), on the hills
overlooking the plain. They went on to the site of Catania, where they
found all they needed to turn a small Sicel village into a substantial
settlement. They chose as their founder a man named Eurarchus and
named the settlement Katane. The date was around 728.[2]

In the Greek era, Katane never possessed the ability to unite the
local Sicel and Greek communities into a unified force to defend
itself. The city was overshadowed by its more powerful neighbour,

Syracuse, which came to dominate eastern Sicily. Unlike Syracuse, which had strong, natural defences, Katane was vulnerable to attack from the sea and fell to hostile forces on many occasions. In 476 Hiero I of Syracuse took Katane, renaming it Aetna, putting his son in charge and exiling the city's residents to Leontini. Fifteen years later the exiles recaptured the city. During the Athenian War of 415–413, when the Athenians laid siege to Syracuse, Katane supported Athens and became the Athenians' base of operations. After the Athenians' defeat, Katane paid the price for this alliance when it was captured by Dionysius I, who sold its residents into slavery. During the Greek wars with Carthage, Katane was occupied by the Carthaginians, and was among the first cities to surrender to the Romans. After further destruction during the civil wars of Rome, Katane went on to flourish under the Romans, demonstrating that given peaceful conditions, the city could prosper from its agriculture.

SANT'AGATA, CATANIA'S PATRON SAINT

Christianity came early to Sicily, either from Rome or directly from the Middle East. It may have been initiated in the Jewish communities or among the slaves brought to the island in large numbers by the Romans. Syracuse became an important centre for the early Christians whose extensive catacombs, second in scale only to those in Rome, can still be seen today. The earliest burials took place there around the year 200.

Sant'Agata (St Agatha) was one of the first recorded Christian martyrs in Sicily. Agatha, from a noble family in Catania, was a young girl of thirteen when she was brought before the Roman governor, Quintian, to answer for her Christian faith. This followed a decree from Decius, the Roman emperor, ordering a persecution of the Christians. According to legend, when she refused to renounce her faith she was subjected to torture, during which her breasts were mutilated. After receiving a vision of St Peter, Agatha recovered, but was then condemned to be burnt. Miraculously, the fire did not harm her, while an earthquake caused the Romans to flee the city. Agatha died in prison on 5 February 251.

A year later, Catania was threatened by an eruption of Mount Etna, with molten lava streaming down the mountain towards the city. The Catanese recovered Agatha's silken veil from her tomb and took it to the advancing lava. When the lava met the sacred relic, it stopped in mid flow, saving the city from destruction. From that point, the cult of Agatha spread rapidly throughout Sicily and on to the wider Christian world.

The saint's body, representing an important Christian relic, was taken to Constantinople in 1039 by George Maniaces, a Byzantine general who had temporarily recaptured eastern Sicily from the Arabs. Two soldiers brought the body back to Catania in 1126 where it has remained ever since.

St Agatha is a hugely popular figure in Catania, celebrated on her feast days in February and August each year. Spectacular festivities, attended by up to 300,000 people, take place during the first week in February when a gigantic float containing the saint's relics is drawn through the city, culminating in a firework display.

Agatha was among the first of the patron saints to be adopted by her city, a practice which later became common across the island. The patron saint's role was perceived as protecting the community and, when required, interceding to God on its behalf. The insecurity of the population in the face of natural disaster and oppression was among the reasons for this development. People felt in need of protection and preferred an intimate relationship with their own saint to a more distant one offered by an authoritarian church. The patron saint fitted into the Sicilian pattern of life based around family and close-knit community.

REBIRTH AS A BAROQUE CITY

In January 1693, a powerful earthquake hit eastern Sicily causing destruction in fifty-eight cities, from Catania to Ragusa. In total, more than 50,000 people died, while coastal areas were hit by an after-shock of giant waves. Following the collapse of buildings, disease spread among the surviving population.

Catania, along with Noto, was one of the places worst hit by the earthquake. It was reduced to rubble, with the old buildings destroyed except for the medieval Castello Ursino and parts of the Norman cathedral. The Spanish authorities were quick to organise a programme of reconstruction under the direction of Catania's bishop.

It was decided to rebuild the city on its old site using a grid plan, a method of town planning which goes back to the ancient Greeks, as can be seen, for example, in Selinunte. The grid plan incorporated wide streets running at right angles to each other, interspersed with large squares and public buildings. As well as representing an improvement in layout, the plan's increased open spaces offered some protection against damage from earthquakes. In the nineteenth century, a British visitor to Catania, Colonel William Light, was so impressed with the city's plan that, as the first surveyor general of South Australia, he applied a similar approach to the city of Adelaide.

The style of architecture adopted for Catania's reconstruction took a new direction in 1730 with the arrival of Giovanni Battista Vaccarini, an architect from Palermo. Vaccarini had been trained in Rome and was imbued with the artistic ideas of master architects such as Bernini and Borromini. The grandeur and monumental qualities of Roman baroque architecture formed the basis of his vision for Catania. He gave the city its unique modern character and uniformity through the creation of impressive street facades together with grandiose churches and municipal buildings. The city's open and sunny aspect suited the use of the local black lava stone which added an elegant touch to his buildings. On his arrival, Vaccarini worked closely with two architects already working in the city, Giuseppe Palazzotto and Francesco Battaglia. Vaccarini's most famous work, the façade of the cathedral of Sant'Agata, dominates the Piazza Duomo in the city's centre. Facing the cathedral and also built by Vaccarini, in 1736, is a fountain consisting of an obelisk supported by an elephant.[3]

Vaccarini and Rosario Gagliardi were Sicily's most talented architects of the eighteenth century. While Vaccarini's career was spent in Catania, Gagliardi worked exclusively in Noto and the surrounding district. Both were sons of carpenters, and although contemporaries, there is no evidence that they ever met. They both added new elements to the late baroque style and left strong imprints upon the cities in which they worked. The results, however, were very different, reflecting the characters of both the architects and the cities. While Noto was built in golden stone, exuberant and imaginative in style, Catania's architecture was grandiose and sombre, using black stone, in a style appropriate for a big city.

Vaccarini died in 1768, but reconstruction work in Catania continued throughout the eighteenth century. When Brydone visited the city in 1770, he noted: 'The whole city was rebuilt, after a new and elegant plan, and is now more handsome than ever'.[4]

THE MODERN CITY
Catania developed rapidly as the main commercial centre of eastern Sicily in the second half of the nineteenth century. It lay in the island's most progressive region, along with the province of Ragusa, where society was more open and forward looking, and where crime was less endemic than in the west. Catania's rich agricultural hinterland led the way in terms of investment, reform and modernisation. As a result, early in the twentieth century Catania replaced Palermo as the most important port on the island for overseas trade.

During the First World War, Sicily was cut off from its export markets and the island's economy stagnated. In the following years, emigration soared due to unemployment, with most emigrants going to North America, Argentina and Brazil. Yet in the inter-war years, Catania continued to expand and develop its trade. Edward Hutton, the English travel writer who visited the city in 1926, found it the most prosperous in Sicily and was impressed by its vivacity.[5]

The Second World War brought more destruction to Sicily through allied bombing of the major ports, including Catania's. Following the Allied invasion of Sicily in July 1943, some of the fiercest fighting of the campaign took place on the plain of Catania for control of the bridge over the River Simeto.

Catania consolidated its position as Sicily's leading commercial centre following the war. Building upon its strengths as a wholesale market for fish and agricultural products, it added capacity for manufacturing and technology. Catania's university, the oldest in Sicily, became the training ground for new generations of skilled workers.

The city has good communications, being served by motorways which head along the coast in both directions and across the island to Palermo. The airport is one of the busiest in southern Italy, handling nearly ten million passengers in 2017, compared to Palermo's less than seven million. Catania's port deals with much of Sicily's export trade, as well as offering a ferry service to mainland Italy and berths for cruise ships.

VISITING CATANIA

First-time visitors should make their way to Piazza Duomo, the heart of the city. It is a large open square containing the cathedral and other public buildings, where the city's two main streets meet at right angles. Running east towards the harbour is the Via Vittorio Emanuele and running north, the Via Etnea. Overlooking the square, the cathedral is impressive in scale, its conservative lines softened by decorative elements such as statues and free-standing columns. Vaccarini's façade completed the work done by Palazzotto on the cathedral's structure.

The interior is spacious and simple, with a chapel of St Agatha, to whom the cathedral is dedicated, to the right. Facing the cathedral is Vaccarini's curious fountain on which stands an elephant, the symbol of Catania, carved in black lava stone, supporting an obelisk. Both the elephant and the obelisk are thought to be ancient but much restored.

Behind the cathedral is the church of St Agatha, also by Vaccarini. The façade contains some fine decorative details in the capitals, celebrating the saint's virtues, the palms of martyrdom, the lilies of virginity and the crowns of eternal life. On the other side of the cathedral, in Via Dusmet, stands the Palazzo Biscari, one of the finest private palaces in Catania. West of the cathedral lies an elegant baroque street, Via Crociferi, which is filled with eighteenth-century churches and palaces.

One of Sicily's famous writers, Giovanni Verga, is remembered in a small museum in the house where he lived at No. 8, Via Sant'Anna, a ten-minute walk from Piazza Duomo, heading west. In his short stories, such as the collection entitled *Vita dei campi* ('Life in the fields'), Verga described the hard life of peasants in realistic terms. One of the stories, *Cavalleria Rusticana,* became the subject of an opera by Pietro Mascagni. By 1884, Verga was considered the greatest living Italian writer.

There are few ancient remains due to the damage done by earthquakes and volcanic eruptions. Among the surviving monuments are two from Roman times, the Roman Theatre and Amphitheatre. The theatre, which dates from the third century AD, held 7,000 spectators and was probably built on the site of a Greek theatre. Underlying the importance of Catania in Roman times is the exceptionally large amphitheatre, which could hold 16,000 spectators. Built from blocks of lava it dates from the second century AD.

Another important monument that survived the earthquake of 1693 is the Castello Ursino, a castle built for Frederick II in the thirteenth century. It is now a museum holding a rich collection of finds from the prehistoric era to the eighteenth century.

Further to the north, in Piazza Carlo Alberto which leads off Piazza Stesicoro, is a vast, colourful street market known as *Fero ò Luni* (the Monday fair), open every day except Sunday. Almost every conceivable item of domestic use is on sale here, from clothes to kitchen utensils, together with a huge selection of fruit and vegetables. A sign of the times is the fact that many of the stalls are in the hands of the Chinese community. A lively fish market can be found on the western side of Piazza Duomo.

In Piazza Stesicoro stands a statue of Vincenzo Bellini, who was born in Catania on 3 November 1801. He developed rapidly as a composer of romantic operas in the *bel canto* style, and by the age of thirty had produced two favourites of the international repertoire, *La Sonnambula* and *Norma*. Most of Bellini's career was spent first in Milan and then in Paris, where he died aged thirty-four. His body was returned for burial in Catania in 1876, when he was given a state funeral.

The memorials to Bellini include a museum holding mementos of his life and the scores of some of his operas, and the house where he lived for sixteen years. The city's opera house, the Teatro Massimo Bellini, puts on a full operatic repertoire including the composer's work. Bellini's operas can sometimes be seen in Taormina, at the outdoor Greco-Roman theatre, in a spectacular setting facing Mount Etna and the Ionian Sea.

MOUNT ETNA

The largest volcano in Europe, Mount Etna reaches 3,300 metres in height and has a base circumference of 150 kilometres. Visible for miles, its huge outline dominates the eastern coastline of Sicily. To the Phoenicians and Greeks who explored Sicily in the eighth century BC, Etna represented a primeval force, a sinister place inhabited by gods, and a source of fear. The name Etna, originally Aetna, possibly derives from the Phoenician *athana*, meaning 'furnace', or from a composite of the Greek and Latin for 'to burn'.

Today, local people refer to Etna as *Mongibello*, a combination of the Italian *monte* and the Arabic *gebel,* both meaning mountain, or simply as *à muntagna,* the mountain.

It is among the most active volcanoes in the world and its violent eruptions have brought disruption to surrounding areas since ancient times. Thucydides recorded the first eruption for fifty years in 425 BC, noting that there had been three eruptions in total since the Greeks arrived in Sicily. In 396 BC a flow of lava reached the sea and blocked the Carthaginian advance on Syracuse. Eruptions have tended to occur in clusters, with the majority concentrated in ancient times, the Middle Ages, and more recently in the twentieth century. The worst of all happened in 1669 when large parts of Catania disappeared below the flow of lava. The latest eruption took place in 2017, when a BBC reporter and a group of tourists ran down the mountain as they were pelted by rocks, dodging burning boulders and scalding steam. On this occasion no one was injured, and no damage was done to the city.[6]

The power and unpredictability of the volcano has produced many legends. One concerned the philosopher and scientist, Empledocles, who in the fifth century BC was supposed to have thrown himself into the crater, either in the pursuit of knowledge or because he wished to be worshipped as a god. His claim to divinity was undermined by leaving one of his sandals on the edge of the crater. Another, quoted by Aristotle and Seneca, concerned the heroic action of two rich brothers, Anfinomius and Anapias, who were faced with molten lava pouring into Catania. While everyone around them was salvaging valuable possessions, the brothers carried their aged parents out of danger on their backs. According to the legend, the lava respected such filial loyalty and spared them, while many others perished on the same road.[7]

Since 1981, the countryside around Etna has been designated a regional park containing villages, farms and a *strada del vino*, a wine trail that leads around the vineyards. The lower slopes of the mountain are intensely cultivated with oranges, lemons, tangerines, pistachios, apples, olives and vines. Further up the mountain there are forests of oak, pine, chestnut and beech filled with wildlife. Among the birds are hoopoes, woodpeckers, red kites and the occasional golden eagle, while pine martens, porcupines, hares and foxes abound. Nearer the summit the volcanic zone begins which, apart from flowers in the spring, is one of desolation, filled with black lava and clinker, some of it hot to the touch.

The southern approach is via the village of Nicolosi to Rifugio Sapienza, from where a cable car departs for the summit. The northern approach is via Linguaglossa, a ski resort, from where the climb can be made on foot. The ascent of Etna is well worth pursuing, for apart from the interest of the volcano itself, the views from the summit are magnificent, extending as far as the Aeolian islands. The view varies according to weather conditions, with the quantity of cloud and the direction taken by smoke from the craters affecting visibility. There are strong winds, possibly carrying volcanic ash, and low temperatures to contend with at the top of the mountain. These conditions have led some travellers to say that they prefer to see Etna from a distance. Despite the difficulties, to climb Mount Etna remains an essential part of any serious traveller's visit to Sicily, accomplished among others in Roman times by the emperor Hadrian and the philosopher Seneca, and more recently by Goethe and Gladstone.

TAORMINA, SICILY'S TOP INTERNATIONAL RESORT

Taormina is a small town built on a rocky plateau some 200 metres above sea level, on the east coast of Sicily. It is famous for its magnificent setting overlooking the Ionian Sea, with panoramic views of Mount Etna and a long stretch of coastline. Behind the town rise peaks on which perch an Arab castle and a cluster of houses that make up the village of Castelmola. Below the town, cliffs descend to the sea forming small coves with sandy beaches.

Like Capri in the Bay of Naples, Taormina attracted international visitors in the late nineteenth century. The picturesque town with its famous Greco-Roman theatre appealed to artists and intellectuals and it has been filled with visitors, including the rich and famous, ever since. An annual film festival, which began in 1955, increased the town's reputation. Its international status was enhanced when it was chosen in 2017 as the location for a meeting of the leaders of the G7, the world's most advanced countries. It is one of the top tourist attractions in Sicily, with some 800,000 visitors in 2017.

In Taormina one enters an exclusive environment remote from the real Sicily, consisting of smart hotels, fine restaurants and international boutiques. The theatre is used as a setting for evening concerts of both popular and classical music, as well as for opera productions. Taormina is a place in which to relax and enjoy events, food, walks and incomparable views of the mountains and the sea.

THE HISTORY

Taormina was founded in the turbulent period following the defeat of the Athenian expedition to Sicily in 413 BC. The Athenians, who had attempted to capture Syracuse, had been supported by the smaller Greek cities, Katane (Catania), Leontini (Lentini) and Naxos. In the aftermath of the Athenian war, when the Carthaginians invaded Sicily, Dionysius I seized control of Syracuse and took revenge on the Greeks who had supported Athens. Naxos, the oldest Greek colony, was destroyed and its land granted to the Sicels. In 396, assisted by the Carthaginian general Himilco, the Sicels established themselves on the spur of a hill, *Monte Tauro* (Bull Mountain), and named their new city Tauromenion. Four years later it came under the control of Dionysius who settled some of his mercenaries in the city.

Tauromenion was refounded as a Greek city in 358, with the arrival of the survivors of Naxos and their descendants, by Andromachus, father of the historian Timaeus. Andromachus was renowned as an opponent of tyrants who established the rule of law. When Timoleon arrived in Sicily from Corinth to remove the tyrants, Tauromenion became his initial base of operations. Peace continued in the city under Hiero II, who ruled eastern Sicily from Syracuse.

Once the Emperor Augustus brought peace to Sicily, Tauromenium, as the Romans called it, was among the six cities granted the status of *colonia*, which brought full Roman citizenship. There followed a period of rebuilding and the resettlement of Roman personnel. Tauromenium flourished under the Roman Empire, due in part to its famed wine, favoured by the Romans.

Little is known of the city in the Middle Ages other than that its Byzantine fortress was one of the last to fall to the Arabs in 902 and that it was taken by the Normans in 1079. In 1410, the Sicilian parliament met here to choose a king on the extinction of the line of Peter of Aragon.

Under the Spanish, Taormina experienced a long decline, until it was discovered by travellers in the late eighteenth century. Once established as part of the Grand Tour, Taormina began to attract international visitors and developed as a resort.

INTERNATIONAL VISITORS
In the late nineteenth and early twentieth centuries, during the period known as the Belle Époque, Sicily became a fashionable destination for the elite of European society. Royalty and other celebrities flocked to Palermo where they were lavishly entertained in the palaces of the Sicilian aristocracy. Taormina, discovered by Patrick Brydone and Goethe in the late eighteenth century, became popular with these visitors and was soon hosting the rich and famous, including the kings of England and Spain, the German Kaiser, Richard Strauss, Oscar Wilde and Guy de Maupassant. It became a resort for the elite as well as attracting artists drawn to its spectacular scenery. The town became so popular that overcrowding in its narrow streets became a problem, noted in 1900 by Douglas Sladen, who wrote:

Taormina suffers from artists badly – they swarm and have made models dear and independent. The town is, of course, full of artists' bits. Many of the shops sell their pictures. Taormina is the artists' town of Sicily.[1]

The arrival of a German photographer, Wilhelm von Gloeden, added a touch of notoriety. Von Gloeden moved to Taormina, set up a photographic studio, and began to exhibit shots of naked Sicilian boys in albums destined for a gay audience. Using props such as wreaths and amphorae, the photographs suggested a setting from antiquity. By 1893, von Gloeden was exhibiting his work internationally. His work, which was suggestive rather than pornographic, struck a chord among classically educated homosexuals in northern

Europe. In societies where homosexuality was not accepted, the Mediterranean presented an idealised image of youth that combined physical attraction with a romanticised nostalgia for the ancient world. As in the case of Capri, made famous by writers such as Norman Douglas, sexual and cultural tourism went together.

An international community grew in Taormina made up of English, Americans, Germans and Scandinavians. Some of these residents built themselves mock-Gothic villas, leading to overbuilding in parts of the town. Others added gardens which helped to improve the environment. The most famous English resident was Lady Florence Trevelyan, a friend of Queen Victoria, who left the royal household due to her relationship with the queen's son, the future King Edward VII. Florence settled in Taormina in the 1880s, married a local doctor, Salvatore Cacciola, and created a magnificent garden filled with exotic plants and birds, which she left to the town.

The flow of visitors to Taormina was halted firstly by an earthquake, which in 1908 destroyed Messina, and then by the outbreak of the First World War. In the interwar years, visitors returned, among them Edward Hutton, who described his reaction to the town as follows.

Taormina in truth is not a place for sightseeing but for *dolce far niente,* for basking in the sun between a stroll and a stroll, always with that marvellous panorama before one, of which who can tire, changing as it does with every mood of the sky, with every hour of the day.[2]

The secret of Taormina's perennial attraction is the way that Etna rises before it with its overwhelming and dominant presence. D. H. Lawrence, who with his wife Frieda lived near Taormina in 1920, was more critical, however. He was not impressed with the English visitors and found Etna's huge presence threatening and forbidding, referring to it as a wicked witch.[3] He and Frieda left Sicily for Sardinia where he wrote his travel book, *Sea and Sardinia.* During the interwar years, visitors continued to arrive, including King George V and Ernest Hemingway.

Following the Second World War, Taormina resumed its role as an international resort. Famous visitors, including Bertrand Russell and Tennessee Williams, stayed at a guesthouse run by an English resident, Daphne Phelps, who published an entertaining account of her life in Taormina in *A House in Sicily*. In the 1950s, an annual film festival became established where movies and documentaries were judged competitively. A star-studded event attended by celebrities from the film world, it further raised the town's international profile. The list of visitors to Taormina in the 1950s and '60s included Cecil Beaton, Jean Cocteau, Salvador Dali, Winston Churchill, Orson Welles, Rita Hayworth, Marlene Dietrich, Greta Garbo, Cary Grant, Harold Acton, Evelyn Waugh, Elizabeth Taylor and Richard Burton.

At the same time, Taormina continued to attract artists and writers, its attractions summarised by Lawrence Durrell:

> However blasé one is, however much one has been prepared for the aerial splendours of the little town, its freshness is perennial, it rises in one like sap, it beguiles and charms as the eye turns in its astonishment to take in crags and clouds and mountains and the blue coastline.[4]

MODERN TAORMINA

Taormina exists on its tourist trade (for which it is well-organised) and remains busy from Easter to mid-October. The attraction of the old town lies in its medieval churches and palaces, its quaint small streets and its Roman monuments. Access from the motorway is provided via a tunnel leading to two large car parks situated near the main gates, the Porta Messina and the Porta Catania. There is also a cable-car connecting the town to the coast.

Corso Umberto, the main street, runs across the town parallel to the coast, linking the gates and three central squares. It is a prime shopping thoroughfare offering everything from designer clothes and accessories, to jewellery, antiques, local pottery and confectionery. Side streets contain open markets for fruit, vegetables and household goods. At the southern end of the Corso, near Porta Catania, stands a fourteenth-century palace, the Palazzo Duchi di Santo Stefano, by the remains of the old Jewish quarter. Medieval palaces with Catalan-Gothic decorations can be seen here, along with a twelfth-century clock tower.

The first of the town's squares, Piazza Duomo, contains the cathedral, founded in the thirteenth century, and a fountain from 1635, one of the town's symbols. Above the fountain stands a creature with the body of a bull and the head and shoulders of an angel, a reference to Monte Tauro (Bull Mountain) near which the city was built. Through the Porta Cuseni lies the Casa Cuseni, run by Daphne Phelps in the 1950s as a guesthouse.

The next of the squares, Piazza IX Aprile, got its name from the date of an uprising against the Spanish Bourbon government in 1860. Filled with cafés, the square contains the seventeenth-century church of San Giuseppe (St Joseph), which holds paintings of the life of the Virgin Mary by an unknown Flemish artist. To the left of the church are steps that lead to the heights above the town and the Castello Saraceno (Arab Castle) and the village of Castelmola.

Piazza Vittorio Emanuele, the third square, is the site of the ancient Greek *agora* and the Roman forum. Today it is a popular meeting place filled with bars and restaurants. Nearby is the seventeenth-century church of Santa Caterina and a museum of Sicilian handicrafts. Roman remains are to be found here including a small, covered Roman theatre known as the Odeon from the first century AD, together with fragments of public baths and the forum from imperial times.

From the square, Via Teatro Greco leads to the Greco-Roman theatre with its breathtaking view of Mount Etna and the coastline. The original theatre was built by the Greeks, probably in the third century BC in the time of Hiero II, a supporter of the arts who ruled eastern Sicily from Syracuse. Inscriptions on the seats of the theatre, comparable to those in Syracuse, support this theory. The Greek theatre at Akrai (Palazzolo Acreide) was built in the same period. Taormina's ancient theatre had its seating carved out of the hillside, with a portico built along the top, and was the largest in Sicily after that of Syracuse.

The theatre one sees today is Roman, for it was entirely rebuilt in imperial times. Its Roman renovation is shown by the brickwork, a building technique which was introduced in Augustan times. It was built over different periods and is in a remarkably good state of preservation. The position chosen by the Greeks was appreciated by the Romans, who left gaps in the arches to accommodate the view. Initially the Romans used it as a theatre. Then, in the second or early third century AD, they adapted it to serve as an amphitheatre for gladiatorial games. For this purpose, the seats were cut back, the stage was removed, and an underground room was built to hold the cages of wild animals.[5]

In the modern era, the theatre's role is to entertain international visitors. The film festival, known as the Taormina Film Fest, is an annual event in July, when film stars and other people from the movie industry briefly take over the town. During the rest of the summer musical events are staged to suit all tastes, ranging from concerts by Sting and Elton John to classical symphonies, jazz sessions and operas by Bellini, Verdi and Mozart. Attendance at one of these events on a warm evening, with the ancient theatre floodlit against the night sky, is a magical experience.

Below the theatre, to the south, lie the extensive Giardini Pubblici, the public gardens, containing a range of Mediterranean plants and trees. Originally laid out by Florence Trevelyan, they offer a superb view of the Ionian Sea.

NAXOS

On the coast below Taormina stretches a long sandy beach on which an isthmus ends in a rounded promontory. This is a famous beauty spot known as Isola Bella. The surrounding bay is protected as a nature reserve. To the north, in another sandy bay, lies the fishing village of Mazzarò, and to the south, the resort town of Giardini Naxos which is popular in summer and is filled with hotels facing a wide bay.

Near Giardini, at Capo Schisò, is the site of Naxos, the first Greek colony in Sicily. This is where the Greek adventure in Sicily began, leading to a civilisation on the island that lasted for over 500 years. The city was founded in 734 BC by men from Chalcis in Euboea, led by Thucles. Among the settlers were men from the Ionian island of Naxos, hence the name chosen for the settlement. Naxos was never a large colony but served as an initial base from which the settlers set out to found new cities, Katane and Leontini, which were closer to the fertile plain. Naxos was an important religious centre, with a renowned altar to Apollo, the god to whom the city was dedicated.

Little remains of the ancient city except for a long stretch of an early wall built with polygonal blocks of stone using a technique common in the eastern Mediterranean. The archaeological museum, housed in a fort, contains finds from the site including pottery of the eighth century BC from the Ionian island of Naxos.

13

MESSINA, THE PORT WITH
CONNECTIONS TO MAINLAND ITALY

Messina is famous as the port city in Sicily closest to mainland Italy. Backed by hills that lead up to the Peloritan mountain range, the city looks outward towards the sea, maintaining contact with the Aeolian islands, the ports of mainland Italy and beyond. It lies on the east coast close to the north-eastern tip of the island. A narrow strip of sea, the strait, only three kilometres across at its narrowest, separates Sicily from mainland Italy. On the other side of the strait, clearly visible from Messina, is the city of Reggio Calabria. Today Messina is a busy port which maintains commercial and tourist links with the mainland and is the usual point of arrival in Sicily for visitors by car and train. It is Sicily's third largest city, after Palermo and Catania, with a population of 238,000.

Messina has been important since ancient times both for its location and for its well-protected, deep-water harbour. These advantages enabled it to prosper and to play a vital role in communications, especially at times when Sicily and southern Italy were united under the same government. The harbour helped the city to develop as an important centre for trade around the Mediterranean.

These natural advantages, however, brought their own dangers. Being so close to the mainland, Messina was often the place where invading armies landed and where armies, defeated on the island, sought their escape. Examples include the Normans who took Messina at the start of their invasion in 1061 and the German and Italian forces which withdrew to the mainland via Messina in 1943. Under these circumstances, which were repeated many times, Messina suffered hardship and destruction from sieges and bombardments.

In addition, the region has been subject to natural disasters including extreme weather conditions, epidemics and earthquakes. The worst was the earthquake of 1908 which destroyed most of the city. While Messina was rebuilt and repopulated, and its ancient monuments restored, it is effectively a modern city.

In the long run, Messina's fate has been tragic. While for sustained periods the city led a prosperous existence, military conflicts and natural disasters were always around the corner. As a result, there is little continuity in the history of Messina, leading it to be called a city without memory.

MYTHS AND LEGENDS

On a fine day, the setting of Messina seems idyllic. The city is well-laid out, with widely spaced streets lined with low buildings. The centre of the city faces a busy seafront filled with shipping. Over the brilliant blue of the strait can be seen the hills of Calabria, while the air is fresh with wind from the sea. Appearances, however, can be deceptive, for the strait of Messina has always held the potential for violence. High winds and dangerous currents have posed a threat to sailors since antiquity and this small stretch of water is where the earthquakes originated which on several occasions destroyed Reggio and Messina.

The origin of the strait lies in some great geological upheaval, possibly an earthquake, which burst through the earth's crust, separating the island from the mainland. The spirit of this dramatic event is captured in a legend, according to which the strait was created by Neptune, god of the sea, when he dealt the earth a great blow with his trident. Whatever happened, the creation of the strait was an important development which allowed ancient navigators to hug the coastline on their journeys of discovery.

It was probably from such navigators that Homer learnt of the risks that they faced from treacherous currents, storms and rocky coastlines. In the *Odyssey,* Homer dramatised these perils in the myths of Scylla and Charybdis, female monsters who preyed upon ships passing through a strait, thought to be that of Messina. Scylla, who had twelve feet and six heads, lurked in a cave on a high rock from which she grabbed sailors as they passed by. Charybdis, on the other side of the strait, created a giant whirlpool into which ships were sucked and submerged.[1]

Another myth anticipated the future disasters of Messina. It concerned a young, expert diver, called Colapesce. Cola being short for Nicola, his name translates as Nick-fish. Colapesce was asked by King Frederick II to discover what lay below the city. He duly dived down and saw that it sat upon a reef supported by three columns, one broken, one damaged and one intact. In making his report, he foresaw an unhappy future for Messina.[2]

THE HISTORY

After the foundation of the Greek cities of Naxos and Syracuse, Messina was founded around 730 BC by pirates from Cumae. Thucydides tells us that they were joined by settlers from Chalcis, in Euboea, and that the founders were named Perieres from Cumae and Crataemenes from Chalcis. The name given to the city was Zancle, meaning sickle, referring to the semi-circular strip of land which protected the harbour.[3]

As the Greek cities in Sicily expanded, due to the fertility of the land, they founded further settlements across Sicily. Following this pattern, Zancle established two new cities on the north coast, Milazzo and Himera. Anaxilas, tyrant of Rhegium (Reggio), across the strait in Calabria, colonised Zancle in the fifth century BC with settlers of mixed origins, renaming it Messana, after his hometown in Greece. The Carthaginians destroyed the city at the end of the third century BC. It was subsequently rebuilt with the support of Syracuse and was then occupied by mercenaries known as the Mamertines, in the employ of Agathocles, tyrant of Syracuse.

During the civil wars in Rome, Sextus Pompey was based in Messana, which was sacked by Octavian. The long Roman era which followed was one of relative prosperity for the city. Under the Byzantines and the Arabs, mulberry trees were planted in the surrounding hills to supply the growing silk industry which flourished until the nineteenth century.

Al-Edrisi, the Arab geographer to the Norman king, Roger II, was impressed with Messina on his tour of Sicily in 1150.

Messina is among the finest and the most prosperous cities in Sicily. It has a large and well-protected port which can accommodate any size of ship. Travellers and merchants from many nations, both Muslim and western, visit the city to do business in the extensive markets. In the hills behind, there are iron mines and many windmills. Along the coast are fine beaches and gardens producing abundant fruit. The strait, which separates Sicily from the mainland, is difficult to navigate and in high wind produces currents that are dangerous to shipping.[4]

Messina took on increased importance in Norman times as a base for the crusaders heading for the Holy Land. In 1190, the English and French crusader armies arrived in Sicily. The English were led by their king, Richard I, the Lionheart, whose relations with Tancred, the King of Sicily, were fractious. Richard was incensed at the treatment of Joanna, his sister and widow of the previous King of Sicily, William II, and sacked Messina in revenge. Richard and Tancred then met and came to an amicable agreement. Tancred supplied Richard with ships for his expedition to Palestine. According to the legend, Richard in return gave Tancred King Arthur's famous sword, Excalibur, which had recently been discovered in England.

In the fifteenth century, as the Aragonese strengthened their hold on Sicily, foreign merchants became established in Messina. They included Catalans, Genoese, Flemish and Venetians who developed trading links around the Mediterranean and with northern Europe. It was into this environment that Messina's most famous son, the painter Antonello, was born around 1430. Antonello benefited from Messina's overseas connections and was trained in Naples.

Under Spanish rule in the mid-sixteenth century, Ignatius Loyola founded the first Jesuit college in Messina which became the city's university. In August 1571, the combined fleet of the Holy League, formed by Pope Pius V and financed by Spain, collected at Messina. There were ships from Spain, Naples, the Papal States, and Genoa as well as from Sicily. Commander of the fleet was John of Austria, brother of the Spanish king, Philip II. The aim was to confront the Turks, who ever since taking Constantinople in 1453, had been expanding their empire at the expense of the Christian states of western Europe. The Battle of Lepanto which followed was a decisive victory for the League and marked the limit of the Turkish advance. Serving in the League's fleet was Miguel de Cervantes, the future creator of Don Quixote. Wounded in the battle, Cervantes returned afterwards to Messina where he spent six months recuperating. Messina's importance as a naval port led to a revival in the city's fortunes. It flourished in the seventeenth century as the second city of Sicily, becoming the rival of Palermo.

EARTHQUAKES AND WAR
In January 1693, eastern Sicily was hit by an earthquake which damaged fifty-eight cities. Catania and Noto were both reduced to rubble. The damage to Messina, which was more limited, was aggravated by giant waves hitting the coast. A plague epidemic followed in 1743 and another earthquake forty years later. When Goethe visited Messina in 1787, he found the city still in a state of shock. Along the seafront, he noticed how the palaces which were

four storeys high had been damaged, leaving gaps like missing teeth in the curved façade.

When the Spanish Bourbons set out to re-take Sicily after the revolt of 1848, they targeted Messina, subjecting the city to a four-day artillery bombardment which set much of the city centre on fire. Having captured Messina, they went on to take Catania in similar fashion. Palermo, fearful of a similar assault, quickly capitulated.

The worst disaster came with the earthquake of 28 December 1908, whose epicentre lay in the strait of Messina. It was short lived, but very powerful, and was followed by a tsunami which engulfed the coastline with shattering effect. It struck at night when the population was asleep, causing maximum casualties. Virtually the entire city was destroyed, killing around 80,000 people, or half the population of the city and outlying areas. Reggio Calabria also suffered badly with around 25,000 casualties. Many of the survivors chose to join the thousands of Sicilians seeking a new life in America. Messina was rebuilt in the same location, with lower buildings, on carefully constructed foundations. An influx of migrants followed, from Sicily and the mainland, so that by the census of 1911 the city's population had reached 127,000.[5]

In July 1943, the Italian campaign of the Second World War started as the British and Americans landed on the south coast of Sicily. In thirty-eight days, the German and Italian forces on the island were defeated and pushed back towards Messina from where around 100,000 of their troops succeeded in withdrawing to Calabria. During the Sicilian campaign, Messina and the other major ports on the island were subject to saturation bombing by the Americans. Major General John P. Lucas, of the US Seventh Army, noted upon entering Messina that the city had been largely destroyed, with virtually no houses undamaged and few habitable.[6]

During their retreat to Messina, the Germans laid many mines which took months to clear. Post-war reconstruction was a slow process and the 1950s saw more mass emigration from the island to the industrial cities of northern Europe and to the Americas.

THE MODERN CITY

Messina's main activity is to provide the ferry service over the strait. Since the end of the nineteenth century, trains have reached Sicily via this service, which lands at the main terminus at the southern end of the harbour. From here there are railway connections with other coastal cities on the island. This is also where cars arrive by ferry, while for foot passengers, there is a hydrofoil service. Most of the traffic is with Reggio Calabria, although there are also connections with Salerno, to the south of Naples, and the Aeolian Islands.

Most people arriving in Messina do not stay long in the city but continue to other destinations in Sicily, making it a place of transition. In addition to running the ferry service, Messina is a busy commercial and naval port with connections across the Mediterranean. The controversial project to build a bridge over the strait, the subject of much planning and discussion in the past, is currently on hold.

Messina is also known for its wine, famous since Roman days, its olives and citrus fruit. It is important for fishing, especially for swordfish. The strait, with its fast-flowing currents, has been well-stocked with swordfish since ancient times. The swordfish, which can measure two metres in length, one third consisting of the sword, come close to the shore in the breeding season which lasts from June to August. The ancient fishing method was to post a lookout up a mast on a fast, narrow boat with six oarsmen, while a fisherman wielding an iron-tipped harpoon balanced on a plank. While the boats are now motorised and the planks have been replaced with metal platforms, much of the ancient technique is still in operation. In season, swordfish play an important part in the local cuisine.

The historic centre, with its view of the harbour, the strait and the hills of Calabria beyond, retains its fascination. At the harbour's entrance stands a tall column, on top of which is a statue of the Virgin Mary, known as the *Madonna della Lettera* (Madonna of the Letter). At the base of the column, carved in large letters, appear the words in Latin, *Vos et ipsam civitatem benedicimus*

(We bless you and the city itself). The story goes that Messina, which was an early convert to Christianity, sent ambassadors to Jerusalem in AD 42. There they met St Paul who introduced them to Mary herself. She wrote a letter for them to take back to the senate of Messina, promising to act as the city's protector. This story, despite the disasters which later befell the city, is celebrated each year in June.

At the heart of the city lies the Piazza Duomo with the Norman cathedral, founded by Count Roger, and consecrated under Henry VI and Constance in 1197. It has been well-restored and retains much of its medieval character, including some carved stone portals. It contains a statue – the copy of a Byzantine original – of the Madonna giving her letter to the ambassadors. There is also a statue of John the Baptist by Antonello Gagini. Mosaics with the figure of Christ have been reconstructed. Adjoining the cathedral stands a tall campanile, reconstructed from old designs. It contains a series of colourful, mechanical figures which appear at the chimes for midday and tell stories from the city's past including the Madonna's letter.

In the same piazza stands an elaborate fountain created in 1553 by the Florentine sculptor, Giovanni Angelo Montorsoli, one of Michelangelo's students. It features several levels of statues, including nymphs and angels, and a representation of four rivers. It is capped by the figure of Orion the hunter, the legendary founder of Messina, together with his dog, Sirius.

In Via Garibaldi, not far from the cathedral, stands the church of the Santissima Annunziata dei Catalani (Holy Annunciation of the Catalans), a twelfth-century Norman church which has undergone many alterations. In the nearby Piazza Catalani, there is a statue of John of Austria, by Andrea Calamech from 1572, commemorating his victory at the Battle of Lepanto.

In Piazza Unità d'Italia, to the north of the cathedral, is another fountain by Montorsoli, in fact a copy of the original which can be found in the regional museum. A fountain of Neptune, it features a giant figure of the sea god clasping his trident, caught between Scylla and Charybdis, the two mythological monsters who guarded the strait of Messina.

A panoramic route leads from behind the university, following the course of ancient fortifications, via the Botanical Gardens, to the church of Cristo Re (Christ the King). This church, which overlooks the city with its huge dome, is a shrine to the victims of war and of the earthquake of 1908. From the piazza in front of the church, there is a magnificent view of the city, the harbour and the strait.

THE REGIONAL MUSEUM
Along the seafront towards the north runs Viale della Libertà, on which can be found the Museo Regionale (Regional Museum). The museum occupies a late-nineteenth-century building, an old silk mill, and holds works of art salvaged after the earthquake of 1908. Entrance to the museum is by a path bordered by wildflowers and miscellaneous pieces of statuary. There is much to admire here in terms of paintings and sculpture from the twelfth to the eighteenth centuries, including works by local artists. There are sculptures by Antonello Gagini, Francesco Laurana and Giovanni Angelo Montorsoli, as well as archaeological finds from the ancient city. The most important works are by two artists of international fame, Antonello da Messina and Caravaggio.

Antonello, who was born in Messina and spent most of his life in the city, was trained in the cosmopolitan environment of Naples. Here he assimilated the techniques of the Flemish, Provençal and Venetian masters to produce portraits and altarpieces of rare quality. His work is ranked among the best of fifteenth-century Italy. Fortunately for posterity, much of his work became spread around galleries throughout the world and thus escaped destruction in the earthquakes. Here can be seen his *Madonna col Bambino con i santi Gregorio e Benedetto* (Madonna and Child with Saints Gregory and

Benedict), an example of his best work from 1473. There is also work by Antonello's school.

Caravaggio, after escaping from prison in Malta in October 1608, spent around a year in Sicily where he left some of his last masterpieces. In Messina, he created two altarpieces, displayed in the museum. Both are large canvases, dark and brooding in character, reflecting the artist's mood at the time, for he was on the run from the Knights of Malta.

The *Resurrezione di Lazzaro* (Resurrection of Lazarus) concentrates the viewer's attention on the moment when Christ, with a commanding gesture, orders Lazarus to rise from the dead. In *Adorazione dei pastori* (Adoration of the Shepherds), the humble figure of Mary and her child are set in a scene of simple poverty.

14

CEFALÙ, A SEASIDE TOWN WITH
A NORMAN CATHEDRAL

Cefalù occupies a dramatic position, poised between rock and sea, on the north coast of Sicily some seventy kilometres east of Palermo. In front is the Tyrrhenian sea, while directly behind the town rises the square shape of a huge crag, the Rocca, which dominates the landscape in a similar way to Monte Pellegrino near Palermo. Cefalù took its name from a local dialect version of the ancient Greek, *kephaloidion,* meaning point or headland. This is entirely appropriate as the environment here, with its old harbour, limpid sea and rocky coastline, is distinctly Greek in character. The old town consists of a cluster of houses packed closely together at the base of the Rocca, facing the sea. At its heart lies Piazza Duomo, at the far end of which stands the cathedral, with its elegant portico and two tall towers in yellow stone. The cathedral was built on a higher level than the piazza so that it rises above the rooftops, visible from miles away.

It was the Normans, after they captured Cefalù in 1063, who expanded the town around the base of the Rocca, and who, under King Roger II, began the building of the cathedral. Al-Edrisi, Arab geographer to Roger II, described the town as: 'A fortress-city on the sea, with markets, baths and mills all within its walls. A spring that comes out of the rock provides drinking water, sweet and fresh, for the population. The fortress of Cefalù is built by a tall mountain, difficult to climb because of the high, rugged coastline.'[1]

Cefalù was a favourite place of Vincenzo Consolo, a Sicilian writer who came from Sant'Agata di Militello, which lies down the coast towards Messina. Consolo moved to Milan and, in a career that lasted from the 1960s until his death in 2012, published works of historical fiction and travel writing steeped in the culture of Sicily. He wrote of the discovery of a small town, Cefalù, compact in its structure, which had miraculously preserved its historical inheritance. For Consolo, Cefalù represented a point of reference, a small world rich in content, where his discoveries never ended.[2]

THE OLD TOWN

Two main streets run north-south across the town, Corso Ruggero across the bottom of Piazza Duomo, and Via Vittorio Emanuele next to the seafront, linked by nine parallel smaller streets in an ancient grid system. The smaller streets are cobbled and carry decorative paving stones in various shapes. The town's coat of arms also appears, a design consisting of three fish facing a central circle which represents a loaf of bread. Via Vittorio Emanuele was formerly known as Via Fiume, for a river once ran here and the *lavatoio*, the old wash house, is still to be seen halfway down the street. Here fresh water runs along channels cut into the rock past stone blocks on which women used to beat their garments. Due to the ingenuity of this irrigation system, the *lavatoio* is thought to have Arab origins. Nearby is the last of the city gates to have survived, Porta Pescara, which leads to the seafront and the old harbour.

The old harbour, or the Marina, as it is known, is bordered by a breakwater which stretches out into the crystal-clear sea to protect the area where boats were moored. While there are still a few small boats in evidence, the sandy beach is now given over to holidaymakers and their families enjoying ideal swimming conditions. Behind the beach stands the outside wall of the old town, with houses and apartments built haphazardly on top of the Spanish ramparts. The tall façade contains a profusion of windows, balconies, supporting arches, terraces and roofs that rise above the beach and rocks below. From the apartments built in the wall, and from the restaurants and bars at ground level, a breathtaking view is afforded of the sea and the bay curving around with the green hills beyond. It is an atmospheric location used to good effect in *Cinema Paradiso*, a film made by Giuseppe Tornatore in 1988 about his native Sicily.

Heading down Via Vittorio Emanuele away from the Porta Pescara, one emerges from the old town onto a long promenade, the Lungomare Giardina. This follows the curve of the bay above the sandy beach and is where many of the hotels are situated. On the eastern side of the Rocca is the modern harbour filled with yachts and holiday craft. Cefalù, along with Taormina, was one of the first places in Sicily to become an international resort and is popular with the English, French and Germans. It is well-organised and, due to the wide bay where much of the tourist infrastructure is situated, can absorb large numbers of visitors.

THE CATHEDRAL

In its cathedral, Cefalù holds one of the great Norman monuments of Sicily. It was built before the cathedrals at Palermo and Monreale and like them displays a fusion of Arab and Norman architecture. Along with Monreale, and the Palatine Chapel and Church of the Martorana in Palermo, it is decorated with colourful mosaics. Cefalù was added to the list of UNESCO World Heritage Sites in 2015.

The cathedral overlooks a piazza flanked by old palaces and backed by the sheer face of the Rocca. It stands in a raised position, high above the piazza, and is reached by a flight of steep steps. Two towers, subtly different in design, rise on either side of a façade consisting of a double row of blind arcades above three arches. The towers, with their square shapes, narrow windows and pyramid roofs, recall the Arab fortress-palaces. All this was constructed in sand-coloured stone which glows in the sunlight. Palm trees in the piazza complete the exotic picture.

In common with other medieval churches, the cathedral has a founding legend. According to this, Roger found himself in a storm at sea in danger of his life when returning from southern Italy. He took an oath that, if he survived, he would build a cathedral at the place where he landed and dedicate it to the Saviour and to Saints Peter and Paul. When the storm subsided, the ship came ashore at Cefalù. The legend hides the true motive for founding the church and a bishopric at Cefalù. This was to please Pope Anacletus and was probably part of the 1130 settlement which led to Roger being crowned King of Sicily and southern Italy with the pope's support. As Otto Demus, an expert on the Norman churches of Sicily, observed, the founders wished to conceal their political aims under a cloak of miracle and devotion.[3]

Roger took a personal interest in the building and laid the foundation stone on 7 June 1131. He then ensured that the cathedral was magnificently endowed with land and serfs. A palace was built for the king in the town, possibly on the site of the building in Corso Ruggero known as the Osterio Magno. Later Roger expressed the wish to be buried in his cathedral in Cefalù and had a sarcophagus prepared for himself.

Building the cathedral employed Arab craftsmen and took place in stages, with the core completed in Roger's time and additions made during the reigns of William I and II. The towers and the façade were added in 1240 and the portico and arches, the work of Ambrogio da Como, in 1471. The interior is in the form of a Romanesque basilica with many later additions. Down the central nave sixteen ancient Roman columns support Arab-Norman arches. The wooden roof bears traces of paintings in the Islamic style, showing court scenes like those in the Palatine Chapel in Palermo. In the chapel to the right of the altar is a statue of the Madonna and Child by Antonello Gagini from 1533, and to the left, a painted crucifix by Tommaso de Vigilia. The stained-glass windows high in the nave were added during restorations carried out in 1925–32.

The mosaics are the cathedral's crowning glory. They cover the apse and the wall above the altar with a variety of figures that stand out against a golden background. They were the work of master craftsmen from Byzantium brought over to Sicily by Roger II, and, as an inscription indicates, were completed by 1148. In a strict hierarchy, there appears a huge image of Christ, below which are images of the Virgin Mary and four archangels, the twelve apostles, prophets and saints. The cathedral is thus a triumphant blend of Norman, Arab and Byzantine-Greek artistic talent.

Dominating the mosaics is the Christ Pantocrator (the Almighty), who looks down, his right hand raised in blessing, his left hand holding a book open at a text in Greek and Latin from St John's gospel that begins: 'I am the Light of the World'. In a portrait rich in symbolism, the solemn, bearded figure projects authority but also compassion and sorrow, while two loose locks of hair across the forehead imply something more personal, indicating that he is both God and human. His robe is of purple and gold, the colours of divinity, while his mantle is blue, the colour of humankind. This image of Christ has been widely praised. Although not produced in the Byzantine Empire, this apse mosaic of the Christ Pantocrator is one of the most beautiful and famous in the world.[4]

The cloisters of the old monastery, which are from the twelfth century, are to be found to the left of the cathedral's entrance, at the end of an alleyway. Like the cathedral, the cloisters represent a precursor to Monreale, on a smaller scale. In the centre of the cloisters were originally four gardens, each representing a theme from the Old or New Testament and with a fountain in a corner. A series of twin columns line the cloisters, with capitals bearing elaborate decorations linked to the themes of the gardens. The side wall of the cathedral is visible from the cloisters and shows Islamic-style patterned decorations like those on the cathedral walls at Palermo and Monreale.

Roger II's wish to be buried in his cathedral at Cefalù was ignored by his son, William I. He was buried instead in Palermo's cathedral where his tomb can be seen today. Under William II, Cefalù fell out of favour, with precedence going to Monreale.

THE MANDRALISCA MUSEUM

Enrico Pirajno, Baron of Mandralisca, who came from Cefalù, was an archaeologist, a naturalist and a collector of paintings and ancient artefacts. He took an active part in defying the oppressive Spanish Bourbon regime, became a deputy in the Sicilian government of 1848 and served in the first government of unified Italy. His marble tomb can be seen in the church of the Purgatory in Corso Ruggero. A museum occupies Mandralisca's former house, in the street bearing his name, which links Corso Ruggero to Via Vittorio Emanuele. Its collection reflects the baron's broad interests and includes ancient coins from the Greek era, pottery from the fourth century BC and a mosaic from the first century BC. The baron's interest in seashells is represented by a collection of 20,000 specimens. A library of 6,000 volumes includes books on Cefalù from the seventeenth century.

Mandralisca found some of his finest pieces on the island of Lipari, where he carried out excavations. One is a vase from the fourth century BC on which appears the picture of a fishmonger wielding a large knife and about to carve up a tuna for a client. The buyer has money in his hand and appears to be negotiating a price with the seller, a scene still familiar today in street markets across Sicily.

The gallery on the first floor displays paintings by Pietro Novelli, Antonello de Saliba, Francesco Bevelacqua, Giovanni Sogliani and the school of Pietro Ruzzolone. The outstanding exhibit is the *Ritratto d'uomo* (Portrait of a Man) by Antonello da Messina, from around 1470. Mandralisca found it on Lipari, being used in a pharmacy as part of a cupboard door. It is a small painting, oil on wood, featuring a mature looking man with a half-smile that engages the viewer in a hypnotic way.

Consolo, in his historical novel, *The Smile of the Unknown Mariner*, tells the story of Mandralisca, his fascination with the arts of Sicily, and of his gradual involvement in the uprisings against the Spanish Bourbons.

THE ROCCA

Getting to the top of the Rocca, which stands at 270 metres above sea level, requires care and stamina. It is a steep climb, taking about an hour, up a narrow path that begins in Percorso Pedemontana, a street that follows the side of the Rocca, not far from Piazza Garibaldi. The area on top is strewn with fragments of walls, buildings and water cisterns from many different eras. Its high position meant it was a suitable location for religious rites and it is linked to various ancient myths.

The Rocca was occupied from prehistoric times and through antiquity served as a place of refuge. There are remains of a wall linking the Rocca to the port below. Traces of a Sicel community from the ninth century BC have been found. The megalithic blocks of stone, known as the Temple of Diana, are probably the remains of an ancient sanctuary dating from the fourth or fifth century BC. The foundation of a castle from the twelfth century can be seen on a peak overlooking the sea. Part of a defensive wall is also visible. The son of Charles of Anjou, the Frenchman whose rule of Sicily was overthrown by the Sicilian Vespers, was apparently imprisoned here.

CASTELBUONO AND THE MADONIE MOUNTAINS

Inland from Cefalù lies a protected nature reserve, the Parco delle Madonie, which extends from the lower hills near the coast, with their vineyards and olive trees, to the high peaks of the mountains beyond. The higher ground, which contains extensive pine and beech woods, takes on an alpine character. Mountain streams flow from gorges down into the valleys which are filled with pastures for sheep and cattle. The park of the Madonie demonstrates the variety of Sicily's countryside, for this kind of territory is more usually associated with northern Italy.

The region of the Madonie has always had a close relationship with Cefalù, the countryside providing fresh produce and the town offering both a market and a port. In the fourteenth century, this relationship became closer with the emergence of the Ventimiglia family. This occurred in the aftermath of the Sicilian Vespers, when the French were thrown off the island. The Ventimiglia, who came originally from Liguria in northern Italy, established themselves as the most powerful family in northern Sicily, providing the island with viceroys, admirals and governors. Their counterparts in Palermo were the Chiaramonte. In Cefalù, the Ventimiglia base was at the Osterio Magno in Corso Ruggero. In the Madonie region, they built themselves a castle at Castelbuono.

Castelbuono lies in a fertile valley surrounded by green hills, some twenty kilometres from Cefalù. For a small provincial centre, it contains a remarkable collection of fine buildings and works of art. While the origins of the town are Byzantine, it was under the Ventimiglia that it made its mark. The town's main monuments include the Ventimiglia castle, which has a chapel brilliantly decorated in stucco attributed to Giacomo and Giuseppe Serpotta.

A characteristic of the inland towns in Sicily is their cleanliness compared to the coastal cities. Castelbuono, which is no exception, makes a feature of its refuse collection by using donkeys. Employing a hardy breed of donkey from Ragusa, the weekly, door-to-door service is described as donkeys in the service of the environment.

15

THE HILLTOWN OF NOTO,
A BAROQUE MASTERPIECE

Noto is the capital of Sicilian baroque for the richness and originality of its architecture. Rebuilt on a new site after the old town was destroyed by the earthquake of 1693, it was laid out according to a grid plan which allowed free rein to the late baroque style. The result was an urban environment of rare beauty. Theatrical and dazzling in the sun, with its richly ornate churches and palaces, Noto is a baroque masterpiece. The Sicilians call it a *giardino di pietra* (a garden of stone).

It lies some thirty kilometres south-west of Syracuse and is reached by the motorway flanked by the ridge of the Hyblaean Mountains. Beyond the motorway, the state road 115 winds its way up to Noto and then on to the baroque towns of Modica and Ragusa.

THE HISTORY
In antiquity and throughout the Middle Ages, as well as after being relaunched in its baroque splendour under the Spanish, Noto was an important provincial centre. It maintained this position until decline set in during the nineteenth century. Little is known of the town's history due to its scarce records, most of which were destroyed by the earthquake.

Noto Antica (Ancient Noto) stood on Mount Averia, some ten kilometres away from its present site. Its origins were Sicel, who were well established in the mountainous region of eastern Sicily. In its early expansion, Syracuse established outposts to protect itself, one of which was Helorus on the coast (near Noto Marina), another at Noto, named Neaiton by the Greeks. In the mid-fifth century BC, the town was briefly the centre of a revolt against Syracuse by the Sicels, led by Ducetius. When Hiero II ruled eastern Sicily from Syracuse in the third century BC, Neaiton enjoyed a period of prosperity.

Renamed Netum, under the Romans the town's status was enhanced, along with Messana (Messina) and Tauromenium (Taormina), by being made one of the *civitates foederate,* cities linked directly by treaty to Rome and benefiting from a tax-free status.

The town's importance continued under the Arabs, who divided Sicily into three administrative districts. Noto became the capital of the Val di Noto, responsible for the south-eastern corner of the island, in which role it prospered from agriculture, silk production, tanning factories and fishing. Its position was maintained in Norman times, as witnessed by al-Edrisi, who visited Noto during the reign of King Roger II.

A well-defended hilltown, among the finest on the island, it covers a large area and is an important centre with well-ordered markets and palaces protected by towers…Its rich province covers highly productive territory.[1]

After being rebuilt, Noto continued to be a centre for agriculture and fishing, the wealth of the region helping to finance the recon-struction programme.

The nineteenth century saw a change in Noto's fortunes. In 1817, the Bourbon king of Sicily made Syracuse the provincial capital, reducing Noto's importance. Further decline came with the closing of the monasteries in 1866, for the town was an important ecclesiastical centre. As the economy contracted, so residents left, and the fabric of the city became neglected. Much restoration work has been carried out since, including on the cathedral. Modern Noto remains, however, more a destination for visitors and the scene of local festivals, than a thriving residential centre. In 2002, Noto was included among eight baroque towns in south-eastern Sicily as a UNESCO World Heritage Site.

THE REBIRTH OF NOTO

The rebuilding of Noto was made necessary by the earthquake of 1693. During the nights of 9 and 11 January, two seismic shocks of great violence devastated cities from Catania to Noto. Two of the island's three administrative districts were affected, the Val Demone, which included Messina, and the Val di Noto, which extended from Catania to take in Syracuse and the south-eastern corner of the island. Catania and Noto were both reduced to rubble and the centre of Syracuse badly damaged. Over 50,000 people died, with thousands more injured and made homeless. According to a letter sent to the Spanish viceroy, in total fifty-eight urban centres were affected, twenty of which were virtually destroyed. Noto was so badly affected that it was decided to rebuild the city on a new site further down the hill.[2]

This disaster occurred at a time when the baroque style of architecture, which had been established in Palermo since the early seventeenth century, was at its peak in Sicily. Architects and craftsmen had honed their skills over the years, some with training in Rome, and had developed designs unique to Sicily. The period following the earthquake saw a construction boom in eastern Sicily, with city centres rebuilt in the late baroque style.[3]

Immediately after the earthquake, the viceroy, the Duke of Uzeda, set up a central administration to handle reconstruction with Giuseppe Lanza, the Duke of Camastra in charge. Two committees, made up of churchmen and aristocrats, were established to oversee the work. Led by a local nobleman, Giovanni Battista Landolina, the city's elders adopted a plan based on a grid system centred on three main streets, incorporating squares that housed public buildings.

Palaces for the aristocracy were located centrally, while secondary streets on the periphery were designated for the working population. In the case of Noto, the rebuilding was a unique experiment, a whole city reconstructed in a consistent style.

The town plan drew upon experience that went back to the ancient Greeks, who used grid plans for some of their cities, an example of which can be seen at Selinunte. Also influential was the work of a Venetian architect, Vincenzo Scamozzi, who published a treatise on the ideal city in 1615. When implemented, the plan created a town of extraordinary harmony.

The leading architect in the reconstruction process, whose work was influential across the Val di Noto, was Rosario Gagliardi. Other architects who played an important part were Vincenzo Sinatra and Paolo Labisi.

Work at Noto began in February 1693 and by the 1750s Noto was on the way to recovery with its population up to 10,000. The full story of Noto's rebirth as a baroque city is told by Stephen Tobriner in his book, *The Genesis of Noto.*[4]

EXPLORING NOTO
The approach to the city is down Viale Marconi, a broad promenade shaded by ficus trees. In the nearby public gardens stands a bronze statue of Noto's patron saint, San Corrado. He was a nobleman from Piacenza in central Italy who on a hunting trip lit a fire that destroyed local property. In penance he became a hermit, and, moving to Sicily lived in a cave in the hills above Noto, dying in 1351. At the end of the promenade stands a commemorative arch, the *Porta Reale* (Royal Gate), built in 1841 for the arrival of the Bourbon king, Ferdinand II.

Through the arch one enters Corso Vittorio Emanuele, the city's central artery, which runs east-west for a kilometre, dividing Noto Alta to the right, from Noto Bassa to the left. Even a prior visit to other baroque towns does not prepare one for the first glimpse of Noto. Built in the local limestone, the magnificently decorated buildings glow with a golden colour in the sunshine. The style of the city is light and spacious, in contrast to the medieval towns with their dark alleyways. The roads are wide and straight, linked by side roads which run at right-angles, with open space created in the squares.

The first building of note, at the beginning of the Corso, is the church of San Francesco all'Immacolata (St Francis of Our Lady) designed by Sinatra. Next to it is the monastery of San Salvatore with a façade attributed to Gagliardi. On the other side of the Corso stands the small church of Santa Chiara by Gagliardi, whose elegant interior contains a marble statue of the Madonna by Antonello Gagini.

In the centre of the Corso stands the *Piazza Municipio* (Town Square) with the *duomo* (cathedral) on the north side and the town hall, the Palazzo Ducezio, to the south. The cathedral, dedicated to San Nicolò was begun in 1746, the work of Gagliardi and Sinatra. The approach is especially impressive, up a long series of steps as wide as the building itself. The centre of the elaborate façade is supported by columns and crowned with statues, on either side of which stands a campanile. The lightness of touch is maintained in the interior of the cathedral. The Palazzo Ducezio, by Sinatra, has an original design featuring a series of arches at ground level, topped by a balustrade and a classical first floor.

Next to the cathedral is the Bishop's Palace and the Palazzo Sant'Alfano Landolina, once the property of the town's leading family. Further down the Corso from the cathedral lies Piazza XVI Maggio, containing the church of San Domenico, with its curved façade by Gagliardi. The square also holds an ancient bronze statue of Heracles from Noto Antica. Via Nicolaci, which runs off the Corso, is famous for the Palazzo Nicolaci, attributed to Labisi, with its array of balconies. These balconies, fronted by ornate metalwork, are supported by exotic stone sculptures which include winged horses and a variety of mythological figures.

Noto is famous for its festivals, and Via Nicolaci is the location for a spring flower festival, on the third Sunday in May, when the entire street is laid with intricate designs made from flowers. Other festivals include those of the patron saint, San Corrado, in February and August, when processions carry a statue of the saint through the streets. There are celebrations at Easter, a baroque festival in May, and concerts of classical music in July.

At the renowned Caffè Sicilia in the Corso, Noto's desserts, cakes and ice-creams are on offer along with *Moscato di Noto,* the local dessert wine.

Noto Antica, the ancient city destroyed by the earthquake, is to be found off the road from the modern city leading to Palazzolo Acreide. The remains of ancient walls, bastions, churches and palaces are memorials to the city's former status. The site is reached through rocky territory, like the area around Pantàlica, where remnants of prehistoric settlements have been found. Noto Antica itself holds traces of the Sicel, Greek, Arab, Christian, Byzantine and Spanish eras. There is little left of the buildings, for due to the remote location and the lack of supervision, the site has been systematically looted over the years.[5]

THE GULF OF NOTO

Noto Marina, the city's old port and source of wealth through its fishing industry, is now a holiday resort. Along the coast, south of Noto Marina, lies the nature reserve of Vendicari. It is an unspoilt area of low scrubland, wildflowers, rock, sand dunes and freshwater lagoons, the home of varieties of birds including flamingos, cormorants, herons and storks. On the shoreline stand the remains of two buildings, a Swabian tower dating from the thirteenth century, built in the same period as the Maniace Castle in Syracuse, and from more recent times, a *tonnara* where tuna fish was processed.

Facing the coast is a landscape with strong echoes of the ancient world. Here flows the Asinaro river where the Athenian general

Nicias surrendered to the Syracusans in 413 BC after his troops had been decimated in battle. Two ancient sites are located nearby.

The first of these is Eloro, ancient Helorus, one of the early outposts settled by Syracuse around 650 BC. The settlement was named after the river of the same name. It is to be found just north of Vendicari, approached down a narrow lane that wends its way through olive groves. The site contains the remnants of a section of ancient wall, gates, part of the marketplace, a small theatre and sanctuaries to Demeter and Kore and to Asclepius. It was important in ancient times both for the religious significance of its sanctuaries and for its position as a coastal look-out point.

The second is the Roman Villa del Tellaro, to be found just off the Noto-Pachino road, close to the Vendicari reserve. Tellaro is the modern name for Helorus, the river mentioned above. The villa, which dates from the fourth century AD, was discovered in the 1970s. It is significant for the elaborate, coloured mosaics which decorate its floors. A typical Sicilian farmhouse, a *masseria,* was built over the remains of the villa in the eighteenth century and this structure has been preserved. The mosaics, now restored and open to the public, are rich in content and colour. They include scenes from classical Greece, a dancing satyr, a lively hunt featuring a lion, a formal banquet and numerous illustrations of animals and birds. There are separate sections decorated with geometric and floral patterns. Although on a much smaller scale than the Roman villa at Piazza Armerina, the Villa del Tellaro contains mosaics of comparable quality and represents an important monument to the Roman era in Sicily.

RAGUSA AND MODICA, BAROQUE HILLTOWNS ABOVE A SPARKLING COASTLINE

The province of Ragusa, in the south-eastern corner of Sicily, contains some of the most spectacular scenery on the island. The province extends from the Monti Iblei (the Hyblaean Mountains), with its peak of Monte Laura at 986 metres, through an ancient landscape containing rivers and deep gorges, to a sparkling coastline facing Africa. Along the coast lie fishing villages and holiday resorts made up of rows of low-lying white buildings with small harbours and sandy beaches.

The population of the province, which is around 320,000, is spread among twelve towns, all of which are decorated in the local baroque style. The urban scenery of the province is among the finest in all Italy. This is where, according to the art historian Anthony Blunt, some of the best examples of Sicilian baroque are to be found. These towns, with their cupolas and campaniles, sit astride peaks in the rocky landscape divided from one another by steep valleys. Flights of stairs weave their way through the towns leading up to flamboyant church façades, the most remarkable being those designed by Rosario Gagliardi. In 2002, UNESCO recognised the quality of the baroque architecture in the Val di Noto, which extends from Catania to the province of Ragusa, naming eight cities as World Heritage Sites, among them Ragusa and Modica.[1]

This scenery, both urban and maritime, is used as the setting for the Italian TV series featuring Inspector Montalbano, based on the novels by Andrea Camilleri. Hugely popular in Italy, the series spread to reach international audiences. The province of Ragusa, made famous by the TV series and where most of its episodes were filmed, has become known as Montalbano territory.

THE HISTORY

Human habitation of the province began in prehistoric times, with ancient tombs visible in the rocks. In the nearby province of Syracuse lies the site of Pantàlica, an ancient settlement with origins in the thirteenth century BC. The earliest recorded people in the Ragusa province were the Sicels, who came from mainland Italy, and who established themselves in eastern Sicily in the eleventh century BC. It was from the Sicels that Sicily took its name, while the Hyblaean Mountains were named after a Sicel goddess, Hybla. After the Greeks arrived on the island and established settlements around the coast, the Sicels moved further inland, with their king, Hyblon, granting territory near Syracuse to the Greeks on which to build another city, Megara Hyblaea.

Many of the different people who ruled Sicily left their mark on the province. Kamarina was founded by Greeks from Syracuse in 599 BC, as an outpost of their city, when the whole of south-eastern Sicily was Syracusan territory. The town of Chiaramonte Gulfi, to the north of the province, stands on the site of a staging post used by the Greeks of Syracuse on their way to the coast. Kaukana shows signs of both Roman and Byzantine civilisations. It was from the port of Kaukana that the Byzantine general, Belisarius, sailed in AD 533 to defeat the Vandals in North Africa.

In the Middle Ages the Normans built estates here, as did the Chiaramonte, a powerful family based in Palermo who became the Counts of Modica. It was the Normans who introduced one of their favourite saints to Sicily, George, who became a patron saint in both Ragusa and Modica. The county became famous for its agriculture, which because of its geography developed differently than in most of Sicily. The combination of hilly country with a central plateau and a narrow coastal plain was more suited for mixed farming than for growing grain. As a result, local farms produced cattle and other livestock, as well as olives and wine. This kind of farming led to greater independence for agricultural workers than elsewhere on the island and the county gained a reputation for liberal attitudes and a crime-free environment.

Ragusa was badly hit by the earthquake of 1693 and lost half its population. For the work of reconstruction, the Spanish rulers of Sicily, together with the church and the aristocracy, chose the local baroque style, giving Sicily's skilled architects and craftsmen the opportunity to design major new projects. By this time Sicilian baroque had matured into a style of architecture and sculpture with original features of its own which were rich in exotic decoration.

Mussolini, who visited Sicily in 1924, made a personal intervention in Ragusa, declaring it capital of the province in 1926, while at the same time redefining its borders. Up to this point Modica had been the capital. According to local legend, the reason for this was the lack of an adequate turnout to welcome Mussolini at Modica's railway station, during the Duce's tour of eastern Sicily. Being a liberal-minded city, its residents showed their disapproval of the Fascist government by refusing to give Mussolini his usual rapturous welcome. This was taken as an insult and the status of *Capo Provincia* was taken from Modica and granted to Ragusa.

Today Ragusa, the smallest province on the island, is also one of the wealthiest. Oil was discovered here in 1953 and is now drilled offshore and piped to refineries at Augusta on the east coast. The quarrying of stone as building material continues as it has for centuries. The tradition of mixed farming goes on, with dairy farming and the production of livestock taking place on the plateau below the hills. Typical products include milk, pork and cheese known as *caciocavallo*. Wine is widely produced, with the town of Vittoria renowned for the quality of its red wine, *Cerasuolo*. Intensive market gardening is carried out on the coastal plain, producing fruit and vegetables, including cherry tomatoes in large quantities.

Tourism, which is thriving and includes an increasing number of foreigners with holiday homes, has recently been helped by the opening of the airport at Comiso to international traffic. The airport, which is less than twenty kilometres from Ragusa, has direct flights to London, Frankfurt, Brussels and Dublin, as well as to cities on the Italian mainland. Another boost to tourism is the so-called *Treno Barocco*, a train which runs on Sundays in the summer months, from Syracuse and calling at Noto, Modica and Ragusa, enabling visitors to see the most famous baroque towns in a day's outing. Other attractions are the frequent feasts and saints' day celebrations when elaborate processions can be seen parading through the streets.

VISITING RAGUSA

Ragusa has two separate centres, the upper town, Ragusa Superiore, and the lower, Ragusa Ibla, linked by a flight of over 240 steps and by a steep road full of hairpin bends. Ragusa Superiore is laid out with wide streets according to the reconstruction plan which followed the earthquake. The imposing cathedral of San Giovanni Battista (St John the Baptist), with its wide façade and fine campanile, dominates the middle of the town. Close by is the archaeological museum, containing a statue of a Sicel warrior from the seventh century BC as well as Greek and Roman artefacts. Above the cathedral is a vantage point, known as the Rotonda, which provides panoramic views over the lower town.

Ragusa Ibla, with ravines on either side, occupies the site of the ancient Sicel settlement, Hybla Heraea, and that of the medieval town that was destroyed by the earthquake of 1693. It is the more spectacular of the two centres and contains thirteen baroque monuments listed by UNESCO. Built in golden stone, it consists of small squares, churches, narrow streets, crumbling palaces, ornate balconies and sudden, breathtaking views over the countryside. This is a place to be explored on foot, with cars left at the lower street level. Starting at Piazza della Repubblica, where the two centres meet, a winding street leads through the middle of Ibla to the Giardini Iblei, the public gardens. Close to the piazza is the church of Santa Maria dell'Idria, which was originally built for the Knights of Malta. The church has a richly decorated interior while its blue tiled dome has become one of the symbols of the town.

At the heart of Ibla stands the cathedral of San Giorgio designed by Rosario Gagliardi, the leading architect of the late baroque era, whose work can be seen across the Val di Noto. The three-tiered façade of the cathedral fills one end of Corso XXV Aprile, a wide street containing palm trees, cafés and two decorative buildings, the Circolo di Conversazione and the Palazzo Donnfugata. The cathedral's interior contains statues of St George, one by the Gagini school, as well as Gagliardi's original plans for the building. Among the palaces of note are the Cosentini, known for the grotesque figures supporting the balconies; Battaglia, with its classical façade and La Rocca, famous for its six balconies.[2]

MODICA

Like Ragusa, Modica consists of an upper and a lower town, Modica Alta and Bassa. There is also a third, modern centre for commercial activity. The town lies on the road some fifteen kilometres before Ragusa when approaching from Ispica and Noto. The town's social centre in Modica Bassa is Corso Umberto, a wide street containing several fine palaces, laid out in the reconstruction period. On either side lie alleyways and courtyards recalling the town's medieval past. On the right can be seen the remains of the castle of the Counts of Modica. From the Corso, a series of steps decorated with statues of the apostles leads up to the church of San Pietro, whose broad façade topped by more statues looks out over the town. Two more churches are of interest, the church of the Carmine, containing sculpture by the Gagini school, and the church of Santa Maria di Bethlemme, which has a Palatine Chapel in the Arabo-Norman style.

Steps climb steeply towards Modica Alta, along a road lined with palaces and the church of San Giovanni Battista at the highest point. The cathedral of San Giorgio, possibly designed by Rosario Gagliardi, was built on the site of a Norman church. It is one of the outstanding examples of Sicilian baroque, with an unusual curved façade, and stands at the top of a flight of 250 steps. The view of the old town from outside the cathedral is exceptional.

Modica was the birthplace of Salvatore Quasimodo, who won the Nobel Prize for poetry in 1959. He takes his place among Sicily's writers who achieved international fame including Pirandello, Lampedusa and Sciascia. Quasimodo wrote lyrical poetry about Sicily while working far from home in northern Italy.

The town has a vibrant economy based on agricultural produce which provides a robust local cuisine. The best-known local product is Modica chocolate, now produced on a large scale. It is unusual in that it is based upon an ancient Aztec recipe, brought to Sicily by the Spanish. It contains no fat, unlike most chocolate bars, and comes in a variety of natural flavours such as orange, lemon and almond. A good place to try it is the Antica Dolceria Bonajuto, founded in 1880, to be found at No 1, Corso Umberto.[3]

SMALLER TOWNS AND THE SEASIDE
The smaller towns of the province are full of character. Scicli, not far from the sea, lies between two gorges and has some of the most striking architecture. Around the central Piazza Italia cluster churches and palaces of note including the church of San Matteo (St Matthew) and the Palazzo Fava. Wrought-iron balconies supported by fanciful creatures carved in yellow stone are a feature of the town. Strange heads appear on the façade of the Palazzo Beneventano, the most extravagant of the palaces. The church of

San Bartolomeo stands out for being the only one from the fifteenth century to have survived the earthquake.

On the high ground above Ragusa stands Chiaramonte Gulfi, originally built in the early fourteenth century as an outpost to protect Modica from the north. Panoramic views of the province can be seen from here. The town centre contains fine baroque buildings around a core of medieval side streets.

Close to Santa Croce Camarina, on the coast, are two small archaeological sites, Kamarina and Kaukana. Kamarina was an outpost of Syracuse in the ancient Greek era and Kaucana has Roman and Byzantine origins. Their archaeological sites and museums can be found nearby.

Other towns of interest include Ispica, Comiso and Vittoria. All contain significant monuments from the baroque era. Comiso was the birthplace of another well-known Sicilian writer, Gesualdo Bufalino, who died in 1996.

For seaside holidays there is a choice of locations along the province's eighty-five kilometres of coastline. Centres such as Donnalucata and Punta Secca stretch along the seafront with their traditional low, white houses. Fishing boats go out in the evenings to maintain the supply of fresh fish to the many small restaurants. The sea is clear and the environment in summer is hot. The temperature can reach over forty degrees centigrade while the *scirocco*, the south wind, makes it feel even hotter. The most developed resort is Marina di Ragusa, which has a yacht harbour and a seaside promenade lined with palm trees. Smaller holiday centres include Scoglitti and Sampieri, which were once fishing villages, while one of the best sandy bays is to be found at Cava d'Aliga.

THE MONTALBANO TRAIL

The success of the Montalbano TV series has led to an increased interest in the province. Italian fans, landing at the airport, ask taxi drivers to take them to Vigàta, the fictional town where much of the action takes place. In practice, the sets used in the TV drama are often composite, drawing upon images from different places. Certain locations can be identified, as Maurizio Clausi makes clear in his book, *I luoghi di Montalbano* (Montalbano's places). Montalbano tours have become a popular feature of the local tourist trade.[4]

Punta Secca, a cluster of houses behind a small harbour near Santa Croce Camarina, is the main location for the filming of Marinella, where Montalbano lives. The white tower of the lighthouse is instantly recognisable from the opening sequence of the TV drama, which was broadcast from 1999 to the present day. Montalbano's apartment, with its terrace overlooking the beach, is a busy B&B when they are not filming. The small restaurant favoured by the inspector, known as *Enzo a Mare* on TV, can be found along the seafront. Some of the scenes in the fictional Marinella are also shot in Donnalucata.

Scicli is the principal location for Vigàta, where Montalbano has his office. Several central streets are used for the set, together with the town hall which acts as the inspector's headquarters.

Ragusa Ibla features prominently in the TV drama. The opening sequence includes aerial shots of the town and surrounding hills. The square in front of the cathedral of San Giorgio is where Montalbano can be seen heading for his usual caffé. In the nearby Piazza Pola is a palace, next to the church of San Giuseppe, which is sometimes used as the inspector's office. The restaurant named *La Rusticana* (*Calogero* in the TV series), in Corso XXV Aprile, is where Salvo and Mimì like to have lunch and enjoy a glass of Grillo, their favourite white wine.

Andrea Camilleri, author of the novels on which the TV series is based, came from Porto Empedocle, which lies further along the coast near Agrigento, and lived in Rome. In the Sicilian literary tradition, his work is steeped in the character and social mores of the island. The context of the stories, in which Montalbano and his small team of policemen fight crime and corruption, is contemporary

Sicilian life with its political problems, mafia background and huge differences between rich and poor. The stories explore how the traditional Sicilian way of life is changing to meet the pressures of the modern world, including increased tourism and the influx of refugees from Africa and the Middle East. The books thus provide not only entertainment but also a way to increase understanding of the island.[5]

PALAZZOLO ACREIDE, ANCIENT AKRAI, A BAROQUE HILLTOWN

Palazzolo Acreide is a small town in the Val di Noto, some forty kilometres inland from Syracuse, which contains several interesting features. It combines the attractions of baroque architecture in its squares, churches and palaces with the archaeological site of an ancient Greek city and the remains of a sanctuary to an obscure ancient goddess. In addition, there are traces from the Roman, early Christian and Byzantine eras. Little is known of the history other than that gleaned from the archaeological sites.

Rebuilt following the earthquake of 1693, it is an example of a well-kept town near the mountains which has preserved much of its traditional way of life. The name Palazzolo comes from a Norman castle, mentioned by the Arab geographer al-Edrisi, which once stood here. Acreide is derived from Akrai, the name of the Greek city, the site of which lies just outside the town. The region was inhabited from prehistoric times as is evident from the nearby necropolis of Pantàlica.

The road from Syracuse leads up to countryside that is very different from the coastal plain. Climbing slowly, the road reaches a plateau with open vistas, olive groves divided by low stone walls, rocky hillsides and deep gorges along the rivers. The air is clearer and the heat less intense than by the sea and a visit is like a trip back in time to a life lived closer to the land. This is an agricultural region, famous for raising horses and for its produce such as olive oil, cheese and meat, and which offers a robust country cuisine.

Beyond the town lie the Hyblaean Mountains, whose name comes from Hybla, a Sicel goddess. The Sicels, who gave their name to Sicily, inhabited eastern Sicily before the arrival of the Greeks. Under the Greeks, who rapidly dominated the Sicel population, the region became part of the Syracusan hinterland, established for defensive purposes as well as for supplying the city with food and livestock.

PALAZZOLO ACREIDE

Palazzolo Acreide was badly damaged by the earthquake of 1693, along with fifty-seven other urban centres across eastern Sicily. The town was slowly rebuilt in the eighteenth century in the late baroque style by craftsmen under the direction of architects such as Paolo Labisi, who helped rebuild Noto. As a result, the compact historic centre is filled with decorative churches and palaces, rows of elegant town houses, ornamental gateways and elaborate wrought-iron balconies. A feature of the architecture, as in Noto, is the stone carving of grotesque figures to support the balconies. Some of the most imaginative are to be seen on the Palazzo Judica in Corso Vittorio Emanuele.

The central square, Piazza del Popolo, is dominated by the façade of the church of San Sebastiano by Labisi. Other churches of note include the church of San Paolo, the town's patron saint; the Immacolata (dedicated to the Virgin), which contains rich decoration and a statue of the Madonna and Child by Francesco Laurana; the *Chiesa Madre*, or Mother Church, which holds a painting by the school of Pietro Novelli; and the Annunciata, with a marble altar by Antonello Gagini. The church of the Annunciata originally held Antonello da Messina's painting of the Annunciation, now to be seen in the Bellomo museum in Syracuse. Along with seven other cities in the Val di Noto, Palazzolo Acreide was made a World Heritage Site by UNESCO in 2002.

In Via Machiavelli is a museum, the Casa Museo, dedicated to the old rural economy which demonstrates local traditions of food

production and agriculture. It was created in the 1970s by the poet
and anthropologist, Antonino Uccello. It contains a collection of old
implements and utensils, located in a seventeenth-century house
complete with workshops and courtyards, a memorial to a working
way of life that sustained the region for centuries.

Near the entrance to the town lies the monumental cemetery,
built in the 1890s, which contains elaborate tombs, family vaults
and statues by local stonecutters. On a clear day the cemetery
offers a fine view of Mount Etna. Since ancient times this region
has been a place of strong religious beliefs, still evident today in the
celebrations of the saints' days when the population turns out to
watch processions through the streets. The main celebration is that
of the town's patron saint, St Paul, on 28 and 29 June. A festival to
St Sebastian, a saint popular across the region, takes place on 9 and
10 August.

THE ANCIENT CITY OF AKRAI

The archaeological site of Akrai lies just outside the town, away
from the modern buildings. Akrai, an outpost of Syracuse, was
founded by the Syracusan Greeks in around 664 BC, an event
which may have coincided with the end of a war with the Sicels.[1]
The name Akrai comes from *akros,* the Greek for edge or extremity,
referring to the town's position dominating a hilltop. After being
abandoned for centuries, the site was rediscovered in the 1550s
by Fazello.

According to the Sicilian archaeologist, Luigi Bernabò Brea,
who carried out excavations here in the 1950s, the site Akrai was
chosen for strategic reasons. A comparison can be made with the
Castello Eurialo, the great fortress of Dionysius. Just as the Eurialo
dominated the ridge of hills behind Syracuse, protecting the city's
rear, so Akrai, at the high point of the city's hinterland, gave Syracuse
protection in depth. Possession of Akrai provided the Syracusans
with access to the inland routes to the Greek cities on the south

coast, Gela, Agrigento and Selinunte, as well to the Sicel cities of the interior.[2]

Akrai was at its most prosperous under Hiero II, who ruled Syracuse from 269 to 216 BC. The site contains a well-preserved Greek theatre dating from this period, in miniature compared to that in Syracuse with seating for around 700. It lay forgotten until unearthed by Fazello on his tour of the island in the 1550s. It was rediscovered in 1824 by a local archaeologist, Gabriele Judica. The semi-circular *cavea* contains tiered seating cut from the rock of the hillside, divided into nine segments by eight staircases. The theatre was remodelled by the Romans when the existing paving of the orchestra was laid.

Adjoining the theatre is the *bouleuterion,* a small council chamber for the senate which governed the city, consisting of a semi-circle of seats in three tiers. Originally it faced the *agora,* the marketplace, which was the centre of political and civic life.

A temple to Aphrodite, the main deity of Akrai, stood on the top of the hill overlooking the city. Only fragments of its foundations remain today. Two more temples once stood nearby. The ancient walls, which date from between the fourth and the second centuries BC, consist of huge blocks of stone. In these walls there once stood a gate to the east with the route for Syracuse and a gate to the west for Selinunte. From the western gate, the route led through the centre of Sicily (via Caltagirone), reaching the south coast at Gela.

The site contains traces of several civilisations following the ancient Greeks, including the Roman, early Christian and Byzantine. The elaborately worked caves and catacombs, first used by the Greeks for religious cults, were extended in the early Christian period. In the fourth and fifth centuries AD this area became the most important Christian centre on the island after Syracuse. The catacombs were further developed by the Byzantines, after the arrival of the Arabs in 827, to be used as living quarters and burial sites.

There is a Roman relief carving from the first half of the first century BC, showing a soldier making a sacrifice. The site also contains two *latomie*, or quarries, known as the Intagliata and Intagliatella, which supplied the stone to build the city.

The inland route, linking Akrai to the south coast, continued to be used for centuries. It was followed by the Arabs in AD 827, when they invaded Sicily and first tried to capture Syracuse. On their way through to Syracuse, the Arabs sacked Akrai. On this occasion, Syracuse managed to hold out, not falling to the Arabs until 878. This route may also have been taken by Caravaggio, on his way to Syracuse, after he landed on the south coast of Sicily in 1608.

THE SANTONI OR SANCTUARY TO THE GODDESS CYBELE

Outside the archaeological site of Akrai, next to the old road to Noto, can be found a unique monument. Known locally as the Santoni, having once been mistaken for saints, the monument consists of twelve statues representing the ancient cult of the goddess Cybele. They are the remains of a sanctuary for one of the most mysterious goddesses of antiquity, that of the Magna Mater, the Great Mother. It is thought to have been the principal centre of this cult in Sicily.

The cult of Cybele came originally from Phrygia in Anatolia where it represented the state goddess. Comparable to the Harvest-Mother goddess, Demeter, who was revered in Sicily, Cybele added some exotic traits of her own, including orgiastic rituals, a lion-drawn chariot and a following of eunuch priests. Her cult spread to mainland Greece and then to the Greek colonies in the west, including Sicily. Here she was associated with mountains, city walls, fertile nature and wild animals, especially lions.

The large sanctuary is located on a rocky hill overlooking a path with two flat, semi-circular areas at each end. Circular stones, which probably formed the foundations of altars, can be made out. The sculptures are found in twelve niches carved into the rock, eleven at one level, and one on a lower level. Most of the niches contain a similar, seated female figure, the goddess Cybele, accompanied by lions, a panther and a drum, in different states of preservation. One of them contains a life-sized statue of the goddess. Other figures associated with the cult also appear, such as Hermes and Attis, the latter being a younger priestly attendant. Identification of the goddess in the niches as Cybele comes from comparisons with her representations elsewhere in the Greek world, especially in Athens.

The reason for building the sanctuary at Akrai remains a mystery. A possible connection lies with Corinth, the mother-city of Syracuse, which had a temple to Cybele. When Dionysius II, ruler of Syracuse, went into exile in 344 BC he moved to Corinth where he became a priest of the goddess. According to Bernabò Brea, Dionysius may have introduced the cult to Syracuse. The sanctuary itself, however, was probably created later, sometime towards the end of the fourth century or during the third century BC. So far, this sanctuary with its many figures and detailed carvings is the most comprehensive presentation of the cult of Cybele to have survived from the ancient world.[3]

MARSALA, ANCIENT LILYBAEUM, A PORT CITY FAMOUS FOR ITS WINE

Marsala is a port city with a population of 83,000 in the far west of Sicily, built on a coastline characterised by sand dunes, marshes and lagoons, the haunt of herons and flamingos. Its economy is largely based upon agriculture, especially wine production. Sea salt is also produced in large quantities, in salt pans to be seen along the coast. While tourism is on the increase, there is far less than in the cities on the east coast.

Marsala's claim to fame lies in two different historical periods. In ancient times, when it was called Lilybaeum, it became the leading Carthaginian city in Sicily, after nearby Motya (Mozia) was destroyed by the Greeks. Lilybaeum then continued as an important city and naval base under the Romans. In the nineteenth century, Marsala's economy took off on the back of an international wine trade established by British traders. The most important event in the city's history took place in 1860, when Garibaldi and his *Mille* (Thousand) landed at Marsala at the start of the campaign to free Sicily from the Spanish Bourbon government.

The city's fascination lies in its ancient origins, its position on the sea, and its historic centre filled with churches and decorative squares. Among the collection in the archaeological museum is the core of a Punic warship, sunk in a great naval battle with the Romans, and a marble statue of Venus from the second century AD.

Marsala makes a convenient base from which to visit ancient sites and other places of interest in south-west Sicily. Mozia, the site of ancient Motya, is located nearby, while the Egadi islands of Favignana, Levanzo and Marettimo lie just off the coast, facing the city. To the south is the fishing port of Mazara del Vallo, and further along the south coast, the ancient Greek site of Selinunte.

THE HISTORY

Lilybaeum was a small settlement, probably of Sican origin, situated on the promontory of Capo Boeo, which came under Phoenician and then Carthaginian control. Its Phoenician name, Lilybaeum, means 'looking at Libya', due to its position facing the North African coast. It lay only ten kilometres south of the Carthaginian city of Motya. After Motya was destroyed in 397 BC by Dionysius I, tyrant of Syracuse, during the Carthaginian-Greek wars, it was never rebuilt. The few survivors who escaped Dionysius's army were settled in Lilybaeum, which became a prosperous naval base famous for its harbour, and the leading Carthaginian city in Sicily.

While Lilybaeum's position was protected on three sides by the sea, there were no natural defences on the landward side. Learning from their defeat at Motya, the Carthaginians walled off the approach by land, building towers and fortified gates at short intervals, and protecting the walls with a series of deep ditches. Underground passages allowed the defenders to launch surprise attacks. The Carthaginians adopted tactics used by Dionysius, making giant catapults capable of hurling missiles onto advancing troops. These fortifications proved strong enough to repel Dionysius when he returned to besiege the city.

Lilybaeum's defences became so strong that no army succeeded in capturing the city. It was the one place which held out against Pyrrhus, who in 276 attempted to take the whole of Sicily for the western Greeks. It successfully defied the Romans for ten years during the first Punic war. The city only surrendered as part of the peace treaty which followed a great Roman naval victory fought off the Egadi islands. In 241, following the treaty, the Carthaginians withdrew from Sicily.

Under the Romans, Lilybaeum was an important administrative and naval base. It was from its harbour that Scipio sailed with his army to defeat Hannibal at the Battle of Zama, in North Africa, in 202. It became the seat of one of two quaestors, appointed by Rome to oversee grain shipments and the payment of taxes, the other being Syracuse, the seat of the Roman governors. Cicero, who in his assignment as quaestor came to Lilybaeum in 75 BC, found it a prosperous city with a large community of Roman citizens.[1]

The early Christian community grew from small beginnings in the second half of the third century to a significant size by the fifth century. Christianity became well-established across the island after the Byzantines took Sicily in AD 535.

Under the Arabs, Lilybaeum lost in importance to Mazara, another port city, situated at the mouth of the river Mazara on the south-western coast. After the Arabs landed at Mazara in AD 827, at the start of their conquest of Sicily, Mazara became their initial base. When under Arab rule the island was divided into three districts, the western district was called the Val di Mazara, with its administrative head at Mazara. Once Palermo became the Arab's capital of Sicily, this role passed to Palermo. The name Marsala is derived from the Arabic, though opinions differ on the origin, which may have been *Marsa Allah,* meaning Harbour of God, or *Marsa Ali,* the reference to Ali being unknown.

At some stage during the Arab domination of the island, Marsala was destroyed and abandoned, to be restored under the Normans by Count Roger, according to al-Edrisi, the Arab geographer to King Roger II. When Edrisi visited Marsala, he found it repopulated and thriving, filled with shops and markets, and with visitors from North Africa. He noted gardens and public baths and ample supplies of fresh water.[2]

The cathedral was originally built under the Norman king, William II, in 1176–82. It was dedicated to Thomas Becket, the archbishop of Canterbury murdered on the orders of the English king, Henry II. According to legend, a ship carrying marble columns to England, destined for a church in honour of Becket, was wrecked off the west coast of Sicily. The residents of Marsala took it as an omen and, appropriating the columns, dedicated their cathedral to Becket, who died in 1170. There was a connection to Becket through William's English wife, Joanna, who was Henry II's daughter. Joanna venerated Becket, possibly to assuage her father's guilt, and supported memorials to him. Becket is remembered, for example, in the cathedral at Monreale. Becket also had the support of members of the English clergy, attracted to Sicily by the Normans, who included Walter of the Mill, archbishop of Palermo, and Richard Palmer, bishop of Syracuse.

The importance of Marsala declined in the Spanish era. In 1575, to protect the city from Barbary pirates, the harbour, famous since antiquity, was blocked up. When in the nineteenth century it was re-opened, this was done on the southern side of Capo Boeo.

In the late eighteenth century, the city's fortunes changed when an English entrepreneur, John Woodhouse, began to ship Marsala wine, fortified with alcohol, to Liverpool. His product was comparable to madeira, port and sherry which were already popular in England. Woodhouse's enterprise took off when in 1798 a large order was placed by Nelson for his fleet. During the Napoleonic Wars, when from 1806 to 1815 Sicily became a British protectorate, the city thrived on the wine trade. More English merchants arrived in Sicily, notably Benjamin Ingham from Yorkshire, who established an international business in Marsala wine supplying both England and America.

On 11 May 1860, Garibaldi, with his army of a thousand volunteers, landed at Marsala with the aim of overthrowing the rule of the Spanish Bourbon government in Sicily. The landing heralded the start of the campaign which eventually led to the unification of Italy. It had been a perilous journey in two antiquated steamships, the *Piemonte* and the *Lombardo*, during which the expedition narrowly managed to avoid a squadron of Neapolitan ships. Fortunately for Garibaldi, the harbour at Marsala was undefended and the presence of two British warships deterred the Neapolitans, once they arrived, from attacking the invaders. As a result, the thousand men and their equipment were disembarked successfully. Garibaldi and his men made their way into the city where a document was signed to the effect that the Bourbons no longer ruled Sicily and that Garibaldi was declared the island's dictator. The next day, after the word had spread of Garibaldi's arrival, volunteers came forward to join his army and together they set off inland, up the hills to Calatafimi, where the first battle of the campaign took place. The outcome was a decisive victory for Garibaldi which opened the way to Palermo and to the liberation of Sicily.

The two world wars brought economic decline in Sicily, closing the trade in Marsala wine. The city suffered badly from the Allied bombing prior to the invasion of Sicily by the British and American forces in July 1943. The city's fabric was restored after the war, agriculture picked up and tourism began to develop.

THE MODERN CITY
The historic centre of the city stands, in the shape of a rectangle, across the middle of a broad promontory which leads to Capo Boeo, the western-most point in Sicily. In front of the city lies the archaeological park, the site of ancient Lilybaeum, which stretches to the road along the seafront. The city's main streets are laid out in a grid with one street, Via XI Maggio (named after the date of Garibaldi's landing on 11 May), leading in from the seafront and bisecting the city. It is an attractive place to explore with its many churches, lively open market and fine baroque architecture. Robert Camuto, whose book on Sicilian wine was published in 2010, described it as follows.

Old Marsala's historic centre is surprisingly orderly, monumental, and tranquil with its white stone streets, limestone baroque churches and gateways, and ancient Punic ruins. Considering that it is not a major tourist stop, I was astonished to see that the decay of many Sicilian cities seems to have stayed out of Marsala, which at night glows yellow in the beam of spotlights.[3]

Entry to the city from the seafront is through Porta Nuova in Piazza Vittoria. To the left are the public gardens, called the Giardino Cavallotti, filled with giant ficus trees, magnolias and pines. Via XI Maggio leads to the central square, Piazza Repubblica, which contains the cathedral, dedicated to St Thomas Becket. Originally built in Norman times, it has been much restored. The interior contains sculpture by the Gaginis, Domenico, Giacomo and Antonino (respectively the father and two sons of the more famous Antonello). A statue of Thomas Becket, by Antonello himself, is also to be seen here, together with a magnificent marble altarpiece depicting Christ's Passion, with panels set in the walls, which was completed by Antonello. Behind the cathedral is the Museo degli Arazzi, the Tapestry Museum, which displays eight Flemish tapestries donated to the cathedral in 1589 by Antonio Lombardo, archbishop of Messina, who was born in Marsala.

Next to the cathedral, Via Garibaldi runs west towards the Porta Garibaldi, the gate through which the general and his men marched in 1860. Originally known as the Porta di Mare, it was constructed in 1685 to resemble a Roman triumphal arch and is decorated with the royal Spanish eagle. Beyond the gate, the *Via dei Mille* (route taken by the Thousand) leads to the large, well-appointed harbour where Garibaldi landed. The harbour's facilities were improved by the English wine merchants to serve their trade. The city's original harbour lay on the other side of Capo Boeo.

There is much to discover in Marsala, which contains sites and monuments from different eras, but has very few remains of the ancient city. There are catacombs, a necropolis and a Roman funeral chamber with paintings. The church of San Giovanni Battista contains a marble statue of the saint attributed to Antonello Gagini and, below ground, rooms decorated with mosaics.

Near the archaeological park is the church of San Giovanni, beneath which lies the grotto of the Sibyl, a prophetess who in ancient times was believed to speak for the gods and interpret the future. People requiring information entered the grotto to ask the Sibyl who went into a trance before making a reply. The Sibyl of Lilybaeum had a reputation among Carthaginians comparable to that of the oracle at Delphi for the Greeks. This practice ended with the arrival of the Romans.

ARCHAEOLOGICAL PARK AND MUSEUM

Excavations have been carried out to reveal remains of the ancient city in the archaeological park, mostly from the Roman era. The site includes a Roman villa from the third century AD, containing mosaics by Arab craftsmen, the remains of a Roman road and Roman baths.

Along the seafront can be seen the old wine warehouses known as *bagli*. A *baglio* was a fortress-like walled enclosure, some of them with watch towers, built to defend houses and the storage of wine from raids by north African pirates. Some of the *bagli* are still used to store wine, others have become restaurants, while one of them, the Baglio Anselmi, houses the archaeological museum.

The museum contains a collection of material from prehistoric, Phoenician, Carthaginian and Roman times and includes finds from nearby sites including Mozia. The history of ancient Lilybaeum is illustrated on a series of panels. Artefacts displayed include painted vases and plates, statuettes, funerary monuments, stelae and figures of goddesses. The recently discovered, life-sized statue of *Venus Callipyge* (literally, 'Venus of the beautiful buttocks') is thought to be a Roman copy of a Greek original, from the second century AD. The statue is one of the many versions of the goddess who, under the different names of Astarte, Aphrodite and Venus, was venerated by the Phoenicians, Greeks and Romans.

The museum's most prized possession is a Punic warship, the core of which has been reconstructed to give an impression of its original size. It was discovered in 1971 by a team from the British School of Rome led by the English archaeologist, Honor Frost, in the Stagnone lagoon near Mozia. When recovered, it proved to be the remains of a long, fast warship measuring thirty-five metres long by nearly five metres wide. The discovery of a second, similar ship added more material to be analysed by archaeologists.

Such warships were propelled by sixty-eight oarsmen pulling seventeen oars on each side, with two oarsmen per oar. The bow of the ship originally carried a metal blade for ramming the enemy.

The wood recovered around the wrecks revealed some interesting facts. Firstly, it came from locations all over the Mediterranean and secondly, the sections were marked with geometric signs indicating how they should be put together. This evidence of prefabrication and mass production fits what is known of the huge size of the Carthaginian fleet, when a naval battle could involve hundreds of ships. Among the items found near the wrecks were small jars containing traces of cannabis, possibly used in drinks to fortify the oarsmen before battle.

Carbon dating techniques have placed these ships in the third century BC. They were probably casualties of the great naval battle fought off the Egadi Islands, close to Marsala, that ended the First Punic War in 241 BC.[4]

MARSALA WINE

Thanks to the British merchants Woodhouse, Ingham and Whitaker, who worked in Sicily, fortified wine from Marsala was well known in England and America during the nineteenth century. In a poem published in 1846, describing himself, Edward Lear made the following reference:

He sits in a beautiful parlour,
  With hundreds of books on the wall;
He drinks a great deal of Marsala,
  But never gets tipsy at all.[5]

The international trade in Marsala was suspended during the two world wars and did not recover after the Second World War. Prices fell, consumer habits changed, and Marsala went out of fashion, becoming known as a cooking wine. The wine growers of south-western Sicily, used to providing white wine in bulk for producing Marsala, entered a lean period. This trend continued so that by 1990 there were fewer than forty commercial wine producers left in Sicily.

Since then a renaissance in Sicilian wine has taken place, as described by Robert Camuto in his book, *Palmento, a Sicilian Wine Odyssey*. Concentrating upon making local wines, which had a long tradition, new producers entered the market. Several of these, with experience in other territories, introduced new grape varieties and applied techniques learnt in hot climates like Australia. The Sicilian wine trade expanded exponentially led by companies such as Azienda Agricola COS, Benanti, Donnafugata, Planeta, Settesoli and Tasca d'Almerita, so that by 2016 there were nearly 400 commercial wine producers on the island. The result is an exciting renewal in Sicilian wines which are making their mark in international markets.

The producers of Marsala responded by increasing the quality of their products to make an outstanding range of aperitifs and dessert wines. They come in three levels of sweetness, from dry to semi-dry and sweet, and in three colours, *Oro* (gold), *Amra* (amber) and *Rubino* (ruby). All are made in oak casks, the standard wines aged from one to three years, with the reserve wines aged from five to ten years. Among the leading producers are De Bartoli, Pellegrino and Curatolo. Today, as in Edward Lear's time, Marsala is once again being drunk in England.

PART THREE

ANCIENT SITES

Map of
ancient Sicily

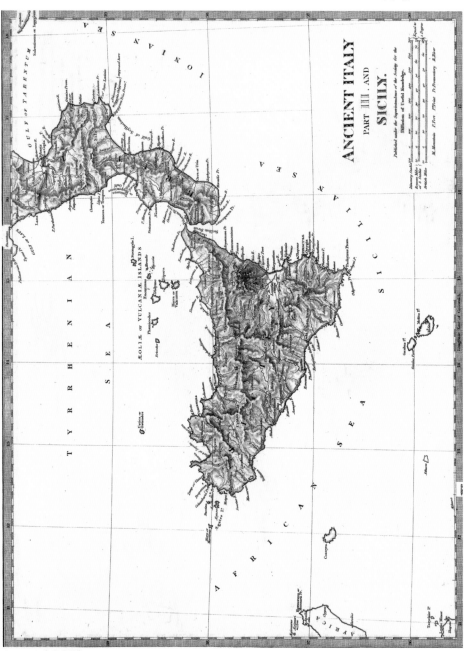

1830, engraving by J&C Walker

Catania's elephant fountain

Catania, the cathedral of Sant'Agata, with façade by Giovanni Vaccarini

1809, etching from Lander und Bolferfunde, Prague

Catania and Mount Etna, 1809

Scopello, with the remains of Arab watchtowers and a *tonnara,* once used for processing tuna fish

Greek temple at Segesta, 1835

1835, engraving by Lemaitre

1838, anonymous lithograph from Poliorama Pittoresco, Naples

Greek Temple of Concord at Agrigento, 1838

Castelbuono, small town in the hills of the Madonie

Ferla, church of San Sebastiano, façade by Michelangelo Di Giacomo

Cefalù, with the background of the Rocca

Norman cathedral
at Cefalù, c. 1840

Palermo's opera house, the Teatro Massimo, designed by Giovan Battista Filippo Basile and completed by his son, Ernesto

The *Triskelion*, ancient symbol of Sicily

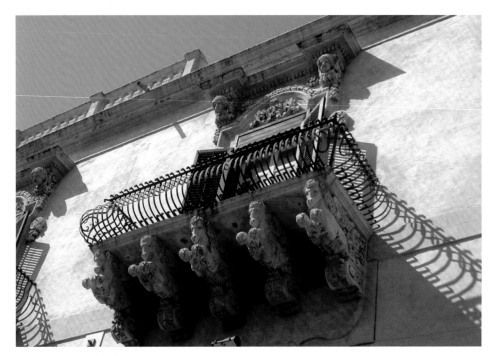

Noto, decorative balcony

Noto, cathedral of San Nicolò, by Rosario Gagliardi and Vincenzo Sinatra

Baroque hilltown of Ragusa Ibla

Ragusa, cathedral of San Giorgio by Rosario Gagliardi

Antonello da Messina, *Vergine Annunciata* (1476-7)

Antonello da Messina, *Ritratto d'uomo* (c 1470)

Statue of Giuseppe Garibaldi at Palermo, by Vincenzo Ragusa

Messina, cathedral square, c. 1840

Marinella di Selinunte, with the remains of a Greek temple visible on the headland

Modica, cathedral of San Pietro by Mario Spada and Rosario Boscarino

Villa Palagonia at Bagheria, built by Tommaso Napoli

The port of Marsala where Garibaldi landed in 1860

INTRODUCTION

Ancient sites are an exceptional feature of Sicily. They form a direct link to the people who inhabited the island and include remains from the prehistoric, Phoenician, Carthaginian, Greek and Roman eras. There are at least sixty ancient sites in total, scattered all over the island, thirty-two of them highlighted by the British Museum.[1] In scale, they range from entire cities, contained in archaeological parks, to individual monuments. Some of the sites are complex and multi-layered in structure with one culture superimposed upon the other, as in the case of the major cities, all of which have ancient origins. Others, located in unspoilt countryside and abandoned since ancient times, have retained their integrity. No doubt there are many more waiting to be discovered.

One of the earliest prehistoric sites is on Monte Pellegrino, near Palermo. Here, in the Addaura caves, wall carvings of dancing men from around 10,000 BC were discovered. For safety reasons, the caves are not currently open to the public. Remains of the Sican, Sicel and Elymian cultures, the peoples who settled in Sicily before the Phoenicians and Greeks, exist in many places. The largest site with Sican and Sicel traces is at Pantàlica, on the Hyblaean plateau in the east of the island. The main Elymian sites are in the north-west at Segesta and Erice.

The Phoenician settlements, which were absorbed into the Carthaginian empire, were located in western Sicily. The principal site is at Mozia, an island off the coast near Marsala.

The Greek sites are the most spectacular, containing impressive monuments to Hellenic civilisation in their temples and theatres. According to the British Museum, Sicily boasts some of the largest and best-preserved Greek-style temples in the Mediterranean.[2] There are also substantial remains of defensive walls and fortifications. The main Greek sites are at Agrigento, Selinunte and Syracuse, on the southern and eastern coasts, with smaller sites situated inland and along the other coasts.

Roman remains are fewer than the Greek, for the Romans adapted the Greek cities to their own use, rather than building anew. For that reason, Roman sites are often to be found superimposed upon the Greek, as in the case of the theatre in Taormina. The outstanding Roman sites include the Villa del Casale at Piazza Armerina and the amphitheatre at Syracuse. From the Roman era also come early Christian sites such as the catacombs in Syracuse.

Complementing the ancient sites are the archaeological museums, which are among the best of their kind in Europe. Started in the early nineteenth century, they were developed to contain outstanding collections of Sicilian antiquities. The museums, with their array of artefacts, play an essential role in the understanding of the ancient sites and of how their inhabitants lived. The most comprehensive archaeological museums are to be found in Palermo and Syracuse, both of which have regional coverage, Palermo for the west and Syracuse for the east of Sicily. There are important museums linked to individual sites at Agrigento, Gela, Marsala, Mozia, Kamarina, Naxos and Morgantina. The major cities, like Catania and Messina, and the hilltowns of Noto and Ragusa, all have their own museums. Several smaller sites also have museums of interest.

The late nineteenth and early twentieth centuries saw a huge advance in the knowledge of ancient Sicily. The pioneers of archaeology in Sicily in this period were Antonio Salinas and Paolo Orsi, who worked respectively in western and eastern Sicily. They carried out excavations which unearthed more material from ancient times than ever before. Building upon earlier collections, they went on to develop the archaeological museums in Palermo and Syracuse, which were named after them. Two Englishmen made contributions to archaeology in the early twentieth century, Joseph Whitaker, who excavated the site at Mozia, and Alexander Hardcastle, who worked in Agrigento.

In recent times, the archaeology of ancient Sicily has made further progress under the leadership of men like Luigi Bernabò Brea, a specialist in the prehistoric era, and Vincenzo Tusa, who worked on the Punic, Elymian and Greek eras. Foreign schools of archaeology from America, Canada, Britain, France and Germany have also made significant contributions.

The ancient historians are a rich source of information on the sites and their original inhabitants. Thucydides included a passage in which he described Sicily before the arrival of the Greeks. It appears at the beginning of Book Six of his *History of the Peloponnesian War*, as an introduction to the account of the Athenian expedition. Based upon the work of Antiochus of Syracuse, who wrote a history of Sicily from earliest times to 424 BC, it opens with references to the early settlers, the Sicans, Sicels and Elymians, as well as to the Phoenicians.

Thucydides goes on to outline the chronology of the foundations of the Greek cities. He does not provide dates but uses comparisons. For example, Naxos is described as the first Greek city to be founded, with Syracuse in the following year, and so on.[3] Applying a reference from Herodotus, historians calculate that the foundation of Megara Hyblaea took place in 728 BC. This allows dates to be applied to Thucydides's chronology, indicating that Naxos was founded in 734 and Syracuse in 733.[4] The pattern described is one of colonisation in stages, starting on the east coast, then extending to the southern and northern coasts, as well as inland. While these foundation dates are open to question and should be taken as indicative, the overall pattern is convincing.

Other ancient writers who contributed to our knowledge of the ancient cities include Diodorus, who covered many key events from the Greek era, Pindar, Cicero, Livy, Plutarch and Polybius.

Tommaso Fazello, who personally rediscovered some of the sites, described them in his book published in 1558, while travel writers from Brydone to Durrell, listed in the introduction to Part II on Cities, all had something interesting to say on the ancient sites and their monuments.

Works by modern historians and archaeologists put the ancient sites in context, adding historical background to descriptions of the individual sites. Margaret Guido's *Sicily: An Archaeological Guide*, first published in 1967, remains the best introduction. A thorough review of the sites appears in R. Ross Holloway's *The Archaeology of Ancient Sicily* while the background is provided in Robert Leighton's *Sicily before History* and Luigi Bernabò Brea's *Sicily before the Greeks*. The British Museum's publication, *Sicily, Culture and Conquest,* published in 2016 to coincide with their exhibition on Sicily, is a mine of information on both the sites and the collections in the museums.

———

The following articles provide profiles of six of the principal ancient sites ranging from the prehistoric to the Phoenician/Carthaginian, the Elymian, Greek and Roman.

2 0

PANTÀLICA, A PREHISTORIC
SETTLEMENT

Pantàlica, the site of a substantial prehistoric settlement, is located on high ground on the Hyblaean plateau, some forty kilometres inland from Syracuse. Nothing remains of the settlement except for possible traces of a palace. The site is famous for its necropolis, which contains over 5,000 tombs carved into the rock, each one leaving a gaping hole like an open window in the rock face. It is a place with strong echoes of the past, which has been called a city of the dead, a huge cemetery of an ancient people who left little record of their civilisation. It was made a World Heritage Site by UNESCO in 2005.

The site is part of the wider nature reserve of the Anapo valley and is set in remote, mountainous countryside. This is wild and rugged territory, the domain of birds of prey and other wildlife, dominated by rocky hillsides and Mediterranean *macchia*, interspersed with deep gorges at the bottom of which flow the Anapo and Calcinara rivers.

THE HISTORY
The history of Pantàlica is lost in the mists of time. Historians are faced with fragments of evidence from legends and literary sources such as Thucydides. Archaeology, however, has shed some light on the subject. The pioneer was Paolo Orsi, who in 1886 came from northern Italy to become director of antiquities in Syracuse. In a

career lasting forty-five years, he carried out excavations across the province and founded the archaeological museum in Syracuse. He discovered much of what we know today about eastern Sicily in ancient times. Orsi's work was continued in the 1950s by Luigi Bernabò Brea and further developed in the 1990s by Robert Leighton. Due to their efforts, an outline has emerged of how the settlement may have evolved.[1]

Pantàlica was inhabited for around 600 years, from 1250 to 650 BC, with the first inhabitants being the Sicans, who were among the earliest immigrants to Sicily. The island, once known as Trinacria, was in their time called Sicania. Homer was aware of this name for Sicily, for in *The Odyssey,* Odysseus leaves Sicania on his way home.[2]

The threat from attack along the coast forced the Sicans to build themselves a secure refuge inland. The chosen site at Pantàlica had excellent conditions for a settlement, with plentiful wood for building houses and abundant fresh water from the rivers. Land suitable for farming lay nearby. It was a natural fortress, situated on the spur of a mountain, and protected on all sides by rocky cliffs and deep valleys. Access was limited to a few narrow paths along the hillside.

Archaeological finds from the larger rock-cut tombs show that an advanced civilisation existed here. There is evidence of trade links with Italy and the eastern Mediterranean, including with Mycenae in mainland Greece. Judging by the number of skeletons found in the tombs, the settlement was densely populated.[3]

New waves of immigrants followed the Sicans to Sicily. Arriving early in the twelfth century BC, the Elymians established settlements in the north-west of the island. Then, around 150 years later, the Sicels came from Italy and, according to Thucydides, challenged the Sicans for supremacy of the island. Arriving with a large army, the Sicels defeated the Sicanians in battle, driving them into the south and west of the island. They established themselves at Pantàlica and other locations in the hills including Ragusa, Modica, Noto and Caltagirone. They also inhabited settlements along the coast. After the wars, a boundary was agreed between the two people. The island took the name Sicelia from the Sicels.[4]

The arrival of the Greeks put an end to Sicel supremacy. Founding new colonies along the east coast in the 730s, first Naxos and then Syracuse, the Greeks soon dominated the Sicels, whom they enslaved and with whom they inter-married. Greek dominance was confirmed when their colonists from Megara were granted territory north of Syracuse by Hyblon, the Sicel king. Here, in 728, the Greeks founded Megara Hyblaea. Around this time the Sicels withdrew to their mountain refuges.[5]

As Syracuse grew in power and status, the city established outposts in the nearby hinterland to protect itself. One of these was Akrai (Palazzolo Acreide), in the Sicel heartland, only twenty-five kilometres from Pantàlica. Established around 664, this may have coincided with the end of a war between the two communities.[6] Once the Greeks were resident close by, the Sicel community began to lose its identity, and Pantàlica became depopulated. It was abandoned around 650.

In the ninth century AD, with the arrival of the Arabs, part of the Byzantine population sought refuge in the mountains and reoccupied the site of the settlement. Tombs cut in the rock were enlarged to create more living space. The name Pantàlica probably derives from the Byzantine period. From Norman times the site was abandoned to be rediscovered by archaeologists in the nineteenth century.

THE SITE

Pantàlica is reached via the state road number 114 from Syracuse to Floridia and then on to the small towns of Sortino or Ferla, which lie on either side of the site. Several footpaths provide access to the site itself. Ferla offers convenient access through the town to a car park from where one proceeds on foot. The site contains over 5,000 rock-cut chamber tombs spread over steep slopes in several large groups. The path from Ferla reaches the site below the north-west necropolis, which holds tombs from the Sican period, dating from the thirteenth to the eleventh centuries BC. The tombs are cut into the rock face, laid out in rows, with the empty black spaces leaving an eerie impression. Finds discovered there by Orsi, which are held in the museum at Syracuse, include amphorae, knives, mirrors, pottery and fibulas (safety-pins for fastening cloaks), as well as signs of metalworking, fragments of bronze tools and kitchen utensils.

The path continues to the centre of the site where the remains of a building, possibly a palace, can be found. The foundations show that it consisted of several rooms and was constructed out of large blocks of stone. Affinities with Mycenaean buildings have been noted. It is known as the *Anaktoron*, or the prince's palace. Moulds for making axes and other weapons in bronze were found inside one of the rooms. This may have been the residence of a local ruler. There are doubts, however, about the origins of the building, as signs of restructuring indicate that parts of it date from Byzantine times.[7]

The path continues until it reaches a deep gorge with the river flowing below. A series of steep steps offers access down to the river where it is possible to swim. To the right of the path are the tombs in the southern necropolis from the Sicel period in 850–730 BC. Further signs of the Byzantine occupation exist inside caves along the path, some of which contain wall paintings.

A visit to Pantàlica is an opportunity not only to view the tombs but also to enjoy the mountain scenery. Filled with wildflowers in the spring, this mountain site is quiet and peaceful, far from the modern cities, a world of its own which guards the secrets of an ancient civilisation.

THE GREEK TEMPLE AT SEGESTA

Segesta's Greek temple, built on a hill overlooking rolling countryside near the town of Calatafimi, is one of the memorable sights of Sicily. It stands in isolation apart from the remains of the ancient city, in full view for miles around. Over the years it has fascinated travellers, among them Guy de Maupassant, who after his visit to Sicily in 1885, described the temple as 'all by itself animating the entire landscape, making it alive and beautiful'.[1]

Segesta, known as Egesta in antiquity, was the capital of a small Elymian state in north-west Sicily. The Elymians, who were established in Sicily before the Greeks, were allies of the Carthaginians. As the Greek presence in Sicily expanded, Egesta faced an increasingly difficult task in defending itself. An immediate threat was posed by Selinus, a Greek city on the south-west coast, whose territory bordered its own. In seeking to defend itself against Selinus, Egesta appealed for help from both Athens and Carthage. The temple was thus probably built for political reasons, during a period of diplomatic activity, to demonstrate publicly the sealing of an alliance with Athens.

THE HISTORY
Before the arrival of the Phoenicians and Greeks in the eighth century BC, three different ethnic groups were established in Sicily, the Sicans in the west, the Sicels in the east and the Elymians in the

north-west. The Elymians, who may have arrived after the fall of
Troy in the early twelfth century BC, became allies of the Phoenicians
and Carthaginians, who were based at Panormus (Palermo),
Solus (Solunto) and Motya (Mozia).² Though small in numbers,
the Elymians gave a good account of themselves, and through the
shrewd use of alliances managed to maintain their independence
through a particularly turbulent period in their history.

The Elymians founded three cities around 600 BC. Their political
and commercial base was Egesta (Segesta) with its port, Emporio,
(Castellammare) on the north coast. Eryx, (Erice) high on a
hilltop on the west coast, was a religious centre; it was home to
the most celebrated temple and sanctuary in Sicily, dedicated to
the goddess of fertility personified by Astarte for the Phoenicians
and Aphrodite for the Greeks. Entella, to the east of Egesta, was
their military base.

As this small state expanded, it came increasingly into conflict
with the Greek city of Selinus, on the south coast, with which it
shared a border. In around 510, a group of Egestans and Phoenicians
defeated an invading force from mainland Greece, supported by
Selinus, who were attempting to establish a Greek settlement on
the west coast. In this battle, Dorieus, the son of the king of Sparta
was killed.

During the Peloponnesian War in the fifth century, when
Athens and Sparta faced each other in a long and brutal conflict,
Athens got drawn into affairs in Sicily. Fearing for its survival
against Selinus, Egesta appealed to the Athenians for help. When
Athenian delegates came to Sicily, they were taken to the temple
at Eryx and shown its treasure as a potential contribution to the
war effort. When the Athenians debated the question of sending
an expedition to Sicily, Egestans were present in Athens, lobbying
for intervention against Selinus.

The Athenians launched their expedition to Sicily, with the
main objective of capturing Syracuse, in the summer of 415 BC. As
the leading city on the island, Syracuse was the key to Sicily. The

Athenians' secondary objective was to help their allies, including Egesta. The expedition was one of the greatest military operations of its day, initially involving 40,000 troops and a fleet of 134 triremes. Soon after their arrival in Sicily, the Athenians learnt that they had been deceived by the Egestans, and that the promised sums of money would not be forthcoming. The siege of Syracuse lasted for two years. It was a hard-fought campaign, which ended in total defeat for the Athenians, with their fleet destroyed and their army annihilated.[3]

Selinus, which had supported Syracuse in the war with Athens, took revenge on Egesta and inflicted a heavy defeat upon the city in 411. The Egestans appealed this time to Carthage. Seeing an opportunity to attack the Sicilian Greeks while they were still recovering from the Athenian invasion, the Carthaginians invaded Sicily in 409. After a nine-day siege, they captured Selinus, leaving the city destroyed, with most of its citizens massacred or sold into slavery.

By engineering the destruction of Selinus, Egesta succeeded in retaining its independence for nearly another hundred years. But by fanning the flames of war between Carthage and the Sicilian Greeks, the Egestans helped to release forces that would eventually engulf them.

THE TEMPLE

The temple at Segesta stands on a hill in a solitary position, immersed in a wild landscape of rock and low scrubland. This position was outside the old walled city of Egesta which stood on the nearby Monte Barbaro. The Doric temple, with its thirty-six columns, fourteen along each side, compares favourably in terms of architectural refinements with those of contemporary Athens. It is an exceptionally fine construction, designed by an unknown architect who was well versed in the techniques of Greek temple building. The columns are shaped to appear in perfectly straight lines when seen from a distance. To obtain this effect, they taper slightly towards the top and curve outwards in the middle, the work of expert craftsmen. Remains of other temples nearby indicate that the original intention may have been to build a group of temples as at Selinus. The building is thought to have been carried out between 430 and 415 BC during a period of diplomatic exchanges between Egesta and Athens.[4]

The question that has long engaged historians, is what made Egesta, an Elymian city, build a grand temple in the Greek style? While the Elymians did become thoroughly Hellenised in their culture, it still seems an unlikely step to take. Both the timing of the building, and its subsequent abandonment, point to the following conclusions: that the temple was built, firstly, to impress the Athenians of Egesta's prosperity and, secondly, to act as a public statement of the growing relationship between the two cities. In the face of the threat from Selinus, it was a way of openly declaring the alliance with Athens.[5]

Following the defeat of the Athenians at Syracuse, the temple was never completed. Allied once again with Carthage, Egesta had no further use for a Greek temple, implying that the motive for its construction was political and not religious.

What is seen today at Segesta is the shell of a temple, with no *cella*, or inner room, no roof, an unfinished floor and unfluted columns. As the archaeologists confirm, these are clear signs of an unfinished building. The deity for whom the temple was intended is unknown and the temple may never have been used for worship.

The remains of the ancient city of Egesta stand on Monte Barbaro across the valley. These consist of a well-preserved Greek theatre from the Hellenistic period with Roman additions, which in its heyday could seat 4,000 spectators; the remains of an *agora* (marketplace) and a *bouleuterion* (council chamber). Fragments of the city's fortifications indicate that the entire hill was originally encircled by walls, interspersed with gates and towers.

THE CITY'S DECLINE

During the Carthaginian-Greek wars which continued in the fourth century BC, Agathocles, the tyrant of Syracuse, took his army to North Africa but failed to capture Carthage. Returning to Sicily, Agathocles turned aggressively to the pro-Carthaginian cities on the island to raise funds to continue his campaigns. He picked on Egesta, and when the city refused to co-operate, he took brutal revenge upon the population. Mass executions were ordered, wealthy citizens were tortured to reveal their treasure, while others were sold into slavery. The city lost its original identity, with its Elymian population dispersed, and new citizens forcibly brought in. Agathocles changed its name to Dikaiopolis (City of Righteousness). Shortly afterwards it reverted to rule by Carthage.

During the First Punic War, Egesta was one of the first cities to go over to the side of the Romans, who rewarded it with a privileged tax-free status, and renamed it Segesta. Under the Romans the city led a largely prosperous existence. In the break-up of the Roman Empire, it was sacked by the Vandals. The city declined in importance under the Arabs and was abandoned by the late thirteenth century.

Few cities have such an elegant reminder of their former glory as Segesta. The temple remains a symbol, for all to see, of the city's short-lived alliance with the Greek world, an alliance shattered by the Athenians' defeat at Syracuse.

SELINUNTE, ANCIENT SELINUS, A GREEK CITY

One of the largest and most impressive archaeological parks in the Mediterranean, Selinunte offers something different to the other Greek sites in Sicily. Here can be seen the outline of an entire ancient city. As it was never built over, and has been left largely abandoned since ancient times, the site is of unique importance to archaeologists. It provides an opportunity to discover how such cities functioned.[1]

The park has an unspoilt setting on raised land facing the sea, where out of season it is possible to wander around the remains of ancient temples, fortifications, city gates and paved streets strewn with pieces of columns, roof tiles and blocks of stone, with few people in sight. Below the park lies the village of Marinella di Selinunte, with a strip of low buildings along the coast. To the east there is a small port filled with fishing boats and holiday craft. To the west, a long stretch of sandy beach ends in a rocky point above which stand a few columns of a Greek temple.

THE ANCIENT CITY

Selinus was a Sicilian Greek city which prospered for over 200 years until destroyed by the Carthaginians in 409 BC. While Thucydides records its date of foundation as 628, archaeological evidence points to an earlier date of 650. Like several other Greek cities,

Selinus, which was built to last, was cut off in its prime in the wars with Carthage.[2]

The most western of the Sicilian Greek cities, Selinus was founded by men from Megara Hyblaea, on the east coast of the island. The first wave of Greek colonisation in Sicily, on the east coast, was followed by a second wave of settlements on the southern and northern coasts, of which Selinus was one. In the case of Megara Hyblaea, one of the motives for founding a new settlement was that being close to Syracuse there was little space for expansion. Megara, the mother-city in Greece, sent a contingent led by Pamillus, to support the new settlement. A Phoenician outpost may have preceded the Greeks on the site.

The location was well chosen, for Selinus was built on raised land with a river on each side, the Selinus (modern Modione) to the west and the Hypsas (Cottone) to the east. The city, like the river, took its name from *selinon*, the wild celery, that grew on the riverbanks. From early days, the leaf of this plant was adopted as the badge of the city and later appeared on some of its coins. A river god of the same name became venerated, in the manner of the Greeks, for whom fresh water was sacred.[3]

The settlement developed into a city consisting of a central acropolis containing five temples, with public buildings and an *agora*. Defensive walls surrounded the city with the main gates inland to the north. On the hill to the east, a separate quarter contained three more temples. To the west lay a sanctuary to Demeter Malophorus, the harvest goddess (Malophorus meaning 'bearer of fruit'). The land sloping upwards from the acropolis, known as the Manuzza Hill, contained the main residential quarter. Based on a grid plan, this layout represented an early example of efficient town planning.

Land cultivated on the inland plain provided crops for the city and for export which became the basis of the city's wealth. Harbours for the ships were formed by widening the mouths of the rivers from which communications were maintained with the Greek cities of Sicily, North Africa and mainland Greece.

Diodorus recorded the city's population in the late fifth century as 24,000, which is now seen as an understatement. The scale of the city and its activities, as revealed by archaeology, indicate a population of nearer 60,000.[4]

THE HISTORY

Western Sicily was the preserve of the Carthaginians, who absorbed the Phoenician outposts of Motya (Mozia), Panormus (Palermo) and Solus (Solunto) into their empire. In the north-west, bordering Selinuntian territory, was a small Elymian state with its base at Egesta (Segesta) and a sanctuary at Eryx (Erice). Initially these settlements lived peacefully with one another and the prosperity of Selinus lay in providing Carthage with agricultural produce. But Carthage guarded its port cites in Sicily jealously, and lay just 150 kilometres across the sea, in today's Tunisia. As rivalry grew between Carthage and the Greeks to control Sicily, Selinus found itself in an increasingly exposed position.

As their cities grew, the Greeks sought to expand their territories at their neighbours' expense. At Selinus, this led to confrontation with Egesta over their common borders. After a defeat for Selinus in the sixth century, a series of tyrants took control of the city, replacing the government of the aristocratic landowners who were descendants of the founding families. The tyrants, who relied upon mercenaries in their campaigns, were more aggressive towards their neighbours. Outposts were established along the coast, to the east at Heraclea Minoa and Sciacca, and to the west at Mazara.

During this period, the population of Selinus suffered from an epidemic, probably malaria, originating in the stagnant marshes. Its effects on the community became overwhelming. Empledocles, a scientist and philosopher from Akragas, was called in to help. He solved the problem by cutting channels to keep the water flowing and thus draining the marshland near the rivers. For his intervention, Empledocles was considered the saviour of the city.

During the Athenian campaign to capture Syracuse, Egesta took the side of the Athenians. Following the defeat of the Athenians in 413, Selinus took the opportunity of settling accounts with Egesta, and invaded its territory. This time, Egesta appealed to Carthage for help.

In 409, the Carthaginians invaded Sicily with a large army. Landing at Lilybaeum (Marsala), they made their way around the coast to Selinus. To this force, Egesta added its own contingent of soldiers. When the people of Selinus saw the size of the army drawn up outside their city, they sent urgent appeals for help to Syracuse and Akragas, but none was forthcoming. Fierce fighting went on for nine days, the men of Selinus defending their city desperately, street by street. When the walls were finally breached, a massacre took place with 16,000 of the city's inhabitants killed, 5,000 taken prisoner, while less than 2,600 managed to escape to Akragas. When the news reached Syracuse, ambassadors were sent to the Carthaginians asking them to spare the temples and to release the prisoners. Both requests were refused. The walls and buildings of the city were demolished and the prisoners, including women and children, were held to be taken to Carthage as slaves. Selinus, as an independent Greek city, ceased to exist.[5]

As the war continued, the ruins of Selinus were briefly occupied by a small Greek army led by Hermocrates, a Syracusan general, who refortified the northern gate. The city then became a Carthaginian colony with a few Greek inhabitants. The Syracusans under Dionysius and Agathocles briefly recaptured it, for use as a base for their operations in western Sicily. In 250, during the Second Punic War, the Carthaginians finally destroyed Selinus, removing the population to Lilybaeum (Marsala) to prevent it being taken by the Romans.

THE ARCHAEOLOGICAL SITE

For centuries the ruins of Selinus lay hidden beneath the undergrowth, huge blocks of stone lying amid broken columns half submerged in the marshes, the damage done by war aggravated by earthquakes. For a long time, it was thought that the site lay beneath the city of Mazara. When in the 1550s Fazello set out to write his history of Sicily, he studied the account of the Carthaginian invasion by Diodorus, which led him to rediscover the site of Selinus. Ancient coins bearing the city's name, found at the scene, confirmed its identity.

Excavations began in earnest in the 1820s when two Englishmen, Samuel Angell and William Harris, found pieces of well-preserved metopes, sculptured friezes showing scenes from Greek myths, from one of the temples. The authorities prevented the metopes from being shipped back to England so that the Englishmen had to make do with plaster copies. Harris died of malaria, the curse of ancient Selinus, while in Sicily. The original metopes and other finds can be seen in Palermo's archaeological museum.

Entry to the site is on the east hill, where transport is available in open cars. The first stop is at a group of three temples. As their names are unknown, the temples have been identified with a letter. Temple G, probably dedicated to Zeus, was originally vast, and dates from the second half of the sixth century BC. Piles of stone are all that remain. Temple F, possibly dedicated to Athena, was smaller and predates G by a few years. Temple E was built later, around 470–460, in the city's period of greatest prosperity. It was dedicated to Hera, the wife of Zeus. This temple, in its partially restored state, is among the most beautiful in Sicily.

The next stop with the cars is over the valley to the base of the acropolis, past the high, stepped outer wall which dates from around 540. A broad terrace stands here facing the sea, containing some pieces of Carthaginian origin. There is also a small museum with relics from the Spanish era. Facing inland, one can see the ancient walled city with its clearly marked streets, and a partially restored temple, Temple C, which dates from 560–540, dedicated to Apollo. At the far end of the central street, dividing the acropolis, lies the fortified northern gate. Beyond the gate are more defences, some of which were built after the Carthaginians' capture of the city. Further up the Manuzza hill is the site of the ancient residential quarter.

To the west of the acropolis, on the far side of the riverbed, lie the remains of the Sanctuary of Demeter Malophorus. Demeter was the goddess of harvest, while Malophorus signified the provider of fruit, both vital to a people dependent upon good harvests for their wellbeing. This was an important sanctuary whose background archaeologists are still trying to understand. While it was clearly the site of a Greek cult, evidence of a Phoenician connection has been discovered. Twelve thousand small votive statues, of gods and goddesses were found here, as well as vases, indicating that in its day the sanctuary played an active role in civic life.

Recent archaeological investigations are revealing the workings of the ancient city. In the residential quarter on the Manuzza hill, 2,500 of the city's abandoned houses have been identified. Along the banks of the river, in the valley between the acropolis and the temples on the east hill, excavations have discovered the remains of an industrial zone, where a large quantity of ceramics was made. Eighty kilns have been discovered, along with workshops and tools; the products from here included roof tiles, food containers, tableware and small statues. These volumes indicate a thriving export trade, while imported goods have been identified as coming from Egypt, Turkey, the south of France and northern Italy.[6]

The ancient quarries that supplied the stone for the temples, the Cave di Cusa, can be seen about half an hour's drive away near Campobello di Mazara. Here huge columns have been partially cut out of the rock and other pieces left abandoned. It is a scene frozen in time, from when the city's temple building came to an end with the arrival of Hannibal's army in 409 BC.

THE ARCHAEOLOGICAL MUSEUMS

Most of the finds from Selinunte are to be seen, brilliantly displayed, in the renovated museum in Palermo, the *Museo Archeologico*

Regionale 'Antonio Salinas'. The Selinunte rooms are on the ground floor, reached through two courtyards lined with ancient statues and filled with exotic plants. Upon entry, one is faced with a relief map of ancient Selinus and a matching photograph of the current site, detailing the layout of the city. The rooms that follow contain the metopes, stone panels containing carved figures, that once decorated the temples in a frieze above the columns. These are the finest pieces in the museum's collection, examples of Sicilian Greek sculpture at its best.

Metopes were used to tell the stories of the ancient gods and heroes and these panels include scenes showing Apollo in a quadriga, Perseus killing the Medusa and the marriage of Zeus and Hera. The metopes covered much of the city's lifespan, from the seventh to the fifth centuries BC, and their artistic development can be followed up to around 460.

On the first floor of Palermo's museum can be found a collection of terracotta statuettes, a series of female figures linked to the cult of Demeter and Kore, from the Malophorus sanctuary.

Castelvetrano, the provincial capital close to Selinunte, has a small museum with some fine pieces from the archaeological park. The most interesting is a bronze statue of a youth, the Ephebe, a rare example of fifth-century BC bronze work.

23

AGRIGENTO, ANCIENT AKRAGAS, A GREEK CITY

Agrigento is a hilltop town and provincial capital, with a population of 60,000, located close to Sicily's southern coast. It is famous for being the site of Akragas, which in the fifth century BC was one of the largest Greek cities on the island. The legacy of Akragas is an array of Doric temples, among the finest around the Mediterranean to have survived from antiquity. Agrigento is a busy place, Sicily's top tourist attraction, with over 850,000 visitors in 2017. It was made a World Heritage site by UNESCO in 1997.

Over the centuries, the city has had several names. The Greeks called it Akragas, the Romans Agrigentum and the Arabs Kerkent, which in Italian became Girgenti. In 1927, Mussolini decreed that it should be called Agrigento. The modern town, which is set apart from the main site, suffers from bad planning and ugly apartment blocks, but is worth visiting for its historic centre and remains from the Greek era. Visitors are well served by a variety of hotels on the slopes below the town.

Agrigento overlooks the Valley of the Temples, the archaeological park containing the temples. The view from the hills above has enchanted visitors for centuries. Today, this view is particularly evocative seen floodlit by night, with the temples silhouetted against the background of the sea.

THE ANCIENT CITY

Akragas was one of the later Greek cities to be established in Sicily, its foundation taking place, according to Thucydides, in 580 BC. Its founders were Aristonous and Pystilus and the city took its name from the river nearby.[1] Colonists for the new settlement came from Gela and from the islands of Rhodes and Crete.

The site was chosen for its fertile land, the supply of fresh water, the proximity of a small port and for the protection offered by a steep rock formation to the north. Below this formation, the land sloped down to the sea, with a ridge halfway down divided by two rivers, the Hypsas to the west and the Akragas to the east. This location placed the settlement some five kilometres inland from the sea, about halfway along the south coast between the cities of Gela and Selinus.

An acropolis was built on the rocky hill known as the *Rupe Atenea* (Rock of Athena), containing a sacred enclosure with temples to Zeus and Athena. This was the settlement's original site, from where it gradually spread down the hill into the valley, with residential districts and public buildings. The ridge across the valley became the location for the city's principal temples. The city's perimeter, from the acropolis above to the ridge below, was defended by strong walls interspersed with towers and gateways.

The Akragantines were a remarkable people who created a magnificent city in a short period of time. Their prosperity was built on their agricultural produce which they traded with Carthage. As Diodorus noted, the city possessed extensive vineyards and olive groves, the produce from which was sold to Carthage. As Libya's agriculture was undeveloped at this stage, the Akragantines were able to build a highly profitable export trade.[2]

Their wealth allowed them to develop their interests in the arts, as demonstrated by their architecture and sculpture. Literature also played a part, for the Greek poets Pindar and Simonides both came here. The city was represented by emblems which appeared on their coins. The first was an eagle, the sacred bird of Zeus, representing the rocky hill on which the acropolis stood. The second was a freshwater crab, representing the river Akragas and the river god of the same name. Later, another emblem was added to the coinage, a racing chariot, representing the city's status as a participant in the Olympic Games.

THE HISTORY

Soon after its foundation, Akragas fell under the control of the tyrant Phalaris, who ruled from around 570 to 554. While developing the city and extending its territories, Phalaris acquired a reputation for cruelty, recorded by the poet Pindar. From Rhodes came the practice of placing statues of bulls on high ground. Phalaris built on this tradition by commissioning a great bull made of brass, which he displayed on the acropolis. The brazen bull was designed as a means of execution, to roast its victims alive, with their echoing cries sounding like a raging bull. The metal worker, Perilaos, who created the bull, was tricked by Phalaris into becoming its first victim. Eventually toppled by an uprising, Phalaris may have been the bull's last victim. The story persisted to Roman times, for Cicero noted that when Scipio captured Carthage, he found the brazen bull, and had it returned to its city of origin.[3]

Theron, the next recorded tyrant of Akragas, who ruled from around 489 to 472, presided over a period of dynamic expansion. A dynastic marriage of his daughter, Demarete, to Gelon, tyrant of Syracuse, cemented an alliance with the most powerful city in Sicily. In 480, the combined armies of Akragas and Syracuse defeated the Carthaginians at Himera. There followed a period of prosperity, the victory temporarily removing the Carthaginian threat. Theron emerged as a hero of Greek Sicily, with his praises sung by Pindar in odes celebrating his win in a chariot race at the Olympic Games. Like Gela, Akragas was famous for its horses and sent teams of racing chariots, sponsored by its rulers, to compete in the games in Greece.[4]

In the aftermath of the Battle of Himera, a construction boom took place, using slaves taken as prisoners-of-war. This transformed the city. In the valley below the hill, the Temple of Concord was built, and work commenced on the Temple of Zeus, the largest temple ever constructed in antiquity. Following a grid plan, a residential quarter was developed, together with public buildings and a marketplace. Channels were cut deep into the rock to bring water into the city. A large pond was built, stocked with a variety of fish, and inhabited by swans and water birds.

The rule of Theron and his son was followed by a period of democratic government which lasted for over sixty years. The outstanding figure of this period was Empledocles, statesman, scientist and philosopher, about whom legends abound. He introduced democracy and curbed the privileges of the aristocracy. He improved public health by increasing the flow of fresh air into Akragas and by draining the marshes in Selinus. He is considered the founder of the Italian school of medicine. An original thinker, Empledocles maintained that changes in the world were not governed by any purpose but by chance and necessity. In his philosophy he anticipated Plato. In contrast to his scholarly side, Empledocles suffered from delusions, thinking that he was a god and that he could perform miracles. Legend has it that he died in mysterious circumstances in the crater of Mount Etna. Alternatively, he may have been banished from Akragas and died in Greece.[5]

This was the city's golden age, as its population rose to some 200,000 inhabitants, comparable to that of Syracuse, the leading city in Sicily. Akragas became famous for its extravagance, personified by a leading citizen named Tellias, who on one occasion played host to 500 cavalrymen from Gela. His wine cellar was reputed to hold casks cut out of the rock with the capacity of holding over 1,000 amphorae. Victory at the Olympic Games brought huge prestige which was celebrated in style. In 412, when Exainetos from Akragas returned home having won a chariot race at the games, he was escorted into the city by 300 chariots drawn by white horses.[6]

In 409 the Carthaginians invaded Sicily, bent upon avenging their defeat at Himera and noting the weakness of the Sicilian Greeks after the war with Athens. They succeeded in taking and sacking the Greek cities of Selinus and Himera. Returning in 406, they approached Akragas to see if the city would become their ally. When this was refused, a siege began which lasted for eight months. Supported by troops from Syracuse and Gela, Akragas initially withstood the attack. A successful counter attack was not followed up, and when the Carthaginians intercepted the Greeks' grain supply, the city's fate was sealed. It was abandoned, leaving only the sick and the wounded, most of the inhabitants fleeing to Gela. The Carthaginians captured and proceeded to sack the city. Practically the whole population which had been left behind were killed. Houses were ransacked for valuables and works of art which the rich citizens had collected.

The temples were stripped of their decorations and destroyed by fire. The Carthaginians remained in Akragas through the winter, and before they left in the following year, the remains of the city were razed to the ground. Shortly afterwards, Gela and Kamarina suffered a similar fate.[7]

In the face of the Carthaginian threat, a young general named Dionysius seized power in Syracuse. After he concluded a peace treaty with Carthage, the citizens of Akragas were permitted to return to their ruined city which never, however, regained its independence or former glory, remaining semi-deserted for years.

After the Greeks, led by Timoleon of Syracuse, won a victory against the Carthaginians in 340, Greek Sicily entered a period of regeneration. Akragas was rebuilt and repopulated and entered a period of relative growth and prosperity. Rule from Syracuse continued under Agathocles. A local tyrant named Phintias then took control and extended the city's territories. During the Punic Wars, which began in 264 BC, when Rome fought Carthage for control of Sicily, Akragas was sacked on several occasions. Under the Romans from 210 and renamed Agrigentum, the city was rebuilt and repopulated. Prosperity under the Roman Empire was followed yet again by decline. By the time of the Arabs' arrival in the ninth century AD, Agrigentum had shrunk to a small settlement on the hill.

ALEXANDER HARDCASTLE

Akragas has long fascinated historians and archaeologists. The story of such a magnificent city, among the greatest in the ancient Greek world, destroyed at its peak, resonated down the ages. Fazello, who explored the site and catalogued its monuments in his book published in 1558, described his reactions as follows.

> I have often been to see the site. Looking at the great spectacle, I am amazed not only by the magnificence of the monuments but also by the passage of time and by the swings of fortune that led to the ruin of everything … I spare a thought for the talents and the culture of the men who created it.[8]

In the 1920s, Akragas gained a champion in the figure of an Englishman named Alexander Hardcastle, who became interested in archaeology. Learning of excavations taking place in Sicily, Alexander and his brother Henry arrived in Sicily to see for themselves. They soon fell under the spell of Girgenti with its ancient stone monuments scattered around the hillsides among the almond and olive trees. They bought and restored a house in the Valley of the Temples, which they called the Villa Aurea after one of the gates of the ancient city.

Hardcastle arrived at a time when the site of Akragas was attracting little attention from archaeologists. Recognising the site's importance, he initiated a busy schedule of excavations employing local workmen. A good organiser with an eye for detail, Hardcastle succeeded in restoring the temple of Heracles, excavating the temple of Demeter and identifying the city's perimeter walls. He collaborated with local archaeologists to develop the site and helped to re-organise the museum. He became convinced that the remains of a Greek theatre lay somewhere, waiting to be discovered. In Hardcastle's opinion, a city as large and prosperous as Akragas would surely have had its own theatre. Despite many attempts, he remained unsuccessful in this quest.

Hardcastle's mission in Girgenti ended tragically, for he was bankrupted in the aftermath of the Wall Street Crash of 1929. Having previously shown signs of mental illness, he died in an asylum in 1933. He is commemorated by a bust in the garden of the Villa Aurea and by a plaque at the Sanctuary of Demeter, while the square at the entrance to the Valley of the Temples carries his name. Hardcastle's services to Sicily were recognised by the Italian government who made him a *Commendatore della Corona d'Italia* (Commander of the Crown of Italy).

THE ARCHAEOLOGICAL PARK

The ancient city occupied part of the rocky hill as well as the land between the two rivers, today's Sant'Anna and San Biago, which meet near the coast to flow into the sea. It is a complex site, with the location of the Greek acropolis now occupied by the modern town, and the slopes below filled with modern hotels. Busy roads and car parks cut across the valley, making it difficult to identify the contours of the ancient city. The archaeological park, known as the Valley of the Temples, contains most of the ancient remains.

Several of the most important monuments are connected by the Via Sacra, a path reserved for pedestrians which crosses the valley. At its western end lies a group of temples, the most notable of which is the Temple of Zeus, the Olympieion. This was the crowning glory of Akragas, the largest Doric temple ever built, demonstrating the ambition of the city's rulers. It was larger than the Parthenon in Athens, which it predated by some twenty years.

Between its columns, gigantic male statues known as *telamones* were incorporated to assist in supporting the roof. Diodorus described pediments in which scenes from the battles of the gods and the Fall of Troy were portrayed. Only an impression can be gained of the temple's original magnificence, for today it lies in ruins, its huge blocks of stone strewn across the ground. Its destruction, which began with the Carthaginians, was completed by earthquakes and pillaging in the eighteenth century to build the harbour at Porto Empedocle. The temple dates from around 480–470, probably started before the Battle of Himera, mostly built by Carthaginian slaves following the battle and never fully completed.[9]

Several shrines lie nearby which formed the Sanctuary of the Chthonic Divinities, gods who lived beneath the earth, whose columns became a symbol of classical Sicily. Its origin is probably pre-Greek, part of an earlier Sicel site. The remains of the Temple of Castor and Pollux, or Discouri, can be found here.

At the start of the Via Sacra, a footbridge leads to the Temple of Heracles, which lies largely in ruins and in which traces of fire can be seen. It dates from around 460. Nine of the temple's columns are standing, eight of them thanks to Hardcastle's restoration work.

Further down the Via Sacra stands the Villa Aurea, with bougainvillea overflowing its garden walls, the home of Alexander and Henry Hardcastle in the 1920s. Today it is used for cultural events and special exhibitions. Alexander's bust stands in the garden.

Beyond the villa rises the magnificent outline of the Temple of Concord, the most celebrated of all the site's monuments, dating from 450–440. It is one of the best-preserved Doric temples in existence, with all thirty-four of its columns and pediments in place. Its preservation is due to its having been converted into a Christian church in the Byzantine era. The name Concord comes from a Latin inscription found nearby which has no connection with the temple. The god or goddess, to whom the temple was dedicated, is unknown.

The Temple of Hera Lacinia, towards the end of the Via Sacra, is partly in ruins, with twenty-five of its original thirty-four columns standing. A classic Doric building, it was built in 460–440 and also shows signs of burning. Smaller and earlier than the Temple of Concord, it follows a similar design.

To the north of the Via Sacra are two monuments celebrating Demeter, goddess of the earth, sacred to the ancient Greeks who were dependent upon the harvest for their livelihoods. The Temple of Demeter is partially incorporated in the medieval church of San Biago. Its origin was established when busts of Demeter and her daughter Persephone were found on the site. The temple may have been built by Theron in the aftermath of the Battle of Himera in 480 BC. Hardcastle excavated the site and discovered numerous votive items. He also uncovered a paved road nearby with deep incisions cut by the wheels of passing chariots.

Steps located near the church lead down to an earlier monument, the Sanctuary of Demeter, another site sacred to the goddess, reminiscent of the Sanctuary of Malaphorus in Selinunte. When discovered, it was filled with votive offerings and statuettes. It probably dates from before the founding of Akragas and served as a shrine to the goddess until the sacking of the city in 406.

To the north of the Via Sacra, near the church of San Nicola, lies an extensive enclosure containing remains from the Hellenistic and Roman period. The residential quarter uncovered there relates to the time of the Roman occupation, from the second century BC to the fifth century AD. This was the location of Roman Agrigentum.

In 2017 came the news that Alexander Hardcastle had been waiting for in the 1920s. Traces of a Greek theatre had been found close to the Hellenistic district. The announcement claimed that a theatre from the Hellenistic period had been identified, with a structure extending in a semi-circle facing the valley and the sea. Excavations to unearth the theatre are continuing, aided by archaeologists from Catania and Bari.[10]

THE ARCHAEOLOGICAL MUSEUM

The museum, the full name of which is the *Museo Regionale Archeologico 'Pietro Griffo'*, was opened in 1967 and named after the superintendent of antiquities at the time. It is located north of the Valley of the Temples, on the main road, Via dei Templi. It contains a collection from the sixth and fifth centuries BC, the period of Akragas's greatest prosperity.

The Temple of Zeus is well-interpreted in a room containing a model of the original structure. From the *telamones*, the huge Atlas-like statues which stood between the columns, have been salvaged three heads and a complete, reconstructed figure which stands over seven-and-a-half metres high. There are further rooms containing vases, statuettes and terracotta heads, including a particularly fine head of Persephone. From the temple of Demeter comes a series of lion-heads waterspouts.

Among the statues is a reconstructed figure in marble of a warrior wearing a helmet. Only the head and torso have survived, from around 470, yet it still manages to convey a sense of dynamism. Another is the *Ephebe,* or young man, from the fifth century BC, which is thought to represent a victorious athlete at the Olympic Games. There is also a kneeling figure of Aphrodite and a statue of the river god, Akragas.

In a room containing inscriptions can be found the one referring in Latin to Concordia, the Roman goddess of harmony, which gave its name to the temple. Discovered by Fazello, the inscription had no known connection to the temple.

The coinage of Akragas, which began in the period between the fall of Phalaris and the accession to power of Theron, includes some remarkable designs. The early coins show an archaic version of the eagle and crab emblems combined with the city's name. From 472 designs become more sophisticated, culminating in the best work from 413 to 406, reflecting the splendour of the city at its peak. The most famous coin is a silver *decadrachm* (ten-drachma piece) featuring two eagles standing on a hare and, on the reverse, a four-horse racing chariot with an eagle above and a crab beneath. It may have been minted for the celebrated victory of Exainetos in the Olympic Games of 412. A highlight of the collection is a hoard of fifty-two gold Roman coins from the Second Punic War, which was found buried. Presumably the owner did not survive to recover his treasure.[11]

24

MOZIA, ANCIENT MOTYA, A PUNIC CITY

Mozia is the Italian name for the site of a Phoenician settlement which lies just off the west coast of Sicily. It is situated on a small island, called San Pantaleo, in a protected lagoon known as the Stagnone. Named Motya in ancient times, it was the principal Phoenician and Carthaginian settlement in Sicily from around 720 to 397 BC. Motya was a victim of the Carthaginian-Greek wars for in 397, in revenge for the Carthaginian destruction of Greek cities, it was captured and sacked by an army led by Dionysius I of Syracuse. It was never rebuilt, for the Carthaginians moved their base to nearby Lilybaeum (Marsala).

The island was bought in the early twentieth century by Joseph Whitaker, a member of Sicily's British community, whose fortune came from the wine trade. Whitaker carried out extensive excavations on the island and in 1921 published an authoritative account of Motya's history and archaeology. The island remains the property of the Whitaker Foundation.

The Motya site gives an insight into a little-known culture, as the Phoenicians and the Carthaginians after them left few historical records. When the Romans destroyed Carthage in 146 BC, any surviving archives were lost. As Motya was not built over, its site provides a model of a Phoenician settlement which grew into a fully-fledged Carthaginian city, with its outline and remains of its fortifications still intact. For archaeologists, Motya is one of the most important Phoenician sites in the western Mediterranean.

Excavations have revealed much about the inhabitants' way of life, with the findings displayed in a museum. The most famous exhibit is a statue in white marble known as the 'Motya Youth', which is one of the most admired and celebrated of all ancient Greek or Greek-style statues to have survived.[1]

The site is reached by a boat service which operates from the coast road some ten kilometres north of Marsala. It lies on unspoilt, low-lying land surrounded by the sea and recalls a thriving maritime city destroyed at its peak.

THE ANCIENT CITY

Before the Greeks arrived in Sicily, according to Thucydides, the Phoenicians occupied the headlands and small islands off the coast and used them as posts for trading with the Sicels. After the Greeks arrived in large numbers, initially settling on the east coast, the Phoenicians withdrew to the west of Sicily, concentrating in three settlements, Motya, Panormus (Palermo) and Solus (Solunto). Here they enjoyed the twofold advantage of living close to their allies, the Elymians, and of being only a short sea voyage from Carthage, their city on the North African coast (in modern-day Tunisia).[2]

The Phoenicians were an enterprising people whose origins can be traced back to biblical times, when they were known as the Canaanites. Living under constant threat from powerful neighbours and constrained by a homeland (modern-day Lebanon) that was squeezed between the sea and the mountains, they developed into a seafaring people. Their port cities of Tyre and Sidon were designed as maritime centres, and the Phoenician fleet became the Mediterranean's first naval power. A commercial trade in high-value goods such as metal, glass and jewellery was developed across the Mediterranean, in support of which trading posts were established at strategic points. The most important of these was Carthage, founded, according to legend, by Queen Dido in 814 BC.

The settlement of Motya stood upon a small island, two-and-a-half kilometres in circumference, with a maximum height above sea level of six metres. Situated in the middle of a lagoon, surrounded by shallow water, it was protected from the open sea by a long, low-lying island. Close to the sea and with ample anchorage for their ships, it was typical of the locations chosen by the Phoenicians.

While the origin of the name Motya is thought to be Phoenician, its meaning is uncertain. According to the founding legend, the Phoenician god Melqart (Heracles to the Greeks) was helped during his adventures in Sicily by a nymph named Motya. In gratitude, Melqart founded the city in her name. More prosaically, the name Motya has been linked to a Phoenician word for 'slime', referring to the marshy waters surrounding the city, as well as to a word for 'weaving', referring to the local craft of textiles.[3]

Motya grew from an early trading outpost to be a significant settlement by around 720 BC. During the seventh century, it developed on the back of trade with the Greek and Elymian cities, as is evident from the remains of commercial buildings where fabrics and pottery were produced.

There was also a sacred precinct, known as the *tophet*, where human sacrifice took place. Dating back to biblical times, this practice was reinforced by the founding myth of Carthage, in which Queen Dido committed suicide by throwing herself upon a pyre. When the community was under threat, the Carthaginians sought to please their gods by sacrificing babies, often the new- or first-born, in the fire.[4]

During the sixth century, as Carthage grew more powerful, the Phoenician settlements in Sicily were absorbed into its empire. Motya became the main Carthaginian base in Sicily, the port to which their troops were sent. In this period, Motya was surrounded by a defensive wall, while an artificial dock, called a *cothon*, was built near the south gate. The island was linked to the mainland by a paved causeway one-and-a-half kilometres long.

The city's defences were further strengthened in the fifth century. The surrounding walls were rebuilt, interspersed with square towers, and protected by bastions and gates. Motya became a city-fortress, with a population of some 16,000 inhabitants, filled with finely decorated properties reflecting the prosperity of its citizens.[5]

THE HISTORY

Initially the Phoenicians and Greeks lived peacefully together in Sicily, with the prosperity of the Greek cities, such as Selinus and Akragas, based upon trade with Carthage. Greek merchants lived in Motya, just as Phoenicians lived in the Greek cities. Greek culture had a strong influence on Motya, as is evident in the design of its buildings and coinage.

But as the Greek cities expanded their territories and Carthage became more powerful, so Sicily became increasingly unstable. The island became divided into two zones of influence, with the Greeks in the east and the Carthaginians in the west. The wars which followed brought great destruction upon the island. Following the Carthaginian destruction of five Greek cities (Selinus, Himera, Akragas, Gela and Kamarina), the Greeks retaliated in a campaign led by Dionysius I, tyrant of Syracuse.

In 397, after long preparation which included the hiring of mercenaries, Dionysius declared war and set out with a formidable force to attack the Carthaginians in western Sicily. His army, as described by Diodorus, consisted of 80,000 infantry and over 3,000 cavalrymen from Syracuse, together with contingents from other Greek cities. Leptines, Dionysius's brother, was in command of the navy, made up of nearly 200 warships, supported by 500 transports carrying siege engines and supplies. The transports also carried a surprise weapon, an early kind of artillery unknown at the time in Sicily, in the form of a giant catapult capable of firing boulders and sharply pointed missiles long distances.[6]

Arriving at Motya, he found the causeway, which linked the island to the mainland, destroyed. This he rebuilt and, having put the Carthaginian navy to flight, began his assault upon the city. Fierce fighting took place at close quarters, missiles raining down upon the city.

Dionysius established a routine of attacking by day and of withdrawing his troops before nightfall. Then he ordered a surprise attack by night which succeeded in scaling a damaged section of wall. Desperate fighting ensued, street by street, the Motyans aware that they could expect no mercy after the destruction of the Greek cities. Eventually the Greeks broke through and an orgy of revenge took place.

The city was given over to the troops to plunder, in reward for the hardships of the siege, and was then burnt to the ground. The survivors who were captured were sold into slavery while Greek mercenaries who had fought on the Carthaginian side were crucified as traitors. Leaving a garrison to hold the remains of Motya, protected by his fleet, Dionysius returned to Syracuse taking with him a large collection of booty in gold, silver and other valuables.[7]

The Carthaginians reconquered the territory in the following year. They abandoned Motya and removed the surviving inhabitants to nearby Lilybaeum (Marsala), which became their principal base in Sicily.

JOSEPH WHITAKER

The site of Motya lay abandoned and forgotten for centuries. In Norman times it was occupied by Basilian monks who gave the island the name of San Pantaleo. Later it passed into the hands of small landowners who planted it with vines. Some inconclusive excavations by renowned archaeologists took place in the late nineteenth century but it was an English businessman, Joseph Whitaker, who revealed the site.

Joseph Whitaker was a member of the British family whose fortune was made in the wine trade at Marsala. Dissatisfied with business life, and bored with the social round in Palermo, Whitaker developed an interest in archaeology, becoming an expert in Phoenician civilisation. Motya fascinated him and by 1906 he had succeeded in acquiring the whole island.

Excavations under the direction of Antonio Salinas, the director of antiquities in Palermo, revealed the remains of temples, defensive walls, residential houses, religious precincts, steles with inscriptions (stone memorials) and many domestic items. This material proved conclusively that this was indeed the site of Motya. To display his findings, which amounted to over 4,000 artefacts, Salinas encouraged Whitaker to build a museum.

Whitaker's book, entitled *Motya, A Phoenician Colony in Sicily,* an account of the history and excavation of the site, was published in 1921. It confirmed his important contribution to archaeology in Sicily, which was recognised in London. In the preface to his book, Whitaker summarised the importance of the site as follows:

On no other Phoenician site, perhaps, are so many ruins of an important fortified city still to be found standing *in situ* at the present day as at Motya. Once overcome and destroyed, as it was, by the elder Dionysius, Motya apparently ceased to exist as a town, and such of its ruins as were allowed to remain, first by its Greek conquerors, and later by the Carthaginians themselves when founding the new city of Lilybaeum, were covered up by the protecting soil and debris, and have probably thus remained, untouched by the hand of man, until the present day. In this lies the great archaeological interest and importance of the site.[8]

THE ARCHAEOLOGICAL SITE

A visit to the site starts with a short boat trip from the coast road on the mainland to a quay on the island. The archaeological remains are spread out around the island, which taken together build up a picture of the ancient city. There are no spectacular ancient buildings to rival the temples at the Greek sites.

A path from the quay leads round the island's east coast to the remains of the city's defences from the fifth century, including a stretch of wall, a staircase and a tower. The path continues to the North Gate, its entrances protected by a bastion. Through the gate, though now under water, can be seen the remains of the causeway linking the island to the mainland.

Directly inland from the north gate is a sacred precinct, called Cappiddazzo, dedicated to an unknown god, containing a building with three aisles. To the northwest lies a necropolis with numerous stone sarcophagi. Further south, on the island's west coast, is the *tophet,* another sacred precinct, attended in ancient times by numerous priests and priestesses.

Tophet, which means 'going through the fire,' signified the ritual sacrifice of babies and small animals to appease the gods in times of crisis. This practice appears to have been active from the seventh to the fifth centuries. The sacrifice was made before a bronze statue of the god, Baal, whose outstretched arms received the victim before it fell into the flames below. Funerary urns were found that contained the ashes of human babies. It is likely that these sacrifices were infrequent and that the bodies of dead babies were sometimes used in the ceremonies. The Greeks were repulsed by the practice of human sacrifice, and in his treaty with Carthage in 480, Gelon of Syracuse requested it to cease.

The Carthaginian gods, Baal, the sun-god; Astarte, the moon-goddess; and Tanit, another female deity, are of ancient origin, mentioned in the Bible in connection with the Canaanites. Astarte was shared with the Greeks, for whom she became Aphrodite, and with the Romans, for whom she became Venus.

The remains of residential quarters, spread around the site, show houses built around courtyards, some of them three storeys high. Near the city walls, some houses reached six storeys high. Water was stored in cisterns and brought into the city from the mainland by pipes laid under the sea. A residential complex, called the House of Mosaics, contains a portico and pavements decorated with designs in black and white pebbles in an oriental style.

On the southern coast stands the South Gate, with two protective bastions dating from the sixth to the fourth centuries. Here can be found the *cothon*, an artificial dock cut out of the rock beneath, included within the city's walls. Copied from a larger version in Carthage, the *cothon* is the only known one of its type in Sicily.

THE MUSEUM

The museum is located near the quay where the boats tie up. In front of it stands a bust of its creator, Joseph Whitaker (1850–1936). The museum's collection was formed around the nucleus of Whitaker's finds with the addition of material from the 1960s and '70s. There is much still to be discovered, for only a small part of the site has been excavated. As well as from Motya, the collection includes items from Lilybaeum and Birgi on the mainland. The first room contains a model of the island with panels describing the history and background of the Phoenician civilisation.

The collection includes a large quantity of architectural remnants and decorations such as stone lions' heads and sphinxes, statues and steles with Phoenician inscriptions. Smaller pieces include terracotta ornaments, vases with painted figures, ceramics, amphorae, votive statuettes and jewellery. There are plates with some striking fish designs and a collection of grotesque masks supposedly worn by participants during the sacrificial ceremonies. Military memorabilia include metal arrow heads and lead shot, large quantities of which were unearthed, a reminder of the bombardment of the city during Dionysius's siege. Examples of the city's coinage show the strong influence of Greek monetary design.

The most famous exhibit in the museum is the statue of the
Motya Youth, or *kouros* in Greek, which was unearthed on the site
in October 1979, causing an instant sensation. When a piece of
marble first appeared, the archaeologists working on the dig
thought it must be a fragment. But as the statue slowly emerged
from beneath two metres of soil and rubble, they realised they had
found a substantial piece of classical Greek sculpture. The event is
described by Gaia Servadio, in her book *Motya, Unearthing a Lost
Civilisation.*⁹

Today the statue stands in the Motya museum, 1.82 metres
high, a proud, heroic-looking figure carved out of white marble.
The feet and arms are missing, while the head, which was found
separated from the body, has been replaced. The statue has been
identified as a charioteer by its athletic stance and by its clothing,
a close-fitting sleeveless tunic, which shows off the muscular body
beneath. Supporting this theory are five holes around the crown of
the head, which probably held in place a victor's wreath. It is a work
of great sophistication, probably by a Greek master-sculptor and is
dated from between 470 and 460 BC. The marble, which came from
Aphrodisia near Ephesus, is of the highest quality.¹⁰

The identification and the origin of the statue are unknown
and are the subject of much debate. What was a Greek-style
statue doing in a Carthaginian city? Whom did it represent? The
archaeologist, Vincenzo Tusa, who examined it shortly after it
was discovered, thought it could be a Carthaginian victor at the
Olympic Games. The fact that the statue wore a tunic, compared
to the Greek statues which were mostly depicted nude, supported
this conclusion. Another theory was that the statue represented a
Greek victor, looted from one of the Greek cities such as Akragas
or Selinus. Other theories of the statue's identity abound, including
that it depicts a Phoenician god, a Greek god or a Greek tyrant.
A comparison is made to the Delphi Charioteer, a bronze statue
found in the Sanctuary of Apollo in Delphi, dedicated by Polyzalos,
the younger brother of Gelon, tyrant of Syracuse.

Whatever the origin of the statue, it was prized in Motya and presumably buried when Dionysius's army besieged the city. In this way it was saved for posterity, for original Greek statues on public display were looted by the Romans and disappeared. Most of the Greek-style statues to be seen in Sicily today are Roman copies.

In 2012, the Motya Youth was displayed at the British Museum in London for the duration of the Olympic Games. It drew extravagant praise and was seen as a magnificent memorial to the ancient Olympiad.[11]

25

THE ROMAN VILLA DEL CASALE
NEAR PIAZZA ARMERINA

The outstanding Roman monument in Sicily is the villa situated near the small town of Piazza Armerina in the centre of the island. This Roman villa, dating from the early fourth century AD, is world-famous for its well-preserved mosaic decorations covering 3,500 square metres of flooring spread over forty-five rooms.

The lively and colourful scenes depicted offer an insight into the lives of the Roman aristocracy during the late Empire. Reflecting both public and personal interests, they range from a chariot race and hunt for exotic wild animals to domestic and family matters. In one scene, girls in bikini-like costumes take part in a gymnastics competition. In others, the subjects are nature and mythology, while fantasy is given free rein in scenes featuring children.

The villa is a significant monument in the archaeology of ancient Rome, for no other building in the Empire has yet revealed a comparable array of mosaics. It was made a World Heritage Site by UNESCO in 1997.

A comprehensive account of the villa is provided by Roger Wilson, archaeologist and historian of Roman Sicily, in his book *Piazza Armerina* published in 1983.[1]

ROMAN SICILY
Under the Roman Empire, with the threat of invasion removed, Sicily entered a prolonged period of stability and prosperity. The

island appealed to the Romans, not only for its agricultural produce but also for its Greek culture, and they settled in the major cities, providing a political and military ruling class. Veterans from the legions were granted land on which they developed farms producing a variety of crops. As well as for its grain, Sicily became famous for its wine, especially the variety known as Mamertine from the region around Messina. The cult of Venus Erycina, from a site of Phoenician origin in western Sicily, became popular in Rome with a sanctuary built to the goddess in the city. The emperors Augustus, Caligula, Septimus Severus and Hadrian all visited the island. Sicily became a fashionable place for wealthy Romans to take their holidays, which might include a visit to Syracuse, the ancient Greek city and seat of the Roman governors, and a climb up Mount Etna.

The *latifundia,* the large grain-producing estates, remained central to the agriculture of the island. However, with Egypt, another Roman province, now also supplying grain, the pressure on Sicily to feed Rome was reduced. Under the Empire, the *latifundia* were no longer worked by slaves but by poor tenant farmers who in time became serfs, tied to the land. On the back of cheap labour, huge profits on grain production were made by the estate managers and owners.

Attached to the estates, residential villas were built and sumptuously decorated by wealthy Romans as their country retreats. The remains of three such villas have been discovered, at Tellaro near Noto, at Patti near Messina, and the most substantial, the Villa del Casale, near Piazza Armerina.

THE SITE
The site lies in the Casale district of central Sicily, some five kilometres south of the modern town of Piazza Armerina. It is to be found just off the state road number 117, which links the motorway at Enna to the south coast at Gela. Surrounded by wooded countryside, the site is protected by mountains to the north, with clear views to the south.

In Roman times the road connected Catania, on the east coast, to Agrigentum, on the south coast. The village of Philosophiana, six kilometres south of the villa, acted as a convenient stop-over for travellers. The district around Enna was favoured by huntsmen for its extensive oak forests and mountain streams.

The Roman villa which occupied the site has been variously described as a mansion, a hunting lodge, a pleasure palace and a centre for estate management. In practice, it probably fulfilled all these roles, acting as a luxurious country retreat, a place for entertaining guests and the centre of a busy farming estate. While evidence is lacking, the estate probably extended over territory to the south, in the direction of the sea.

The villa, which was built on a grand scale, covered an area of 150 metres by 100 metres, and was richly decorated. Apart from the mosaic flooring, the walls were painted, the courtyards contained fountains, while statues of Venus, Apollo and Hercules adorned the rooms. The design, which was based on traditional Greek and Roman architectural principles, featured the peristyle, a courtyard with a covered walkway or portico around it, supported by columns.

The single storey building consisted of four inter-connected sections, each one built on a different level due to the slope of the land. The main entrance was through a monumental archway leading to a spacious courtyard decorated with columns. An anteroom led into another courtyard with a central fountain. Beyond the hall lay the entrance to a basilica used for official receptions. Two large rooms, lavishly decorated and used for entertaining, were situated nearby. Surrounding the public areas were the living quarters, spacious baths, both hot and cold, and lavatories. A continuous water supply came into the villa through an aqueduct.

Based on evidence from the remains of pottery and lamps, together with comparisons of material from North Africa, the villa is considered to have been built during the years AD 300–325. This was the period of the Tetrarchy, when four men shared Imperial power, from which Constantine the Great emerged in 324 as sole ruler. As a luxury residence, it may have lasted for 150 years. It was built on the remains of an earlier structure, dating from the first or second century AD.[2]

When the Empire began to break up in the fifth century AD, Sicily was invaded by the Vandals. After the villa was destroyed, a village grew up around its ruins which was abandoned in the twelfth century when the town of Piazza Armerina was founded. At some stage a landslide occurred, covering the mosaics with mud and preserving them for posterity.

The presence of an ancient site near Piazza Armerina was known for a long time. But it was not until the nineteenth century that sporadic exploration began. The first systematic excavations were carried out in 1929 by Paolo Orsi, superintendent of antiquities at Syracuse, who unearthed a section of pavement. The full extent of the mosaics was revealed in the early 1950s by Gino Gentili. Much information on the site is missing, as records of the early excavations were not well-kept. Many questions remain and there are buildings around the villa yet to be examined.

Today, a modern structure has been superimposed upon the site, protecting the ancient building, and providing raised walkways which afford an excellent view of the mosaics.

THE MOSAICS

The artistic quality and sheer diversity of the mosaics leave a powerful impression. In style they are both realistic in the reproduction of events from everyday life and fanciful in scenes allowing the imagination full scope. The craftsmen who created them were masters of their art. From comparisons to Roman villas elsewhere in the Empire – in today's Tunisia and Algeria – it has been concluded that the mosaicists came from North Africa. Several workshops were probably commissioned and brought over to Sicily. The architect providing overall direction may also have been of North African origin. The materials used come from a variety of sources around the Mediterranean.

The scenes depicted in the mosaics can be divided into three groups, those from public life, personal and family life, and mythology.

The scenes from public life include a chariot race, with eight chariots taking part, in what has been identified as the Circus Maximus in Rome. The starting gates have been opened and the chariots are at full stretch. The far end of the Circus is filled with spectators. The action is dynamically portrayed, with one chariot overtaking another and elsewhere a collision taking place. At the end of the race, a judge awards the palm to the victor. This is the most complete visual record of a Roman chariot race in existence.[3]

The long hall, which measures sixty metres, contains the most dramatic scenes of them all, depicting a great hunt for wild animals. In an African countryside, men carrying shields and javelins round up lions and leopards, to be trapped and loaded onto ships. A man is being rescued from an attack by a lioness. Scenes from another province show more animals being captured, including an elephant, a camel and a rhinoceros. The aristocratic figure, richly dressed and seemingly in charge of the hunt, is sometimes taken to be the emperor himself.

In another hunting scene, men on horseback chase deer and the carcass of a wild boar is being brought in, while hounds chase a fox. Falcons stand in readiness to be released. An open-air banquet, complete with roast duck, is being prepared. This scene probably reflects regular hunting trips made into the forest to the north of the villa.

In a fishing scene, four small boats carrying fishermen lie just offshore, in a sea filled with a variety of fish, including sea bream, red mullet and octopus. Dolphins play in the waves.

Celebrated for its contemporary appearance is the scene where nine girls, wearing bikini-like costumes, take part in a gymnastics competition. A tenth girl acts as the judge who is presenting a crown to the victor. One of the competitors carries small weights in her hands as if in a modern gym.

The family scenes are full of caricature and imaginative touches, including a small version of the circus, where the chariots are being driven by children and drawn by geese. In other scenes, cupids are fishing from boats and playing with ducklings.

Mythology is represented by several large and powerful mosaics. In one, a battle is taking place between Pan and Eros, watched by a woman with a young son and daughter. These figures are sometimes thought to represent the Imperial family.

In a scene from Homer with a Sicilian connection, as it is set in a cave on the slopes of Mount Etna, the Cyclops Polyphemus is seated, about to eat a ram. Ulysses, who together with his companions is planning to make Polyphemus drunk, offers him a cup of wine.

A big room, once decorated with statues, contains mosaics showing some of the Labours of Hercules. The dramatic scenes include horses throwing their riders having been shot by Hercules, a giant serpent, the Cretan Bull, the dying Nemean lion and the Hydra of Lerna. A separate set of mosaics depicts the glorification of Hercules.

THE OWNER

The identity of the original owner of the villa, for whom it was built, has been the subject of much speculation. The villa's sheer scale and lavish decoration, together with the huge expense spent on its construction, indicate someone of high importance in the Roman world. Could the owner have been an emperor?

The construction of the villa, calculated to have taken place between AD 300 and 325, is placed during the chaotic period of the Tetrarchy, when four men shared Imperial power, two in the east and two in the west. In 324, Constantine the Great emerged as the sole ruler, reuniting east and west into one empire. A possible connection has been claimed between Maximian, a member of the Tetrarchy and emperor from 286 to 305, and the scenes of Hercules, the presiding spirit in the villa. Maximian and his son Maxentius both adopted the title 'Herculean' and might have commissioned the mosaics featuring the demi-god. It is possible that Constantine inherited the villa after defeating Maxentius in battle. In addition, several scenes of individuals and families in the mosaics, noted above, have been linked to the Imperial family.

While the involvement of these emperors in the story of the villa is intriguing, several factors make it improbable. Firstly, the Villa del Casale was not a unique phenomenon, but one of three luxury Roman villas discovered in Sicily, the others being near Noto and Messina. It was not an exclusive country retreat, but one of several. In addition, its remote location makes it an unlikely choice for an emperor. Furthermore, the period of the Tetrarchy was one of civil war, with each of the leading contenders, at one time or the other, fighting for his life. There would have been little time and one suspects, little inclination, for designing and building a luxury villa in Sicily.

The subjects portrayed in the mosaics point to an owner who had the following characteristics. He would have been an exceedingly rich man who enjoyed entertaining on a lavish scale. Hunting was a favourite pursuit, while both family and nature were important to him. His beliefs were rooted in the traditional pagan religion of Rome, represented by the exploits of Hercules.

The scene of the chariot race, at the Circus Maximus in Rome, may represent a specific event sponsored by the owner. The importance given to the Great Hunt, and the collection of wild animals, indicates that the owner may also have been engaged in the animal trade, supplying the amphitheatres. Such activities involved a huge commitment, in terms of both expense and organisation, by their sponsors. These mosaics may have been designed as tributes to the owner's contribution to these public events in Rome.

The conclusion reached by Wilson is that the owner of the villa was probably a private individual of senatorial rank, possibly a Sicilian, but more likely a Roman aristocrat. Unless more information is forthcoming, the owner of the Villa del Casale will remain anonymous.[4]

PART FOUR

ARTISTS

INTRODUCTION

In its diversity, the history of Sicilian art mirrors that of the island itself. For Sicilian art represents the cultures of the many different people who occupied the island, and as such it includes a range of art forms and influences originating from the eastern Mediterranean, North Africa and the Italian mainland. With little continuous development, Sicilian art should instead be viewed in distinct chapters, each one representing a historical era, Greek, Roman, Arab, Norman and so on.

Two eras stand out for their artistic achievements, the Greek and the Norman. Under the Greeks, Syracuse became one of the most powerful cities in the Mediterranean, admired as a city of art and for the beauty of its temples and public buildings. Under the Norman kings, the rich kingdom of Sicily was ruled from Palermo through a unique blend of cultures, Norman, Arab and Byzantine Greek, represented by the brilliance of its court and the style of its churches and palaces.

Some common elements between eras can be identified, reflected in the art. Female figures, for example, have remained pre-eminent in religion from ancient to modern times. In ancient Syracuse, the symbols of the city were the goddess Athena, whose statue adorned the temple, and the nymph Arethusa. In Christian Syracuse, they were replaced by the Madonna, whose statue adorned the cathedral, and Santa Lucia. The pantheon of gods and goddesses from the Greeks and Romans metamorphosed into the Christian saints, with the practices of patronage, intercession and votive offerings being common to both. The role of the mother goddess, so prevalent in antiquity, was taken over in Christian times by the Madonna, who is revered in many different guises across Sicily.

As yet another foreign power occupied Sicily, so new artistic influences arrived on the island. This led to frequent interchange, with foreign artists arriving to work in Sicily, and Sicilian artists leaving to study and work abroad. Sicilian art developed into a two-way street between the island and the cultural centres of Europe, the Middle East and North Africa. This interchange continued into modern times.

Up to and including the Norman era, the arts in Sicily tended to be dominated by the culture of the ruling power. While local craftsmen were employed to carry out the work, concepts and designs largely followed principles established elsewhere. The Greeks imported their knowledge of building temples, the Arabs introduced their Islamic architecture and the Normans brought in experts from Byzantium to decorate their churches with mosaics. The ruling elite imposed an artistic framework which, under their direction, was realised wholly or in part by Sicilian craftsmen, supported in the earlier times by slave labour. In this way, Sicily became a melting pot of cultures, adapting to foreign influences, while developing its own artistic talent.

Sicilian art found its own voice and blossomed under Spanish domination, encouraged and promoted by the Catholic church. As well as by the church, the arts were sponsored by the viceroys, civic leaders and the aristocracy. This was the period when the patron saints of Sicily, beloved by their local communities, were celebrated in sculpture and paintings. This environment saw the emergence of local artists of talent and originality. A peak was reached in the baroque era with the redesign of the island's city centres. The arts continued to flourish, with a strong Sicilian flavour, through the nineteenth and early twentieth centuries.

Much of Sicilian art history remains unknown. Due to frequent military interventions and natural disasters, works of art were lost altogether or dispersed around the world. Much documentary evidence was also lost. When foreign armies like the Carthaginians and the Romans took control of the island, they systematically looted the Sicilian cities for their art and shipped it back home. The Spanish dismantled ancient Greek monuments to build their coastal defences and harbours. Modern archaeologists and art historians often have their work cut out to discover the background to individual monuments and works of art.

Pioneering work on Sicilian art appeared in the second half of the nineteenth century, done by Gioacchino Di Marzo, a priest from Palermo. His *Delle Belle Arti in Sicilia* (Fine Art in Sicily) covered the development of art, in four volumes, from antiquity to the end of the seventeenth century. It was followed by books on sculptors, especially the Gagini family, and the painter Antonello da Messina. Di Marzo's research in the church archives of Palermo and Messina revealed original documents which enabled him to catalogue many of the artists' works. Di Marzo was the founder of Sicilian art history. Since then many books, on historical eras and individual artists, have been published by Sicilian art historians. [1]

International art historians have made significant contributions, concentrating upon specific periods, monuments and artists. Outstanding examples include Anthony Blunt on Sicilian baroque, Stephen Tobriner on Noto and Donald Garstang on Serpotta. [2] A useful reference on Sicilian artists is provided by Raleigh Trevelyan, in his *Companion Guide to Sicily*, which includes a list of some sixty artists and architects with brief biographical details and a note of their major works. [3]

As the Greek and Norman eras were covered in the author's previous books on Syracuse and Palermo, the articles that follow relate to the period from the Spanish domination to the twentieth century. The articles present profiles of eight leading artists: four painters, two sculptors and two architects, together with an outline of their work. With one exception, all are Sicilian. The exception is Caravaggio, included for the importance of his work, four examples of which he left in Sicily. Caravaggio's paintings in Sicily, some of his last masterpieces, were influential among artists on the island and are today sought out by visitors. The Sicilian artists included were all leaders in their fields, innovators who pushed the boundaries of their art. Their work is prized in Sicily and is on view in many different locations across the island.

ANTONELLO DA MESSINA, RENAISSANCE PAINTER

Antonello da Messina, who lived from around 1430 to 1479, was one of the finest artists of fifteenth-century Italy. He trained in Naples where he assimilated the techniques of foreign artists, especially the Flemish. Through this training, his innate talent and his contacts with mainland Italy, he rose from a provincial background to be an artist of stature in Renaissance Europe.

Antonello had deep roots in his city of Messina. It was where his family came from and he never left it for long. He used the view of the harbour as a background to scenes in several of his paintings, including in two crucifixions. He linked his name to the city forever, by adding to the base of some of his work, the inscription *Antonellus Messaneus me pinxit* (painted by Antonello of Messina).

For most of the fifteenth-century Sicily was under the control of the Kingdom of Aragon, which had defeated the French in the War of the Sicilian Vespers. In 1412, the Aragonese tightened their grip on the island, introducing a system of government run by viceroys, who were based in the island's capital, Palermo. In 1442, Aragon extended its territories to include southern Italy, choosing Naples as its regional capital.

Messina, in Antonello's day, was Sicily's second city, with around 25,000 inhabitants. Lying close to the north-eastern tip of the island, it was built in a semi-circle facing the sea, surrounded by defensive walls. Directly in front lay the strait, a narrow strip of

water only three kilometres across at its narrowest, which divided
Sicily from mainland Italy. Visible on the far side of the strait lay
the town of Reggio. Messina was important for its location and
for its well-protected, deep-water harbour. It was a busy centre
for shipbuilding and fishing, as well as for maritime trade with the
Mediterranean and northern Europe. As a local merchant class
had not emerged, exports such as silk, textiles, wine and olive oil
were handled by foreign merchants. The city hosted a cosmopolitan
mix of people which included Catalans, French, English, Flemish,
Genoese, Pisans, Venetians, Jews and Greeks.[1]

EARLY LIFE AND TRAINING

Antonello was born around 1430 into a well-established family
in Messina. His full name was Antonio de Antonio, born to
Giovanni and Garita, probably Margherita, de Antonio. Giovanni
was a master craftsman, who worked in marble, and who had his
own workshop. Michele, Antonello's grandfather, was a merchant
seaman with his own ship. It was a family of substance which owned
property in the city.

Messina had little to offer a young painter. Trade was depressed
in the aftermath of the war with the French and there was little
money available to sponsor the arts. Palermo was the artistic centre
of the island, where the viceroys lived, and where the restoration
of the island began. It would be another generation before Messina
became a promising place for artists.

As a port city, however, Messina's overseas connections offered
a way out. An apprenticeship was obtained for Antonello in Naples,
at the workshop of Niccolò Antonio, known as Colantonio, a
leading artist in the city. This training period lasted from about
1445 to 1455.

Naples was twice the size of Messina and the seat of King Alfonso
of Aragon. Like Messina, it was a busy trading port that attracted a
substantial foreign community. It was also a lively centre of the arts,

encouraged first by King René of Anjou and then by his successor, Alfonso. Under René, connections had been established with Provence, which were extended to Spain and Flanders by Alfonso. Naples became a melting pot of artistic styles, with artists from different regions of Europe working in the city. Sculptors, who later moved to Sicily, arrived from northern Italy to work on the king's triumphal arch. Among the painters, the Flemish influence was particularly strong, with work recorded in the city by Jan van Eyck and Rogier van der Weyden. Colantonio was strongly influenced by the foreign artists, especially the Flemish. This was the diverse, international environment, filled with artistic exchanges, in which Antonello learnt his craft. His experience in Naples probably led him to experiment with oil paints and to become one of the early Italian artists to work in oil.

THE WORKSHOP IN MESSINA

In 1455 Antonello returned to Messina, where he set up his workshop. He married Giovanna Cuminella, a widow with a daughter named Caterinella. By Giovanna, Antonello had a son, Jacopo, known as Jacobello, and two daughters, Fimia and Orsolina. His first commission, dated 5 March 1457, was for a standard for a religious confraternity in Reggio. Standards were a form of banner used in religious processions and were popular in Sicily. Antonello's workshop produced a variety of them, few of which have survived.

During the 1460s and '70s, Antonello established the foremost artistic workshop in eastern Sicily. It became a family enterprise employing his brother, Giordano, his son, Jacobello, and two of his nephews, Antonio and Pietro de Saliba. Commissions came in from the church in Messina and from cities such as Catania, Noto and Caltagirone, as well as from Reggio Calabria across the strait. They were mostly small commissions, an exception being an altarpiece for the church of the Annunciata in Palazzolo Acreide.

Antonello was an independent artist who assimilated different influences – Flemish attention to detail, central Italian sense of perspective and Venetian love of colour – to great effect. Probably through merchants travelling between Messina and the Italian ports, Antonello's work attracted the attention of patrons in central and northern Italy, where the artistic developments of the Renaissance were happening apace. As these connections developed, commissions arrived from mainland Italy. There is speculation, but little evidence, about Antonello's own travels in Italy. It is likely that he was on the mainland in the late 1450s, when he may have gone to Rome, and again in the 1460s, but the details of his journeys are unknown. The affinity between Antonello's work and that of Piero della Francesca, who worked in Rome in this period, makes such visits probable. While there is no evidence that he ever visited the Netherlands, Antonello's presence in Venice in 1475–76 is well-documented.

THE PORTRAITS

Antonello is famous for his portraits, for which he adopted the model made popular by the Flemish painters, Jan van Eyck and his student, Petrus Christus. This involved presenting the head and shoulders of the subject, either frontally or at a slight angle, dressed in ordinary clothes, against a dark background. A skilful use of light drew the viewer's attention to the subject's face. In the hands of Antonello, a portrait was reduced to its essentials, employing the utmost clarity and simplicity, so that its sole focus was upon the character of the subject.

As artists looked to the ancient world for guidance, they discovered texts that referred to a connection between a man's soul and his bodily features. Various theories emerged, one of which was noted by Dante, to the effect that the soul is apparent in two places, the eyes and the smile.[2] Antonello, who was gifted with psychological insight, developed a way of conveying character and emotion through the eyes and the smile. He excelled at this technique and was an early exponent of the use of the smile in portraits.

An example can be seen at the Mandralisca Museum in Cefalù, which holds Antonello's *Ritratto d'uomo* (Portrait of a Man) from around 1470. It is a small painting, oil on wood, featuring a mature looking man with sharp eyes, wearing an enigmatic smile. This portrait, which has long intrigued viewers, was found in the mid-nineteenth century by Baron Mandralisca, whose private house became the museum. The Sicilian writer, Vincenzo Consolo, was so fascinated with the portrait that he wrote a historical novel around it, featuring Baron Mandralisca, called *The Smile of the Unknown Mariner*. In fact, the sitter, who was never identified, was more likely to have been a merchant than a mariner, due to the cost of the portrait.

Antonello adapted his style of portraiture to create devotional images for private patrons. These included powerful images of Christ in small panel paintings. In one, *Salvator Mundi,* he is presented as the Saviour of the World, his hand raised in blessing. In others, Christ appears as the suffering figure known as *Ecce Homo* (Behold the Man), these being the words spoken by Pontius Pilate as he presented Christ to the hostile crowd, and as *Cristo alla colonna* (Christ at the Column).

Antonello also painted various versions of the annunciation. In the Palazzo Abatellis, which houses Palermo's regional art gallery, is the *Vergine Annunciata* (Virgin Annunciate). This panel painting from 1476–77 presents the Virgin Mary on her own. Her appearance is that of a young Mediterranean girl, wearing a blue mantle over her head, with the shadow of a smile on her face. She does not look at us directly and has one hand raised in a gesture of acknowledgement. The Metropolitan Museum of Art in New York considered this portrait to be among the most compelling and mysterious of all paintings produced in the fifteenth century. The quality of imagination at work is an exalted one, and once seen, this small picture leaves a lasting impression.[3]

ANTONELLO IN VENICE

Antonello's career reached its peak during his visit to Venice in 1475–76. Here he produced ground-breaking work in large compositions and small religious subjects as well as in portraits, proving himself to be at the forefront of artistic development. To his naturalism with human figures and his ability to portray character was added a new monumental quality in large compositions. While he was working in Venice, his fame spread. A humanist scholar, Matteo Colazio, wrote from the city in 1475 claiming that Antonello, in his use of perspective, was one of the very few painters alive who could be compared to the artists of the ancient world.[4]

In Venice, he carried out major commissions for the church. His *San Sebastiano*, the only surviving panel of a triptych for the church of San Giuliano, is dominated by the handsome body of the saint, a powerfully emotive figure set against the precision of a carefully structured Venetian city scene. Antonello's most influential painting was the *San Cassiano* altarpiece, commissioned for the church of the same name. Adopting a novel style of composition, Antonello placed the Madonna and Child upon a central throne, attended by saints and surrounded by an elaborate architectural structure. From the fragments that remain may be seen the realism with which the human figures were represented. Both this altarpiece, and the *San Sebastiano,* are truly Renaissance in spirit and influenced, among others, Giovanni Bellini and Giorgione.

As he was at work on the altarpiece, a letter arrived from Galeazzo Maria Sforza, Duke of Milan, instructing his ambassador to persuade Antonello to become his court painter. Antonello's patron, Pietro Bon, replied that he could only be released once he had completed it, which he considered to be one of the outstanding works of art in or outside Italy. Antonello declined the duke's offer.[5]

Antonello painted other masterpieces during his stay in Venice. These included two crucifixions with a background of an Italianate landscape, portraits ranging from a mercenary soldier to an old man, and the distinctive *San Girolamo nello studio* (Saint Jerome in his Study). This small painting, with its intense attention to detail, shows Jerome at his desk surrounded by creatures and objects filled with religious symbolism.

In September 1476 Antonello was back in Messina in his busy workshop. For another two years, the high-quality output continued. Belonging to this period are more portraits, the *Vergine Annunciata* and a *Pietà,* generally considered to be his last work. Antonello then fell ill and put his family affairs in order. In his will, he recognised his parents, who were both still alive, took care of his wife and left the bulk of his estate including the workshop to his son Jacobello. He died sometime between February and May 1479 at the age of forty-nine.

WHERE TO SEE HIS PAINTINGS
There are thirty-two authenticated works of Antonello's, and a further sixteen attributed to him by various scholars, to be seen today. They are to be found spread between thirty-one cities from Antwerp to Washington DC, with nine in Sicily.

In the Palazzo Abatellis, which houses Palermo's regional art gallery, is the *Vergine Annunciata* and paintings of the three saints, Jerome, Gregory and Augustine.

The Mandralisca Museum in Cefalù holds Antonello's *Ritratto d'uomo* (Portrait of a Man).

Syracuse has two: the first is the *Annunciazione,* displayed at the regional art gallery in the Palazzo Bellomo, while the second, a depiction of St Zosimus that is attributed to Antonello's time in Naples, can be found in the cathedral.

Messina's regional museum holds Antonello's polyptych (multi-panels) of the *Madonna col Bambino con i santi Gregorio e Benedetto* (Madonna and Child with Saints Gregory and Benedict).

In Ragusa, the Palazzo Donnafugata holds a *Madonna col Bambino* attributed to Antonello.

The Antonello trail continues in London at the National Gallery, where five of his paintings are displayed: *Salvator Mundi* (Saviour of the World, also known as *Christ Blessing*), *San Girolamo* (Saint Jerome), *Ritratto d'uomo* (Portrait of a Man), *Crocifissione* (Christ Crucified) and *Madonna col Bambino*, attributed to Antonello.

The Metropolitan Museum of Art in New York holds three: *Ecce Homo* (known as *Christ Crowned with Thorns*), *Ritratto d'uomo* (Portrait of a Man) and a Group of Draped Figures, attributed to Antonello. Washington's National Gallery has the *Madonna col Bambino*, known as the *Benson Madonna*. Antonello's *San Sebastiano* panel is to be found in Dresden and the remains of his *San Cassiano* altarpiece in Vienna.[6]

EPILOGUE

After Antonello's death, Jacobello continued the workshop along with other family members. Although not of his father's calibre, he was a competent artist who completed the workshop's outstanding commissions. One of Jacobello's own paintings survived, a *Madonna and Child* from 1480, to be found in Bergamo. When signing it, Jacobello added the words *filius non humani pictoris* (son of the immortal painter). He died soon afterwards. Antonello's nephews, Pietro and Antonello de Saliba, became proficient artists and continued the family tradition, both doing work in Venice.

Antonello's reputation was slow to develop in Sicily, as most of his best work was commissioned in mainland Italy. In the second half of the nineteenth century, historians in Sicily began to re-evaluate their cultural heritage. Among them was Gioacchino Di Marzo, whose *Delle Belle Arti in Sicilia* (Fine Art in Sicily) included research into the artist's life and gave Antonello the recognition he deserved. Today his paintings are some of Sicily's most prized possessions.

In the cities of mainland Italy, Antonello's reputation was assured, especially in Venice, where his influence was long-lasting. In 1550

Giorgio Vasari, the founder of modern art history, published his book, *Lives of the Artists,* in Florence. The fact that Antonello was included is indicative of his reputation, some seventy years after his death, in the city at the heart of the Renaissance. Vasari described him as a man of acute mind, well-skilled in his art, and went on to claim that having learnt about painting in oils from the Flemish artist, Jan van Eyck, Antonello had introduced the technique to Italy through Venice. For reasons of chronology, historians no longer consider this claim to be valid.[7]

Antonello's international reputation has long been established. It was re-confirmed by an exhibition of his work in 2005, at the Metropolitan Museum of Art in New York, at which Antonello was described as Sicily's Renaissance Master.

ANTONELLO GAGINI,
RENAISSANCE SCULPTOR

Antonello Gagini was Sicily's finest sculptor of the Renaissance. Born in Palermo in 1478, his career spanned thirty-eight years, during which he created statues of classic simplicity and beauty. He was a prolific artist who excelled at large compositions and developed an architect's eye for framing his figures in elaborate settings.

He came from a family of sculptors whose workshop, for much of the sixteenth century, held a virtual monopoly of religious commissions in Sicily. Even today when visiting the island, it is hard to find a town, however remote, that does not contain one of Antonello's statues, typically a Madonna and Child. His celebrity status led to various legends being circulated which emphasised his talents. According to one, Antonello worked with Michelangelo in Rome. According to another, when Caravaggio landed in Sicily, he made a detour to see one of Antonello's works, praising it to the skies.

As a boy, Antonello was trained by his father, Domenico, who had personal experience of the artistic developments taking place in central and northern Italy. Domenico was a pioneer who introduced new forms of sculpture to Sicily and who established the Gagini dynasty on the island. Antonello, the most accomplished artist in the family, built upon his father's work and that of his contemporaries to record even greater achievements. His work was continued by his sons into the late sixteenth century.

DOMENICO'S CAREER

The Gagini family came from Bissone on Lake Lugano, where Domenico was born in the early 1430s, in an area known for its marble quarries. His training took place in Florence where he was listed as a pupil of Brunelleschi. He left Bissone in 1448 for Genoa to work on a chapel in the cathedral. He was then called to Naples, along with other sculptors, to work on King Alfonso's triumphal arch. After the king died, Domenico left for Sicily in 1463 where he remained for the rest of his life. The timing of his arrival in Palermo was fortuitous, for it coincided with a boom in the construction of public buildings and a demand for sculptors.

The Aragonese, after years of conflict with the French, were now in control of Sicily, and with peace established, they set out to consolidate their presence on the island. As part of this process they turned their attention to Palermo, with a population of 40,000 the island's capital and the seat of their viceroys. After the long war with the French, the city was run down and a reconstruction programme was started, sponsored by the state, the church and wealthy aristocrats. The period from 1460 to 1520 saw some of Palermo's most impressive buildings constructed including the Archbishop's Palace, the Palazzo Pretorio, the church of Santa Maria della Catena and the Palazzo Abatellis. The driving force behind the regeneration of Palermo was the city's *pretore* (mayor), Pietro Speciale. The Speciale, a prominent family in Sicily since the thirteenth century, were the barons of Alcamo and Calatafimi. They were used to high office having supplied viceroys in the past, while Pietro's brother served as ambassador to Aragon.

Once established in Palermo, Domenico embarked upon a series of commissions. For Speciale, he contributed to the decoration of the new senate house, the Palazzo Pretorio. Work for the church included decoration of the chapel of Santa Cristina in the cathedral and a portal for the church of the Annunciation. A series of statues of the Madonna and Child was produced for churches in Palermo, Messina, Syracuse, Erice and Marsala.

Sicily, under the Aragonese, was cut off from the artistic developments taking place in central and northern Italy. The predominant artistic style on the island remained that of Catalan Gothic, while the role of sculpture was largely confined to the decoration of buildings. It was through the initiative of individual artists, such as Domenico, that the influence of the Renaissance reached Sicily. Domenico's own artistic development had progressed from the late-Gothic style of Lombardy, via Renaissance Florence to the international environment of King Alfonso's Naples. His fresh approach, natural and humanistic, was avant-garde in Sicily.

Following the death of Alfonso, Speciale brought in experienced craftsmen from Naples to work on the buildings. Sculptors, stonemasons and builders from Liguria, Tuscany and Lombardy arrived in the city. The range of work required of the sculptors was varied. Centred upon the statue, it extended to include altars, altarpieces, decorative arches, relief panels, tombs, fountains, columns and capitals. The preferred material was white marble from Carrara, in Tuscany, which was brought to Sicily by Genoese merchants.

Two of the sculptors who arrived in Palermo pursued careers which overlapped with that of Domenico. One was Francesco Laurana, originally from Dalmatia, the other was Pietro de Bonitate from Lombardy. The three sculptors influenced one another in style and collaborated on several commissions. Laurana, whose Italianised name derived from his hometown of La Vrana, worked in Provence and then in Naples, at the same time as Domenico. Like Domenico, Laurana brought an injection of Renaissance spirit to Sicily. In Palermo, Laurana and de Bonitate created together a decorative arch for the Mastrantonio chapel in the church of San Francesco d'Assisi, one of the first examples of Renaissance sculpture in the city.

As well as handling commissions for the church, Laurana produced a series of portrait busts of aristocrats, the most celebrated being that of Eleonora of Aragon, niece of the king of Spain. This portrait's elegant, oval face with its gentle expression has long fascinated viewers, among them Sciascia, who wrote of it, 'In my opinion, no work, other than this by Laurana, better explains the essence and mystery of sculpture'.[1]

By the 1480s, demand for his services was such that Domenico established a workshop in Palermo, whose output soon reached commercial proportions. Assistants were hired and production was streamlined. When the *marmorari* (marble workers) of Palermo formed a guild in 1487, codifying working practices, they published the names of ten master sculptors with Domenico at the top of the list.

ANTONELLO'S EARLY CAREER

Antonello was born in Palermo in 1478 to Domenico and his second wife, Caterina. Giovannello, Domenico's son by his first wife, was part of the household. As he grew up, Antonello was trained by his father in the busy workshop where he became familiar with the work of Domenico's contemporaries. He was sent on trips to Carrara to manage the supply of marble. It is likely that he also visited Rome, though there is no evidence of any connection with Michelangelo. When Domenico died in 1492, Antonello was fourteen and Giovanello twenty-three. Neither had enough experience to take responsibility for the workshop, and as Domenico had left debts, the workshop was closed.

Antonello's activities over the next few years are unknown. Somewhere he acquired valuable experience, for in 1498 he was working in Messina as a qualified sculptor. He remained in the city until 1508, where he gained the reputation of being the foremost sculptor in eastern Sicily, attracting the best commissions. They included statues of the Madonna and Child for churches in Messina, Catania and Palermo. Antonello's early work closely resembled that of his father, showing an archaic simplicity and feeling for his subjects.

Antonello also developed a novel kind of decorative altar. The concept of this altar, which combined several statues in a large composition known as a tribune, appears to have originated in Naples. Once transferred to Sicily, it became popular with the church, whose various orders competed with one another for the most grandiose designs. Antonello began work on the first of these in 1499, for the church of Santa Maria Maggiore in Nicosia. His design consisted of a marble structure on four levels depicting the dormition, or death, of the Virgin Mary, ringed by the apostles. This commission was not completed until 1511, but in the opinion of the art historian, Gioacchino Di Marzo, Antonello created in it a truly original composition.[2]

It was a breakthrough, for this work led to a similar commission for the church of Santa Cita in Palermo and then to an even greater assignment. This was for a tribune to decorate the apse of Palermo's cathedral. Not yet thirty years old, Antonello had won the most prestigious commission in Sicily.

MATURE WORK

In his maturity, Antonello became an all-round Renaissance artist. He perfected skills in many forms of sculpture, acquired an ability in architecture, and drew the designs for the construction of the tribune. Alive to the ideas circulating in the Renaissance cities of Italy, he pursued an artistic ideal based on natural beauty and classical examples.

The tribune for the cathedral was a project of prime importance for Palermo. The contract for its construction was signed in 1507 by Antonello and Giovanni Paternò, Archbishop of Palermo, in the presence of the Spanish viceroy. Its purpose was to celebrate the Assumption of the Virgin Mary to whom the cathedral was dedicated. Placed immediately behind the main altar and in full view of the congregation, it would provide a monumental backdrop to the cathedral's telling of the Christian story.

To handle this commission, Antonello moved back to Palermo and set up his workshop. He was joined by several promising sculptors from eastern Sicily as well as by others from Carrara. Apprentices arrived who, according to the custom of the day, required board and lodging. Antonello acquired two properties, one near the cathedral, containing the workshop and accommodation for pupils, and a second down by the Cala, the old harbour where the ships docked, providing storage for finished work and the incoming blocks of marble.

In Messina, Antonello had married Caterina, a sculptor's daughter, by whom he had two sons, Giandomenico and Antonino, and a daughter, Giovanella. In Palermo, following Caterina's death, he married Antonina Valena, by whom he had four more children, Giacomo, Fazio, Vincenzo and Florenza. Eventually, as the children grew up, the workshop became a family enterprise, employing Antonello's five sons and a trusted deputy, Fedele da Cavona, who married his daughter, Giovanella.

As work progressed on the tribune, it came to dominate Antonello's life. It was designed on a grand scale, almost sixteen metres high, divided into three tiers of statues contained in niches featuring the apostles and saints, together with the Assumption of the Virgin Mary and the Resurrection of Christ. Later, a figure in stucco of God the Father was added above the whole structure. There were some forty-five statues in total. Antonello worked on the project for the rest of his life, acknowledging that the workload had consumed his youth.[3]

In parallel to the tribune, Antonello's workshop took on other commissions from the church. Its prestige was such that orders came in from all over Sicily. The high volume of production resulted in uneven quality, leading some patrons to stipulate that the finished product must be done by the hand of the master himself. There were statues of the Madonna and Child, scenes of the Annunciation and figures of the saints. When his patron the archbishop, Giovanni Paternò, died in 1511, Antonello carved the effigy for his tomb.

For the church of Santa Maria dello Spasimo (St Mary of the Agony) in Palermo, Antonello created the marble altar over which Raphael's painting, *Lo Spasimo di Sicilia,* was displayed. Ordered by the monks of the church from Raphael, the painting was completed in around 1516 and, having survived a shipwreck, was delivered to Palermo. It shows the moment when Christ fell under the weight of his cross and his mother suffered a spasm of agony, known as *lo spasimo.* In 1622 Raphael's painting was bought by Philip IV of Spain and taken to Madrid.

Later in his career, Antonello's work took on an added complexity. Altarpieces and tombs became larger compositions, contained within decorative frames and illustrated with relief panels to tell a story. An example is the *Altare di San Giorgio* created in 1520–26 for the chapel of the Genoese in the church of San Francesco d'Assisi in Palermo. In the centre is a marble figure of a youthful St George on horseback, killing the dragon with his lance. Figures of the saints appear on the marble surround. Columns, providing a sense of perspective, support a second level on which appears a panel with the Madonna and Child surrounded by angels.

Still at the height of his powers and with the tribune unfinished, Antonello died in 1536, aged fifty-eight. He was buried in the Chapel of the Sculptors, in the church of San Francesco d'Assisi in Palermo where his father, Domenico, was also laid to rest.

The tribune was completed by Antonello's sons, Giacomo, Fazio and Vincenzo, and put in place in 1575. It filled the entire apse of the cathedral, a tall, curved structure, with its gallery of statues resembling a huge theatre set. It was the Gaginis' greatest achievement and remained in place for over 200 years.

WHERE TO SEE THE STATUES
Sculpture by Antonello and his workshop can be found all over Sicily. According to Gioacchino Di Marzo, there are more than

2 2 0 pieces on the island, from single statues to large compositions. Palermo holds over seventy, some of the finest to be found in central locations.[4]

Palermo's Galleria Regionale, in the Palazzo Abatellis, contains Antonello's *Annunciazione, Ritratto di giovinetto* (Portrait of a Young Man) and two versions of the *Madonna col Bambino*. Domenico's *Madonna del Latte*, and a *Madonna col Bambino*, attributed to him and Bonitate, are also here, together with Laurana's portraits of *Eleonora d'Aragona* and of a young man.

The cathedral holds prime examples of the Gagini workshop, including pieces from the tribune, for in the late eighteenth century it was dismantled during renovation. Remnants of the tribune include statues of the saints standing along the nave and at the end of the choir, a *Resurrection of Christ,* and statues of the Apostles, all by Antonello. Near the main entrance can be found a holy water stoup by Domenico. Side chapels contain relief panels by Antonello and a statue of the Madonna by Laurana. In the crypt is the tomb of Giovanni Paternò with the effigy by Antonello.

The Museo Diocesano, in the Archbishop's Palace next to the cathedral, contains rooms dedicated to the sculpture of the fifteenth and sixteenth centuries. There are statues of Palermo's saints, Cristina, Oliva, Agata and Ninfa, by Antonello, Domenico and de Bonitate. The Gagini room holds a model of the tribune and fragments of the structure, including relief panels depicting the Passion of Christ. There is also work by Giacomo and Fazio Gagini.

The church of San Francesco d'Assisi holds Antonello's Altar of St George plus a statue of the saint with illustrative panels. The decorative arch by Laurana and Bonitate covers the entrance to the Mastrontonio Chapel. There are statues of the virtues by Bonitate and a sarcophagus by Domenico.

The church of Santa Caterina contains Antonello's statue of the saint and the church of Santa Cita his decorative altarpiece.

Outside Palermo, visitors exploring the island can track down statues by Antonello in many of the towns. The provinces of Palermo, Messina and Trapani are rich in his work. The cathedral in Marsala contains several statues by different members of the Gagini family. Antonello's statue known as the *Madonna della Catena* (Madonna of the Chain), supposedly admired by Caravaggio, can be found in the church of Santa Maria di Gesù in Caltagirone.

EPILOGUE

The Gagini dynasty continued to leave its mark on the artistic life of Sicily. The family tradition was maintained by Antonello's grandsons and nephews, including Antonuzzo who made a name for himself as a sculptor, while Nibilio and Giuseppe became successful silversmiths and metal-engravers. Collaborators and pupils from the family workshop kept the Gagini school going for many years.

The tribune did not survive. Between 1781 and 1801 Palermo's cathedral underwent drastic refurbishment, prompted by damage from an earthquake. The project was designed by the Florentine architect, Ferdinando Fuga, on the orders of the archbishop, Filangeri, with the support of the Bourbon king in Naples. It superimposed a late-baroque style upon the medieval structure, destroying the character of the original building. The old form of basilica, built by the Normans, made way for an extended interior with the addition of side chapels. The external appearance, with its pointed towers, was altered by the addition of a large dome. As part of these works, the Gaginis' tribune was pulled down and the pieces dispersed.

In Sicily, Antonello's reputation, which was sky-high during his lifetime, was secured for the future by the large body of work which he left behind. In 1883, Gioacchino Di Marzo published his book, *I Gagini. La Scultura in Sicilia nei secoli XV e XVI* (Sculpture in Sicily in the fifteenth and sixteenth centuries). In it, Di Marzo firmly places Antonello among the great Italian artists of his time. Based on documentary evidence, the book contains an inventory of the Gaginis' work and where it can be found.

Internationally, Antonello's acclaim has been more muted, largely because he is unknown outside the island. Douglas Sladen, an expert on the monuments of Sicily, when writing in 1907, recorded his assessment of Antonello as follows: 'It is doubtful that any of the great fifteenth-century Florentines excelled him when at his best'.[5]

CARAVAGGIO, BAROQUE PAINTER

In October 1608, Caravaggio brought off a miraculous escape from prison in Malta, arriving by boat on the south coast of Sicily. He made his way overland to Syracuse where he was met and looked after by his friend Mario Minniti.

The artist's full name was Michelangelo Merisi da (from) Caravaggio, a small town near Milan in northern Italy. He made his reputation in Rome in the 1590s and early 1600s by supplying the church and wealthy private patrons with paintings of great originality and dramatic impact. In his work, conventional biblical scenes took on new realism through strong characterisation and recognisably contemporary settings. For his models, instead of following classical examples, he used people from the streets. Trusting his instincts, he cut through the artistic conventions of his day to present scenes of rare insight.

Adding to the impact of his paintings was Caravaggio's contrasted lighting effect, known as *chiaroscuro,* in which light and dark colouring was used to focus attention on the main scene. The public, unused to seeing reality expressed in religious art, took him to their heart and Caravaggio's paintings became hugely popular.

While his art was becoming the talk of Rome, and he was making friends in high places with people like the Colonna family, Caravaggio was also indulging his wild side. During the years of his greatest creativity, 1600–06, an increasing number of violent incidents involving the artist was recorded by the police. An expert swordsman with a fiery temper, he enjoyed wandering through the rougher parts of the city with a group of friends looking for a fight. Eventually it got out of hand, a man was killed, and Caravaggio was condemned for murder by the pope.

His influential friends obtained refuge for him in Malta, under the protection of the Knights of St John. At first all went well. The Knights' Grand Master, Alof de Wignacourt, was so pleased with his work, especially his portrait, *Ritratto di Wignacourt con paggio* (Wignacourt and Page) and his *Decollazione del Battista* (Beheading of John the Baptist), that he made Caravaggio a full member of his Order. Then an assault took place on a leading knight, a so-called Knight of Justice, who was badly wounded. Caravaggio, who played a prominent part in the assault, was thrown into an underground cell known as the *guva*. Somehow, he managed to escape at night with the use of ropes, avoid tight security in the harbour and board a boat to take him to Sicily. To do so, he must have had help from someone in authority. Wignacourt was furious at his escape and had Caravaggio stripped of his membership of the Order.[1]

It is not known where Caravaggio landed in Sicily, but it may well have been at the port of Terranova (modern Gela). From here, anxious to avoid being followed, he probably took the old road over the mountains, that leads via Caltagirone to Syracuse. According to the legend, in Caltagirone he took the time to visit the church of Santa Maria di Gesù to see a marble statue of the Madonna and Child from the sixteenth century by the Sicilian sculptor, Antonello Gagini.[2]

SYRACUSE

Mario Minniti, who met the artist upon his arrival in Syracuse, was a Syracusan who had worked with Caravaggio in Rome, had been his model, and was now married and the owner of a successful studio in Syracuse. He was able to introduce Caravaggio to the leading men of the city. The timing could not have been better. The city's senate was in the process of restoring a basilica in honour of their patron saint,

Santa Lucia, who was martyred for her Christian faith under the
Roman Emperor Diocletian in 304. Caravaggio, whose reputation
extended to Sicily, was commissioned to paint an altarpiece for the
basilica, to be ready for the saint's feast day on 13 December.

While in Syracuse, Caravaggio was shown around the ancient
monuments by Vincenzo. Mirabella, who studied the archaeology
of ancient Syracuse, published his work in 1613 containing the
first reconstruction of the ancient city. In his book, he recalls that
Caravaggio was particularly interested in one of the quarries with a
tall, narrow shape and exceptional acoustics, thought to have been
used as a prison. He recounts the visit as follows.

> Having personally taken Michel Angelo of Caravaggio, that
> remarkable painter of our times, to see the prison, I remember
> him saying, prompted by his unique talent for portraying nature:
> *Don't you see how the Tyrant, wishing to hear what was being said, made*
> *the prison in the shape of an ear?*[3]

The name, the Ear of Dionysius, is still used today.

Caravaggio's painting for the basilica, *Seppellimento di Santa Lucia*
(Burial of Santa Lucia), was finished in early December. It was a
large canvas, four metres by three, another realistic scene and a far
cry from the conventional religious paintings of the time. Two huge
gravediggers dominate the foreground, with a group of mourners
behind, and in the middle, the small, broken body of Lucia.
Caravaggio worked directly onto canvas with a brush. During
restoration work it was revealed that an earlier version had showed
Lucia's head severed from her body. This must have appeared too
extreme, even if historically correct, and in the finished painting
she is shown with a gash in her throat. As usual, Caravaggio used
contemporary faces for his models. The gravedigger on the left is
thought to be Wignacourt, the Knights' Grand Master, whether
in revenge for imprisoning him in Malta or simply because his
face was easily remembered, is unknown. Other faces in the

painting may include Mirabella, Minniti and a self-portrait of the artist. The bleak atmosphere of the painting, recalling the city's catacombs where the saint was originally buried, owes something to Caravaggio's own mood at the time, for he was in fear of his life from the Knights of Malta.

MESSINA

His work in Syracuse completed, Caravaggio left for Messina, a larger city where he felt safer. He knew, after his escape, that he was a marked man and he went around armed, looking more like a swordsman than a painter, according to a biographer, Francesco Susinno.[4] His behaviour was odd for a man on the run, for he drew attention to himself by throwing his money around and by being rude about a popular local painter. As an artist, his reputation preceded him, and he received a commission to paint an altarpiece for a chapel built by a wealthy merchant, Lazzari. Appropriately, the painting was called *Resurrezione di Lazzaro* (Raising of Lazarus). It was another large, sombre canvas with much dark space, as in his Lucia. Out of the darkness, Christ holds out his hand in a commanding gesture for Lazarus to rise from the dead. In a powerful scene, rich in religious symbolism, the rigid body of Lazarus appears diagonally across the painting, recalling Christ's own body when taken down from the cross.

This painting was followed by a Nativity, known as the *Adorazione dei pastori* (Adoration of the Shepherds), for the church of the Capuchins in Messina. Again, it was a large canvas with a dark background and the light shining upon a small group of figures in the lower half. Here, in an old barn, the humble figure of Mary is seated on the ground, which is covered in hay, holding her baby to her. A group of haggard men looks on, with the outline of a donkey in the background, in a setting of abject poverty. This nativity is one of Caravaggio's most deeply felt and impressively simple works.

In his three paintings produced in Messina and Syracuse, Caravaggio harked back to the world of the early Christians with its catacombs, its background of fear and its expression of simple devotion.

PALERMO

Two biographers, Giovanni Baglione and Pietro Bellori, who wrote respectively in 1642 and 1672, refer to Caravaggio's visit to Palermo. According to Bellori, after leaving Messina, the artist went to Palermo to carry out a further commission, a Nativity for the Oratory of San Lorenzo.[5] As the oratory was dedicated to the saints Lawrence and Francis, both were featured in the painting. It was another large altarpiece known as *Natività con i santi Lorenzo e Francesco*. In it, Mary looks at her new-born child lying on the ground, with the saints in attendance and Joseph seated to one side. Above is a flying angel with a banner proclaiming *Gloria in excelsis Deo*. This painting was in clear contrast to Caravaggio's earlier work in Sicily, more traditional in style and lacking the dark, brooding element so evident in the work carried out in Messina and Syracuse, and it does not match their emotional appeal.

Recent research now suggests that this painting was done in Rome in 1600. This conclusion is based upon the discovery of a commissioning note from 1600 for a painting by the artist, which appears to match the Palermo Nativity, together with the fact there is no documentary evidence from Palermo that Caravaggio ever visited the city. By contrast there is plenty of evidence of the artist's stay in Messina and Syracuse. Stylistically the painting fits the artist's Rome period much better than his Sicilian period. It has also been noted that the model used for Mary in the Palermo Nativity bears a striking resemblance to the model in *Giuditta e Oloferne* (Judith & Holofernes), a painting of Caravaggio's from Rome in the early 1600s. While there is no definite proof, it does seem likely that this Nativity belongs to the earlier period.[6]

EPILOGUE

By the autumn of 1609 Caravaggio was back in Naples where he had been before going to Malta. He was hoping that his friends would get him a pardon from the pope that would allow him to return to Rome. In Naples, upon leaving a notorious inn, he was attacked and so badly slashed in the face that he became scarcely recognisable. This incident had all the hallmarks of a revenge attack, the settling of a vendetta, and was probably the work of the Knight of Justice assaulted in Malta. Caravaggio stayed on in Naples for eight months, weakened by his wounds, where he produced his final paintings.

In July 1610 he left for Rome by boat, ending up at Porto Ercole, in Tuscany. Here he was mistakenly arrested, causing him to miss the connection with his boat. He died shortly afterwards, in circumstances which are unclear, probably on 18 July. The cause of death was most likely a fever, rather than at the hands of the Knights of Malta. He was less than forty years old.

Today, Caravaggio's reputation is assured. His name ranks among the most famous of the Italian painters and he is widely recognised as the best painter of the seventeenth century. His influence upon European art was profound through his realism, the drama in his canvases and his use of *chiaroscuro*. Artists like Rubens, Rembrandt and Velasquez were all deeply affected by his work. His exhibitions cause considerable excitement internationally and are attended by many thousands of people.

Caravaggio's work in Sicily can be seen today at the following locations. In Syracuse, his Burial of Santa Lucia is on show in the church of Santa Lucia alla Badia in Piazza Duomo. It was commissioned for the Basilica of Santa Lucia, in Piazza Santa Lucia, in a district known as the *Borgata*, which is to be found on the far side of the Little Harbour. Here the painting would have been displayed at its best, in its correct historical context.

In Messina, due to damage at the original locations, the Resurrection of Lazarus and the Nativity can be seen in the Museo

Regionale at 465, Viale della Libertà, along with the work of local painters such as Antonello da Messina.

The Nativity, displayed in the oratory in Palermo, was stolen in 1969 and never recovered. Apparently, this was carried out on the orders of a mafia boss, who once he saw the damage done to the painting during the theft, refused to pay for it. According to America's FBI, this theft ranks among the top ten art crimes of all time. To replace it, the oratory had a copy made based on a photograph and images of the picture taken during restoration work done in Rome in 1951. The result is an altarpiece that looks, to the untrained eye, like the real thing.

In 2010 an Italian researcher, Silvano Vinceti, claimed to have found bones from the body of Caravaggio at Porto Ercole. Using carbon dating and DNA checks, he claims to be 85 per cent certain that these are the remains of Caravaggio's body. An interesting conclusion of the examination is that the bones contain a high level of lead poisoning. Much of the paint in those days contained lead. Caravaggio worked on large canvases and was known to have been messy in his handling. Lead poisoning can produce depression, pain and personality disorders. Van Gogh is another painter who is thought to have suffered from lead poisoning and who committed suicide. If confirmed, these findings could provide an important clue to Caravaggio's violent temper and erratic behaviour.[7]

PIETRO NOVELLI, BAROQUE PAINTER

Pietro Novelli was born in Monreale, the village in the hills behind Palermo, famous for its Norman cathedral. Known as *Il Monrealese* after his birthplace, he lived from 1603 to 1647. Novelli was the first of the Sicilian baroque painters and became the island's greatest artist of the seventeenth century. His large religious paintings and portraits of the saints, dramatic and sombre in tone, adorned the churches and palaces of Palermo. While best known as an artist, Novelli was also an engineer and an architect, for which he was recognised by being appointed *Architetto del Regno* (Architect of the Realm). He lived in dangerous times, for both the plague and armed revolt hit Palermo during his lifetime.

In the seventeenth century, Sicily was a Spanish colony ruled by viceroys, with the co-operation of the Sicilian aristocracy. Early in the century the Spaniards redesigned Palermo, imposing a grandiose plan suitable for the city's status as the viceregal seat. The medieval city was divided into four quarters by two roads bounded at each end by a monumental gate. Religious orders built themselves churches, oratories and monasteries, while the aristocrats competed with one another to create the most lavish palaces. Society was permeated by strong religious beliefs, acted out in public ceremonies attended by huge crowds, as with the colourful processions that left the cathedral and made their way down to the seafront. These developments coincided with the start of the baroque era, and it was the baroque, with its theatrical appeal, that became the dominant style of the city. The seventeenth century was a flourishing period for the visual arts in Sicily.

EARLY CAREER

Pietro Novelli was trained as an artist by his father, Pietro Antonio Novelli, an established painter and mosaicist in Monreale, who had studied in Rome. At around the age of 15, Novelli junior was sent to Palermo to work in the studio of Vito Carrera, an artist from Trapani. This was followed by a period with Carlo Maria Ventimiglia, an architect and mathematician, who taught Novelli the use of perspective and the principles of architecture. Ventimiglia, who was close to the viceroy and a friend of princes, offered a way into aristocratic society for the young artist. Access to the ruling elite, backed by his artistic ability and strong personality, played a significant part in the success of Novelli's career. In 1623 his training came to an end and he married Costanza Di Adamo, by whom he had two children, Pietro Antonio and Rosalia.

Two artists had a profound influence upon Novelli in his formative years. The first was Caravaggio, who came to Sicily in 1608 before leaving for Naples in the following year. His fame preceded him, and he received commissions for altarpieces in Syracuse and Messina. Another of Caravaggio's paintings, a scene of the nativity, which may predate his visit to Sicily, decorated the oratory of San Lorenzo in Palermo. The second influence was Anthony van Dyck, who at the age of twenty-five was invited to Palermo by the viceroy, Emanuele Filiberto, to paint his portrait. Work by Van Dyck was displayed in the city, while his altarpiece for the oratory of San Domenico, known as the *Madonna del Rosario* (Madonna of the Rosary), was painted later in Genoa and delivered in 1628.

A year after Novelli's marriage, Palermo was struck by an epidemic of the plague which lasted until 1626. During this time, a quarter of the city's population died, out of a total of 130,000. Among the victims were Novelli's father and the viceroy, Filiberto. Palermo went into a state of siege, with no one allowed in or out of the city, while the plague ran its course. On 15 July 1624, the bones of Santa Rosalia, one of the saints favoured in the city, were found in a cave on Monte Pellegrino and used to stem the spread of the epidemic. When eventually the plague came to an end, according to the archbishop, it was thanks to the intercession of our glorious Santa Rosalia. Rosalia became Palermo's patron saint, a position she still holds today. Her festival in mid-July, known as the *festino*, is the most important event in the city's calendar.[1]

The first recorded works of the young Novelli were frescoes for smaller church institutions in Palermo. They included a full figure representation of Sant'Antonio Abate (St Anthony Abbot), a cycle of frescoes on the life of Giovanni di Dio (John of God), and in 1629, his *Daniele nella fossa dei leoni* (Daniel in the Lions' Den). In the following year, having become a member of the oratory of San Domenico, Novelli decorated the oratory with his fresco, *L'Incoronazione della Vergine* (Coronation of the Virgin). These works, with dynamic figures and a fresh use of colour, announced the arrival of a new artistic talent.

During 1631–33, Novelli made a visit to Rome and Naples. In his travels, he followed in the footsteps of contemporary Sicilian artists and architects, including his father, who took part in an interchange of ideas with the art centres of mainland Italy. There was much to learn, for it was in Rome that the baroque art movement had begun to emerge in around 1600, which then transformed urban landscapes across Europe. In Naples, Novelli worked with the Spanish artist, Jusepe de Ribera, a master of Caravaggio's style of naturalism and chiaroscuro, the use of contrasting light and dark shades. From his time in Italy, Novelli emerged a stronger and more confident artist, with a style of his own which combined both spiritual and worldly elements.

MATURE WORK

From his return to Palermo in 1633 to his premature death in 1647, Novelli was awarded a series of prestigious commissions. He went on to produce a large body of work, the best of which were his oil paintings. So popular did he become that viceroys, nobles and senior officials of the church competed to display his work. For the aristocracy, he painted portraits and a variety of religious subjects. For the church, he provided religious scenes on canvas, as well as frescoes.

As an artist, he transcended his parochial environment by absorbing influences circulating in European art, especially from the Flemish and Neapolitan schools. From Van Dyck came his elegant figures and soft brown tones. From Caravaggio and Ribera came a sense of drama and naturalism, heightened by the chiaroscuro technique. To these elements were added Novelli's own instinct for composition and his ability to portray character. His self-portraits are revealing. They show a man who is both vigorous and intelligent, wearing a stylish beard and moustache, looking every bit the dashing man-about-town. But there is also an underlying sense of melancholy, which is noticeable in much of his work.

Two paintings from 1634 demonstrate Novelli's mature style, the *Madonna col Bambino e San Bernardo* (Madonna and Child with St Bernard) and the *Madonna con il Salvator Mundi* (Madonna with the Saviour of the World). The latter, with its soft colours and the resigned yet sweet expression of the Madonna together with her Child, has been compared to Raphael.

One of Novelli's most celebrated paintings was created for the Benedictine monastery in Monreale, his *San Benedetto distribuisce i pani* (St Benedict distributes bread). In a large composition full of religious symbolism, St Benedict distributes loaves, representing the Catholic faith, to religious orders, the nobles and the public at large. This scene follows a doctrine established at the Council of Trent, where the Catholic church developed its response to Protestantism, whereby the Catholic church should promote the faith to all social classes. To the left of the picture stand the founders of the Benedictine order. In the centre, a noble receives bread from St Benedict. To the right, representing the public, appear portraits of Novelli's family. The beautiful woman, barefoot and wearing a golden dress, and playing with her two children, is Costanza, the artist's wife. Behind her, in profile, appears Novelli's father, who died during the plague epidemic. Novelli, proud and dignified, stands above them in aristocratic splendour, surrounded by his family and pupils.

The expansion of Palermo offered many opportunities for architects and Novelli alternated his painting with architectural work. The viceroy appointed him *Architetto del Regno* (Architect of the Realm) in 1643 and a year later Palermo made him *Architetto del Senato Palermitano* (Architect of the Palermitan Senate). This made him the foremost figure in his field on the island.

A growing threat from the Turks led the Spaniards to fortify the coastal cities of Sicily. One of Novelli's tasks was to oversee the status of the fortifications, and he toured the coastline from Milazzo to Syracuse for this purpose. In Palermo, he worked on the development of the new harbour, contributed to the decoration of the Porta Felice, the city's gate on the seafront, and planned the decorations for the annual festival of Santa Rosalia.

Novelli's later work as an artist included some of his finest. There was a portrait of Moses, conceived as a shrewd old man clasping his tablet of commandments, and depictions of the sacrifice of Isaac and the moment when St Peter was freed from prison by an angel. There was a touching Pietà, with the Madonna looking up to heaven while indicating the dead body of Christ. For the cathedral in Piana degli Albanesi, a small town inland from Palermo, he provided a cycle of frescoes. His last painting was the *Sposalizio della Vergine* (Marriage of the Virgin), a powerfully emotive representation of the Virgin Mary which, according to the art historian Guido Di Stefano, was one of Novelli's most poetic and humanistic pictures.[2]

In August 1647, an armed uprising against the government took place in Palermo. Led by an agitator named Giuseppe d'Alesi, it was supported by low paid workers, such as fishermen and tanners, in a desperate attempt to cut the taxes imposed by the Spaniards. The Norman Palace, the viceregal seat, was stormed by the protestors, forcing the viceroy to flee the city. Before long, d'Alesi was hunted down and killed by the authorities. On the same day that d'Alesi died, Novelli was riding on horseback behind prince Pietro Branciforte, who was attempting to calm an angry mob, when protesters fired their weapons. Novelli was fatally wounded in the arm and died a few days later. In this way, the career of *Il Monrealese* was cut short at the age of forty-four.[3]

WHERE TO SEE THE PAINTINGS

A catalogue of Pietro Novelli's work, published in 1939 by Di Stefano, listed 111 paintings, eighty-five of them in oil, the rest being frescoes. They are mostly to be found in Palermo. There is also a collection of his drawings and sketches for architectural projects. The following is a guide to the locations of Novelli's work, subject to change due to reorganisation of the galleries.[4]

Palermo's Galleria Regionale, in the Palazzo Abatellis, displays the following paintings: *San Pietro liberato dal carcere* (St Peter Freed from Prison), *Comunione di Maria Maddalena* (Communion of Mary Magdalene), *Presentazione della Vergine al Tempio* (Presentation of the Virgin at the Temple), *Beata Vergine nella Gloria* (Holy Virgin in Glory), *Mosè* (Moses), *Sacrificio di Isaaco* (Sacrifice of Isaac) and *Santo Martire* (Martyr Saint).

The Museo Diocesano, in the Archbishop's Palace next to the cathedral, contains a room dedicated to Pietro Novelli, containing: *Annunciazione* (Annunciation), *Pietà* (Mary and the Body of Christ), *San Francesco di Paola* (St Francis of Paola), *San Gaetano*, *Madonna e santi Carmelitani* (Madonna and Carmelite saints), *Madonna con i santi Benedetto e Luigi* (Madonna with the Saints Benedict and Luigi).

The oratory of the Rosary of San Domenico in Palermo contains the fresco of *L'Incoronazione della Vergine* (Crowning of the Virgin Mary) and the paintings *La Pentecoste* (Pentecost) and *Disputa di Gesù con i Dottori* (Jesus Disputes with the Elders).

The church known as the Casa Professa holds *Santi Eremiti* (Hermit Saints) and *Genealogia di Cristo* (Genealogy of Christ) while an *Autoritratto* (Self-portrait) can be found in the Palazzo Mirto.

In the church of Sant'Orsola is Novelli's *Madonna con il Salvator Mundi* (Madonna with the Saviour of the World) while his *San Benedetto distribuisce i pani* (St Benedict distributes bread) is in the Convento dei Benedettini (Convent of Benedict) in Monreale.

The church of San Matteo contains an *Annunzione* (Annunciation) and the *Presentazione al Tempio* (Presentation at the Temple).

Outside of Palermo, other works are located as follows: Agrigento (Museo Civico), Catania (cathedral), Piana degli Albanesi (cathedral of San Demetrio), Ragusa Ibla (Capuchin church).

EPILOGUE

Pietro Novelli made a major contribution to the artistic and civic life of Sicily, which was recognised at an exhibition of his work in Palermo in 1990, sponsored by the Sicilian regional government. He was Sicily's equivalent of the great masters of central Italy. Outside Sicily, his work is not well known.

In his day he was a leading figure, praised by his contemporaries as the famous painter and architect who never lied with his brush nor played tricks with his perspectives, and who found true glory in Sicily and beyond.[5] His tomb lies in the church of San Domenico in Palermo, the burial place of famous Sicilians. In 1900 a bust of Novelli, by Benedetto Civiletti, was placed in Monreale in his memory.

While Novelli's son died young, his daughter, Rosalia, grew up to become an accomplished painter. Trained in her father's studio, she provided works to various churches in Palermo. There are two of her paintings in the church of the Casa Professa, and a signed drawing in the Palazzo Abatellis. A painting of Sant'Anna, attributed to Rosalia, can be seen in the church of San Domenico. The Novellis' work was continued by their pupils and followers, including Giacomo Lo Verde, Antonio Grano and Pietro dell'Aquila.

GIACOMO SERPOTTA, BAROQUE SCULPTOR

Sicily's long tradition in sculpture reached a peak in the baroque era through the work of Giacomo Serpotta. He was a sculptor of genius who worked in stucco to produce a distinctive style of natural, richly decorated figures. Serpotta's greatest achievement lay in his work for three small oratories in Palermo, Santa Cita, San Lorenzo and San Domenico. For each one he was given the task of decorating a congregational hall with a unified design dedicated to lives of the saints. These commissions enabled him to produce a set of co-ordinated sculptures to unique effect. The profusion of figures and the richness of ornamentation represented a new departure in the use of sculpture.

It took Serpotta over twenty years, from around 1685 to 1706, to complete his work in the three oratories. It was described as follows by Anthony Blunt.

> Over the walls flow ripples of the most exquisite plasterwork in the form of decorative frames, imitation draperies, swags of fruit, trophies of armour, life-size allegorical figures set against the wall or in niches, *putti* (cherubs) poised on ledges or tumbling over frames and panels of tiny figures recounting the stories of the saints to whom the oratories are dedicated.[1]

This article examines Serpotta's work in the oratory of San Lorenzo.

SERPOTTA'S EARLY CAREER

Giacomo was born in Palermo in 1656 into a family of sculptors. His father, Gaspare, worked as a sculptor in marble and stucco, while his mother, Antonina, was the daughter of a noted sculptor from Carrara, in Tuscany. Giacomo, and his elder brother, Giuseppe, learnt their craft from their father. After Gaspare died in 1670, his sons were left to maintain the family. Giacomo's first commission, for the decoration of the church of the Madonna dell'Itria in Monreale, came when he was twenty-one. It was followed a year later by a commission from the oratory of San Mercurio in Palermo. With this work in hand, Giacomo set up his workshop in Palermo, specialising in stucco, with his brother, Giuseppe, working alongside him. When he grew up, Giacomo's natural son, Procopio, joined the family workshop. Giacomo, like his brother Giuseppe, never married.

Work in stucco had been practised since ancient times as a minor form of decoration. It was used in the sixteenth century by the Gagini, a celebrated family of sculptors, to decorate their larger compositions. But it was not until the baroque era that the use of stucco came into its own. Statues in stucco, which were light in weight, were suitable for decorating walls and ceilings. Stucco was far less expensive than marble which, in its white form, had to be imported from Carrara. Work in stucco was intricate, for the artist first constructed a model using frames of wood, wire and rags held together by sand and lime. Over the model was applied a surface layer of stucco, consisting of a mix of lime and plaster. To this mix, Serpotta added marble dust to achieve the smooth surface glaze typical of his work. A high level of skill and dexterity was needed as the plaster mix dried very quickly. In his handling of stucco and his modelling of figures, Serpotta created a new art form.

THE ORATORY OF SAN LORENZO

In 1564 a group of Genoese merchants, devotees of San Francesco, founded the Compagnia di San Francesco (Company of St Francis) in

Palermo. Five years later they began to build an oratory for themselves on the site of an earlier church dedicated to San Lorenzo. While there is no historical connexion between the two saints, the Company undertook to honour them both in their oratory. It stands today in Via Immacolatella, close to the church of San Francesco d'Assisi.

Under the Spanish, who in the seventeenth century ruled Sicily as their colony, a powerful form of Catholicism took hold in the island. It was promoted by the religious orders and regulated by the Holy Office of the Inquisition. New churches, chapels and oratories sprung up all over Palermo, with the various religious orders vying with one another to have the most impressive buildings.

An oratory was a confraternity established by an order of the church. It constituted a kind of rich man's club, comparable to a guild, where members could attend ceremonies and services in a private chapel. It served both a religious and a social function. Architecturally, an oratory was a simple construction, consisting of a rectangular congregational hall with large windows down each side above head height and an altar at one end. Benches for the members, who included merchants, architects and artists, lined the side walls.

Caravaggio was commissioned to paint an altarpiece for the oratory. The timing of this commission is unclear. According to a contemporary biographer, Caravaggio visited Palermo in 1609 before leaving Sicily for Naples, having escaped from prison in Malta the previous year. He may have painted the altarpiece on this occasion while in Palermo. Alternatively, recent research points to an earlier date of 1600, in which case it was painted in Rome. The altarpiece, named *Natività con i santi Lorenzo e Francesco* (Nativity with Saints Lawrence and Francis), graced the oratory until 1969 when it was stolen and never recovered.[2]

SERPOTTA'S COMMISSION

In 1699, the Company decided upon a transformation of their oratory in line with the more secular and theatrical decoration then fashionable in Palermo. To carry out the work the Company chose Giacomo Amato and Giacomo Serpotta. Amato, the most distinguished Sicilian architect of his day, included among his work the churches of Santa Teresa alla Kalsa and della Pietà, numerous other chapels and altars, as well as projects for palaces for the aristocracy. He had spent years in Rome and had studied the work of Gian Lorenzo Bernini, the maestro of Roman baroque. Serpotta was well established at the time, with examples of his work sited around Palermo, including at the oratory of Santa Cita. While it is possible that he too visited Rome, it is more likely that Serpotta learnt about Roman baroque from men like Amato, and from engravings which were widely circulated. Under the eyes of these two masters, the oratory was transformed into a marvel of the late baroque.

While the baroque style employed was exuberant and light-hearted to the eye, the underlying intention was serious. According to Blunt, the sculptor was provided with a detailed iconographical plan for the oratory. This plan was complex, full of symbolism, and included references between different parts of the decoration. Serpotta, for his part, left nothing to chance and worked closely with the various artists employed on the project.[3]

Upon entering the oratory, one is surrounded by an abundance of superbly modelled stucco figures. White is the unifying colour, with some items highlighted in gold, and the atmosphere created is both lively and elegant. At one end stands the presbytery containing the altar, above which hangs a photographic reproduction of Caravaggio's *Nativity*. The Company's coat of arms is also prominent. On the wall at the opposite end there is a panel showing the scene of San Lorenzo's martyrdom. On either side of the altar, and down each side wall, appear life-size figures of the Virtues: Virginity, Fortitude, Mercy and Truth, etc., twelve in all. According to Donald Garstang, an expert on the oratory, these figures are true-to-life, aristocratic young women displaying grace, delicacy and exoticism. The joyous element is given free rein in the naked *putti* who play animatedly among themselves along the walls, oblivious to the cares of the world, behaving just like any small children.[4]

The principal theme of the oratory is the story of the two saints contained in the eight *teatrini* (literally 'little theatres') or panels that appear along the walls. Those on the left-hand side, facing the altar, refer to San Lorenzo, those on the right, to San Francesco. In them small, free standing figures are used to present scenes from the lives of the saints, for example Lorenzo's last prayer or when Francesco receives the stigmata. The *teatrini* trace the saints' difficult paths to sainthood and their final union with Christ. Serpotta studied the work of Antonello Gagini, a sculptor active in Palermo in the early sixteenth century, who used this device in the cathedral. Serpotta, however, developed it further, presenting scenes in sequence to form a narrative. The original concept goes back to the metopes in the temples of the ancient Greeks. Through the *teatrini*, we are taking part in a sacred play of eight scenes culminating in the martyrdom of San Lorenzo and the apotheosis (elevation to divine status) of San Francesco.[5] The stories of the saints are illuminated by reference to the Virtues, whose statues are placed next to the appropriate scene. Thus, Mercy and Charity appear on either side of the scene in which Lorenzo distributes goods to the poor, while Penitence and Constancy stand next to the temptation of Francesco.

THE ICONOGRAPHY

A secondary theme is developed in the decorative elements of the oratory. Mask-like figures appear on the seats of the benches, set against the walls, that are either laughing or crying, situated between pairs of eagles and snakes locked in combat. On the left of the mask, the eagle is winning, on the right the snake has the better of the eagle. The designs are intricately worked, using ivory and mother-of-pearl inlaid in ebony and rosewood. While the artist who created these designs is unknown, it is thought that they were made by local craftsmen to a design by Serpotta. The seating is supported by wooden brackets carved into exotic figures by Leonardo Bongiorno, a sculptor from Trapani, in the early 1700s.

In the baroque era, strange masks were widely used as decoration. In Italian the word for such a mask is *mascherone*, referring to a type of distorted face used in baroque architecture. Such faces appear, for example, in fountains and as waterspouts, as well as in paintings and floor decoration. Some include a grotesque element, presenting deformed features that are part-human and part-animal. Their origin probably goes back to ancient Greece, and in the highly superstitious environment of Sicily they were thought to provide protection. These designs thus form part of a tradition in strange facial images.

As Serpotta left no guide to the complex iconography, art historians have had to make up their own minds as to the meaning of the various elements in the decoration. The masks, alternately laughing and crying, are thought to represent comedy and tragedy, while the eagle and snake stand for the classic battle between good and evil. The theme of the masks, also alternately laughing and crying, extends to the stucco work around the walls. In contrast to the masks, the *putti*, who play joyfully without the cares of the world, may represent eternal life. Put together, these images may refer to the Resurrection through the cycle of life, death and rebirth to eternal life.[6]

EPILOGUE

Serpotta completed his work on the oratory between 1699 and 1706. He is thought to have left his mark in the statue of a man wearing a turban and holding a bow with which to play a musical instrument. It stands in a corner of the presbytery and is thought to be a self-portrait. Serpotta loved music and may have liked the idea of being seen in the guise of an exotic musician. He died in 1732, aged seventy-six, after a career lasting for over fifty years. As well as his work in the oratories, he supplied statues to some of the most important churches in Palermo including those of San Francesco d'Assisi, Sant'Agostino and the Casa Professa. Outside of Palermo, his work can be seen in Alcamo, Castelbuono, Trapani and Agrigento.

Giacomo left the contents of his workshop, consisting of his designs and models, the results of decades of experimentation with stucco, to his son, Procopio, whose work can be seen in the churches of San Giuseppe dei Teatini (St Joseph of the Theatines) and the Casa Professa in Palermo. Giacomo's grandson, Giovanni Maria, continued the family tradition, with his statues decorating the façade of the church of San Domenico in Palermo.

The work of Giacomo and his family, while famous in Sicily in their lifetimes, later fell into obscurity. The oratories became neglected and fell into disrepair, exacerbated by war damage. In the 1970s, the oratories were rediscovered by an American scholar, Donald Garstang, who became fascinated with Giacomo's work. Through his book, *Giacomo Serpotta and the Stuccatori of Palermo 1560–1790*, he became the leading authority on the subject. Tireless in his support of Serpotta's work, Garstang succeeded in raising its profile with the authorities, which helped to bring about the restoration of the oratory of San Lorenzo during the period 1999–2004. Garstang's contribution to the city was officially recognised when he was made an honorary citizen of Palermo. In June 2009, his ashes were buried in the cloisters adjoining the oratory.

ROSARIO GAGLIARDI, BAROQUE ARCHITECT

Rosario Gagliardi, who lived from around 1690 to 1762, was a leading Sicilian architect of the late baroque period, who played a major part in the reconstruction of the cities of the Val di Noto. An innovator in ecclesiastical architecture, he excelled at the design of exteriors, developing the curved façade and introducing the three-tiered tower with belfry. His masterpiece was the church of San Giorgio in Ragusa, which became a prototype for the design of churches in south-eastern Sicily.

As an artist, Gagliardi was unusual. While his experience was limited to a remote part of Sicily, he produced work of international standard. He never designed a building in a major city, such as Palermo, and probably never visited Naples or Rome. Yet he produced designs of an originality and sophistication to rival anyone of his age. His work was hugely influential, setting the style in Noto, and widely copied. He left no heirs, but his followers continued his work into the early nineteenth century.

BACKGROUND AND EARLY CAREER

The event which shaped the destiny of south-eastern Sicily during the eighteenth century, and which paved the way for Gagliardi's career, was the earthquake of 1693, in which over 50,000 people died. In total fifty-eight urban centres were affected, twenty of which were destroyed. Among the victims of the earthquake were men from the building trade, which created opportunities for a new generation of architects and craftsmen.[1]

Rosario Gagliardi was born in Syracuse, probably around 1690, to Onofrio Domenico, a carpenter from Calabria, and Maria Condi, from Augusta in Sicily. He had an older sister called Agata.[2] Little is known about his life and character for he had no contemporary biographer and no portrait of him has been discovered. In 1708, Rosario is recorded as acting as executor for an aristocratic family in Noto. In the same year he moved to Noto where, except for occasional visits to other cities in Sicily, he lived for the rest of his life. There he joined his father's profession and became a carpenter. Gaining practical experience on construction sites, his career progressed so that three years later he was referred to as *capomastro* (foreman) and in 1723, on a project in Modica, as *ingegnere* (engineer).

Gagliardi's background was unusual in that he was not trained in the studio of an established architect nor is there any record of him travelling abroad. He made his own way in his profession and evidently had the personal qualities to gain the confidence of his masters.

His intellectual training took place in Palermo; he was present at the Jesuit College in 1726, and may have stayed for a few years, studying mathematics and architecture. Ecclesiastical libraries were well-stocked with treatises and engravings by master architects such as Vitruvius, from ancient Rome, and Palladio, from sixteenth-century Venice, and it is likely that Gagliardi had access to such material. Fashionable at the time was an influential treatise on the ideal city published in 1615 by the Venetian architect, Vincenzo Scamozzi, which advocated a town plan based on a grid system, interspersed with a regular pattern of open squares and institutional buildings.

While in Palermo, Gagliardi will have seen churches designed by architects such as Giacomo Amato, who studied in Rome, as well as admiring the city's monuments like the Quattro Canti (Four

Corners), with its three tiers of statues. When he returned to Noto, it was with the title of architect.

RECONSTRUCTION OF THE CITIES

The reconstruction programme in the Val di Noto was a huge undertaking which continued throughout the eighteenth century. The work in each city varied according to the level of damage suffered. Catania, for example, was completely rebuilt on its original site, on designs by the Palermitan architect, Giovanni Battista Vaccarini. Syracuse, Ragusa and Modica, on the other hand, needed partial rebuilding together with repairs to existing structures.

In the case of Noto, it was decided to rebuild the city on a new site, ten kilometres below the old one. The city's elders, led by the nobleman Giovan Battista Landolina and the Jesuit architect, Fra Angelo Italia, chose a grid system consisting of three main, parallel streets with smaller streets crossing at right angles. The main civic and ecclesiastical buildings were allocated space around open squares with the nobles' palaces accommodated close to the centre. Housing districts for poorer residents were allocated on the city's periphery. As well as improving the quality of life for residents, the grid system, with more space between buildings, provided some protection against earthquakes. This plan was based upon the ideal city advocated in the treatise by Scamozzi.

The stone, which was quarried from hills to the north, added a unique quality to the new buildings, its pale gold colour glowing in the sun to produce a rich effect. Gradually the new city took shape and by 1750 Noto was functioning once more with a population of 10,000.

The architectural style employed in the reconstruction work, which became known as late Sicilian baroque, drew upon a local tradition dating back a hundred years, from when the Spanish rulers of Sicily redesigned Palermo. Starting in the early 1600s, streets in the city were widened and baroque monuments appeared in the central piazzas, while churches and palaces were built in the baroque style. The concept of the city as theatre, as a place for people to congregate and to take part in ceremonies and festivals, became fashionable.

To carry out this work a series of craftsmen emerged, including master builders to manage the sites, stonecutters to prepare the stone, sculptors to create the statues, carpenters to make seating and ceiling decoration and metal workers to produce the ironwork for balconies. They formed guilds and handed down their skills from father to son.

Anthony Blunt in his book, *Sicilian Baroque,* identified three stages in the development of Sicilian baroque architecture. In the first stage a new fantasy in design appeared, while the style remained essentially provincial. In the second, towards the end of the seventeenth century, a more sophisticated style became evident, introduced by architects who were trained in Rome. In the third stage, the Sicilian architects moved on from being pupils to becoming masters of their own creative style, with the work of Andrea Palma in Syracuse, and of Rosario Gagliardi in Noto, Ragusa and Modica, among the finest examples.[3]

GAGLIARDI'S BUILDINGS

On his return to Noto from Palermo in 1726, Gagliardi took up his profession as architect. He went on to play a major part in the rebuilding of the city as well as in designing buildings for many of the smaller centres in the surrounding district. Initially he referred to himself as city architect, while later he signed himself as *architetto e ingegnere della città di Noto e del suo valle* (architect and engineer of the city of Noto and its district).

He resumed his earlier work for the church and monastery of Santa Maria dell'Arco and designed the church of Santa Chiara. The exteriors of both these churches were conservative in design, with flat façades, while the interiors showed an imaginative use of space and some fine decoration. In Santa Chiara, twelve columns encircled the oval interior carrying statues of the apostles, capped by a vaulted ceiling in white and gold. Years were spent on the decoration of Santa Maria dell'Arco, with Gagliardi personally directing the stucco work, woodcarving and metal ornamentation.

As he took on an increasing workload, two younger architects emerged alongside him. The first was Vincenzo Sinatra, who began his career like Gagliardi as a craftsman, in his case as a stonecutter. He worked with Gagliardi on the church of Santa Maria dell'Arco and the two men became close colleagues. Sinatra went on to make his name as the architect of the Palazzo Ducezio, the city hall which faces Noto's cathedral. The second was Paolo Labisi, who came from an aristocratic family in Noto, and whose training was theoretical rather than practical. Labisi worked on many of Noto's buildings including one for the Crociferi Fathers which ran into trouble over costs. Both Sinatra and Labisi owed much to Gagliardi and his original designs.

The first example of Gagliardi's hallmark design, the curved church façade, appeared in 1733 at the Jesuit College in Modica. It was followed by one of his most celebrated buildings, the church of San Domenico in Noto, which was completed between 1737 and 1762. Here the richly decorated curved façade of the church, with both tiers supported by free-standing columns, dominates Piazza XVI Maggio on today's Corso Vittorio Emanuele.

The design of the curved façade was taken one stage further in the cathedral of San Giorgio in Ragusa Ibla, built between 1738 and 1775. Drawings found in the building prove beyond doubt that it was the work of Rosario Gagliardi. Approached by a flight of steps, the cathedral looks down on a central piazza containing palm trees and elegant town houses. The elaborately curved façade, in three tiers, is supported by free-standing columns and rises to a bell tower at its pinnacle. It was Gagliardi's masterpiece, rich and harmonious to the eye, which influenced church design in the Val di Noto into the early nineteenth century.

Earlier baroque churches, such as San Domenico in Palermo, were built incorporating a flat façade with decoration contained in niches. Typically, there was a tower on either side. Gagliardi's curved structure extended the façade to either side, wrapping it around and integrating it into the core of the building. The clusters of columns added to the three-dimensional effect while the bell tower provided a central focus. It was a new concept in church design, unknown in Italy, a form of baroque beyond the baroque.

The origins of the belfry façade, other than from the creative imagination of the architect, are unknown. Precedents which might have had an influence include Andrea Palma's façade for the cathedral in Syracuse and the monument in Palermo known as the Quattro Canti (Four Corners). The nearest examples come from northern Europe, from cities such as Salzburg in Austria. It is worth noting that Sicily was ruled by Austria from 1720 to 1734. While it is known that engravings of architectural designs were freely exchanged, there is no evidence of any architectural connection in this period between Sicily and northern Europe.

A comparable church to that in Ragusa, also dedicated to San Giorgio, was built in Modica between 1761 and 1848. It is one of the most spectacular of the late baroque buildings, dominating the town at the top of 250 steps. Larger than its counterpart in Ragusa, it has a façade of five, rather than three bays, and an entrance through five doors. The curved façade, emphasised by groups of columns, culminates in a tall belfry tower. Opinion is divided as to the architect who designed it. Gagliardi may well have had a hand in the original design, while Labisi is credited with its early implementation.

During his career of over forty years, Gagliardi was involved in many building projects. Best known for his churches, he also designed palaces and civic buildings. Construction of a building was a slow process which could take thirty years or more to complete and might employ more than one architect. As the records are incomplete, an inventory of his work does not exist.

Four churches in Noto can be attributed to Gagliardi with confidence, Santa Maria dell'Arco, Santa Chiara, San Domenico and SS Crocefisso. Based on stylistic evidence, three more are probably his work, San Carlo, SS Salvatore and the plan for San Nicolò (the cathedral).[4]

In the Val di Noto district, the following churches can be attributed to him, San Giorgio, in Ragusa; Santa Maria delle Stelle, in Comiso; Sant'Agata and San Giuseppe, in Caltagirone; and the Jesuit College and part of the work on Santa Lucia del Sepolcro in Syracuse.[5]

THE MAN

Gagliardi left an unfinished treatise on architecture which provides an insight into the character of the man. On the frontispiece appear images of a human body, musical scales and a church. An inscription claims that musical chords adapt perfectly to the rules that govern the human body and civil architecture. It is an illustration of the importance of proportion and harmony in architecture.[6]

The first volume of the treatise contains drawings of churches and their façades, elevations and ground plans. It addresses the question of how best to design a round, square or a pentagonal church. The other volumes contain geometric exercises and detailed designs for column capitals, altars and military installations. The influence of master architects from the past is evident. The picture that emerges is one of a man who combined a thorough knowledge of the theories of his profession with a craftsman's eye for detail.

According to official documents, Gagliardi lived in Noto with his mother and two nieces in a house opposite the church of Santa Maria dell'Arco in Via Speciale. It was a large house, with ten rooms and a courtyard, probably including his studio and library. There is no mention in the records of a wife or children, but he was often asked to be godfather to the children of the craftsmen with whom he worked. One of his nieces married Vincenzo Sinatra and they called their son Rosario.[7]

Gagliardi continued working until incapacitated by a stroke in 1761. He died at the end of the following year, having made Sinatra his executor, and leaving him the pre-eminent architect in Noto.

EPILOGUE

While famous in his lifetime, Gagliardi was forgotten not long after his death. It was not until the 1950s that documents referring to his career were discovered which began to re-instate his reputation. His treatise survived by being handed down from architect to architect and was finally published in 1972. An exhibition of Gagliardi's work in Noto in 2013 marked another milestone in his rehabilitation.

Two art historians spread the word of Gagliardi's achievements to an international audience. The first was Anthony Blunt, whose pioneering work, *Sicilian Baroque,* was published in 1968. The second was Stephen Tobriner, whose book, *The Genesis of Noto: An Eighteenth-century Sicilian city,* appeared in 1982. For Tobriner, who told the story of the city's rebirth together with descriptions of the architecture and profiles of the architects, Gagliardi combined a talent for lively façades with Renaissance planning and Sicilian decoration.[8]

Rosario Gagliardi and his contemporaries, in creating the exotic urban landscape of south-eastern Sicily, gave a magnificent response to the destruction caused by the earthquake. The whole enterprise was a triumph of human creativity over the malign forces of nature, finally recognised by UNESCO in 2002 when it nominated eight cities in the Val di Noto as World Heritage Sites, describing them as representing the culmination and final flowering of baroque art in Europe.[9]

33

ERNESTO BASILE, ARCHITECT
OF THE BELLE ÉPOQUE

Ernesto Basile, who lived from 1857 to 1932, was a leading Sicilian architect during the Belle Époque, when Palermo played host to celebrities from northern Europe. His career coincided with an ambitious building programme in Palermo aimed at making the city a regional capital worthy of the newly united Italy. Ernesto and his father, Giovanni Battista Filippo Basile, were prominent members of a talented class of architects, sculptors, artists and craftsmen who changed the face of the city. It was a period of outstanding artistic achievement.

Ernesto was trained by his father and worked in Rome during the 1880s. From his father, he inherited a concept of architecture that blended the traditional with the modern, which he used to great effect. In Sicily, Ernesto was famous for completing the Teatro Massimo, Palermo's opera house, on a design by his father, and for championing the use of Art Nouveau, known locally as the Liberty style. In Rome, Ernesto rebuilt Italy's parliament building, the Palazzo di Montecitorio, showing that he was rated among the top architects in the country.

THE BELLE ÉPOQUE
After Garibaldi removed the Bourbon government from Sicily, the aristocrats who took control of government in Palermo, led by men such as the Marquis Antonio di Rudinì, ignored the needs of

ordinary citizens and blocked social reform. Instead of improving the city's infrastructure, they introduced a plan for Palermo to take its place among the cultural capitals of Europe. This included the building of two large theatres – an opera house and one for popular entertainment. A new residential district was planned to accommodate the aristocracy, whose palaces were falling into disrepair, and a rising merchant class. Public buildings, gardens, wide streets and spacious squares were created, the port was enlarged, and a railway station was built to the south. This building programme shifted the focus away from the historic centre towards the Via della Libertà, a wide avenue to the north of the city.

The plan worked, for in the late nineteenth and early twentieth centuries Palermo became a fashionable resort for European royalty and other celebrities, in a period known as the Belle Époque. Attracted by the warm climate and exotic environment, visitors were lavishly entertained in the palaces of the Sicilian aristocracy. Evening concerts took place at the Marina, along the seafront, and visits were organised to the Norman monuments and coastal resorts.

The economy was driven by the export of agricultural products, trade in Marsala wine and sulphur, and by merchant shipping. While agriculture remained in the hands of the aristocracy, a small group of merchant families had established thriving businesses. The Inghams and Whitakers, heirs of British merchants from the time of the Napoleonic Wars, dominated the Marsala wine trade. The Florios, a Sicilian family, owned a large merchant fleet and were also active in the Marsala wine and sulphur trades. Smaller family enterprises in manufacturing, such as furniture making, had also developed. These merchants sought new properties and provided much of the finance for construction in the city.[1]

It was a time of extraordinary contrasts, when aristocratic families hosted all night parties for hundreds of guests, while three quarters of Palermo's population of 250,000 had no regular employment. Emigration to the Americas left many of the villages in the interior of the island semi-deserted. In this environment, criminal activity spread through society, with the term *mafia* first being used. These contrasts were noted by a writer from northern Italy, who wrote of Palermo:

> There is profusion and magnificence in all that meets the eye, giving the impression of a prosperous and powerful city. The appearance is not matched by reality. The people are poor and live with a hermit's frugality, there is no real middle class and the rich aristocracy is small. [2]

The First World War brought an abrupt end to the high life of the Sicilian aristocracy. By the end of the war, burdened by debt, many of the leading families, including the Florios, were bankrupt.

GIOVANNI BATTISTA FILIPPO BASILE

Basile senior was born in 1825 in Palermo, where he graduated in architecture. His studies were completed in Rome. A supporter of Italian unity, Basile took part in the 1848 revolution against the Bourbons and joined Garibaldi's campaign to free Sicily. In 1863 he was made professor of architecture at the University of Palermo, in which role he contributed to the city's development plan. Described by contemporaries as a universalist, he combined an eye for traditional Sicilian architecture with a desire for modern solutions. Although steeped in Greek and Roman architecture, he opened a school for industrial art in Palermo.

Two of Basile's early contributions were in public gardens. The first was the Giardino Inglese (English Garden), created in a large space to the north of the city, laid out in an informal style. The second was the Villa Garibaldi, a formal garden in the centre of Piazza Marina, to honour Garibaldi and the Sicilian leaders of the revolts against the Bourbons. The garden contained busts of the leaders and was surrounded by fine wrought-iron railings containing figures of animals in hunting scenes.

Basile's greatest achievement was the design and initial construction of theTeatro Massimo, Palermo's monumental opera house, dedicated to Vittorio Emanuele, the newly crowned king of Italy. His design, which won an international competition in 1868, contained a unique combination of traditional features with the attributes of a modern opera house. The entrance, which led up a grand staircase to a portico with six columns, had the appearance of a Greco-Roman temple. The dome above the auditorium and the external decorations were neo-classical in style. The use of local material, yellow sandstone, gave the building a strongly Sicilian identity. The interior included a huge stage, suitable for putting on operas such as Verdi's *Aida,* and was designed to seat 3,200 people, making it the third-largest opera house in Europe after Paris and Vienna.

The site chosen for the Massimo was at the dividing line between the historic centre and the new district being developed to the north of the city. A large area containing historic buildings, among them churches and convents as well as the Porta Maqueda, an old city gate, was cleared to make way for the new building and a surrounding square. The contractor, Giovanni Rutelli, designed machinery capable of moving the huge blocks of stone used in the construction.

Controversy over the style of the building, together with a lack of funds, led to the suspension of building works in 1882. Basile senior died in 1891 without seeing the completion of his project.

ERNESTO BASILE'S EARLY CAREER
Ernesto was born in Palermo in 1857. From an early age he was trained by his father, with whom he developed a dialogue on the theories of architecture and the search for new styles. He showed precocious talent and having graduated in architecture from the University of Palermo, he gained practical experience by working with his father on the construction of the Teatro Massimo.

He spent most of the 1880s in Rome as assistant to the professor of architecture at the university. Here, at the age of twenty-six, he won a competition for the rebuilding of the Palazzo di Giustizia (Palace of Justice), and while his project was not implemented, it established his credentials as an up-and-coming architect. In 1887, Ernesto married Ida Negrini, by whom he had five children, two girls and three boys. While in Rome, he gained the commission to design the building for the national exhibition to take place in Palermo. His design, which harked back to the Arabo-Norman era, featured domed towers and a colonnade. After his father's death in 1891, Ernesto returned to Palermo where he succeeded him as professor of architecture at the university.

He then won the commission to complete the Teatro Massimo. As the structure was already in place, his role was to oversee the fitting of the interior, the technology for working the stage and the external decorations. Rich furnishings were used for the auditorium, in red and gold colours, with glass for the lighting coming from Murano in Venice. The ceiling was decorated with paintings. To flank either side of the entrance, two large bronze lions carrying female figures were commissioned. The lion on the left by Mario Rutelli, son of the builder, represented *La Lirica* (lyric opera), the one on the right by Benedetto Civiletti, represented *La Tragedia* (tragic opera). In the square facing the opera house, Ernesto added two decorative kiosks, from which to sell tobacco and other items to opera goers. The Massimo was inaugurated on 16 May 1897 with a performance of Verdi's *Falstaff*. Ernesto, who was present on the opening night, received an ovation from the audience.[3]

While the Teatro Massimo was being designed and built, the second theatre identified in Palermo's development plan was completed. Named the Teatro Politeama Garibaldi, it was designed as a popular venue for a variety of productions, with seating for 950 people. The theatre's architecture was inspired by that of ancient Rome, with the entrance through a triumphal arch crowned by a bronze quadriga, a four-horse racing chariot, also by Rutelli. The Politeama was designed by Giuseppe Damiani Almeyda, an architect from southern Italy, who along with the Basile, made a big contribution to the rebuilding of Palermo. Completed in 1874 before the Massimo, it was the venue in the 1890s for two of Giacomo Puccini's operas, *Manon Lescaut* and *La Bohème*, both attended by the composer. The two theatres, the Massimo and the Politeama, offered a new level of entertainment, and their location in spacious squares redefined the centre of the city.

MATURE WORK

By the end of the nineteenth century, Basile had a well-established practice in Palermo. As a professor at the university, he had an important teaching role, and he was in constant demand for building projects. He became president of the *Circolo Artistico* (Arts Club) of Palermo and a member of the *Belle Arti* (Fine Arts) commission which oversaw the restoration of ancient monuments. He kept himself informed on developments in northern Europe and published articles on architecture in academic journals. Basile was an expert draughtsman whose technical drawings were considered works of art. A photograph taken at the time showed a carefully dressed, fastidious-looking gentleman wearing a straw hat, carrying gloves and a cane, a member of Palermo's elite.

Throughout his career, Basile sought new forms of expression in architecture. While respectful of the past, he refused to be constrained by tradition, preferring to use it as a standard by which to judge new concepts. He found the new forms he was looking for in Art Nouveau.

Art Nouveau, which had its peak of popularity from 1890 to 1910, was an international art movement inspired by natural forms, especially the curved shapes of plants and flowers. Its flowing lines and elements of fantasy offered a fresh alternative to traditional design. It became a contemporary fashion which dominated everything from architecture to painting, interior design and furniture. Art Nouveau spread internationally through exhibitions, notably the Paris Exposition of 1900. In Italy, it became known as the Liberty style, so named after the London store which popularised it, owned by Arthur Liberty, who promoted his merchandise in Italian cities. Arriving in Palermo, the Liberty style was enthusiastically taken up by the merchant families for the design and decoration of their houses.

In 1902, Basile won the most prestigious commission of his career, to rebuild the Palazzo di Montecitorio in Rome, the seat of Italy's parliament. Originally built by Gian Lorenzo Bernini in 1650, the palazzo had been taken over as the Chamber of Deputies in 1871, when Rome became the capital of Italy. The building proved inadequate for this purpose and the government called for a redesign.

Basile's solution was to retain Bernini's façade to which he added four, flat-topped corner towers. Internal space was created by filling in the central courtyard and by adding to the back of the building. The surrounding streets were demolished to place the palazzo in an open square, the Piazza del Parlamento. The result retained the grandeur of Bernini's design, lightened by a touch of Liberty style decoration. In the centre of the building, Basile created the Plenary Hall, the deputies' debating chamber, decorated in the Liberty style using wood panelling and a glass ceiling. A lively frieze, containing an epic vision of the history of the Italian people by Giulio Aristide Sartorio, surrounded the chamber. Basile, who was closely concerned with the details of the interior, completed his work on the palazzo in 1918.

In his maturity, Basile handled some 150 projects concentrated in and around Palermo, as well as in other Sicilian cities and mainland Italy. They included institutional buildings for the savings banks of Palermo and Messina, the Palermo headquarters of the Assicurazioni Generali di Venezia (General Insurance Company of Venice) and the town hall of Reggio Calabria. In Palermo, he designed another theatre, the Kursaal Biondo. Smaller assignments included furnishings for the Sicilian merchant fleet and the fitting out of a retail shop for Vittorio Ducrot, the furniture maker. Pavilions and decorations for international exhibitions to be held in Rome,

Milan and Venice were produced. For the Whitaker family, the huge family house built for Benjamin Ingham in Palermo was redesigned as the Grand Hotel et des Palmes.[4]

Basile's most avant-garde work, for which he is famous, came in the building of villas in Palermo and at the nearby seaside resort of Mondello. In this work, which included the villas Basile, Fassini, Ugo and Gregorietti, he was able to give his imagination free rein to develop from the fashionable Liberty style. For Ignazio and Franca Florio, hosts to the rich and famous of Europe, Basile created the Villino Florio, an architectural fantasy which included a circular turret, an open staircase and porticoed entrance. The interior was adorned with Liberty-style designs on wallpapers and fabrics. The Villa Igiea, also owned by the Florios, began as a sanatorium and was converted into a luxury hotel by Basile in 1904. Facing the small port of Acquasanta, to the north of Palermo, the villa was built in yellow sandstone and extravagantly decorated to become the most fashionable meeting place in the city. Its dining room contained extraordinary ornamentation, lined with columns and mirrors, while other reception rooms contained frescoes, chandeliers and the intricately carved Ducrot furniture. The design combined traditional Sicilian touches with an opulence worthy of Paris.

Basile's last years were blighted by the rise of fascism and Mussolini's taste for a brutal style of functional architecture, an example of which was foisted upon Palermo in the form of a huge post office building in Via Roma. Basile, who was criticised by Mussolini for his decorative style, deplored the direction taken by the fascists in architecture, and reverted to a more classical style in protest. Among his last works was a church dedicated to Santa Rosalia, Palermo's patron saint, completed in 1931, a year before he died.

EPILOGUE
The artistic legacy of the Belle Époque is concentrated in the district of Palermo created to the north of the historic centre. Here can be

found the theatres, the open squares, and the architecture of the period. Paintings and sculptures of the Belle Époque, which began the modern era in Sicilian art, can be seen in the city's Galleria d'Arte Moderna, in Via Sant'Anna.

The work of the Basile, both father and son, played an important part in this legacy. The gardens created by Basile senior are favourites with the public. The Teatro Massimo, where many of the world's top opera singers have performed, continues to be admired for its exotic appearance. Today it offers an annual season of opera, ballet and concert performances with seating reduced to 1,350, due to modern regulations. Visitors can see around the opera house on guided tours.

Many of the grand Liberty-style villas that once lined the Via della Libertà were destroyed in the 1960s to make way for cheap apartment blocks, in an illegal construction boom known as the Sack of Palermo. Fortunately, many of Ernesto Basile's buildings survived. The Grand Hotel et des Palmes and the Villa Igiea, designed by him, remain Palermo's top hotels, attracting visitors from around the world. The Villino Florio, which typified the Liberty style, has been restored to its former glory after being damaged by fire. Several of Basile's villas can be seen at Mondello, Palermo's fashionable seaside resort.

In Rome, the Palazzo Montecitorio continues to serve as Italy's parliament building, with seats for 630 deputies.

After the criticism of the fascist years, Ernesto Basile's reputation was restored in the 1950s and '60s. Today he is seen as the Sicilian architect who embodied the artistic achievements of the Belle Époque, blending traditional and contemporary styles, thus contributing to the development of modern architecture in Italy.

34

RENATO GUTTUSO, TWENTIETH-CENTURY PAINTER

Renato Guttuso was one of Italy's foremost painters of the twentieth century. Born in Sicily in 1911, as a young man he moved to Milan, before settling in Rome. In a career spanning over fifty years, he made his name at national level for his dramatic paintings of contemporary events, as well as for his portraits, nudes, still lifes and landscapes. Underpinning his work was a strong commitment to the human rights of ordinary people.

Guttuso's life was full of contrasts. Starting from an impoverished background, he became a partisan against the Nazis in his youth, a lifelong supporter of the Italian Communist Party, an intellectual and friend of artists and writers, and went on to become a highly successful artist. He joined Rome's elite, his studio a salon for the rich and famous, and served as a senator of the Italian Republic.

As an artist, Guttuso remained closely attached to his native Sicily and its social conflicts. Sicily was at the core of his creativity and he returned frequently to renew his connections with the island. Some of Guttuso's most memorable subjects were the landscapes and the people of Sicily, their vitality portrayed in intense colours: the fire of Etna, the deep blue of the Tyrrhenian Sea, the green, orange and yellow of the fruit and vegetation. Sicily was never far from his thoughts when he was painting. As his friend, Leonardo Sciascia, quoted him as saying, 'Even if I paint an apple, Sicily is there'.[1]

THE EARLY YEARS

Renato Guttuso was born on 26 December 1911 in Bagheria, a small town near Palermo. His birth was not registered until 2 January 1912, in Palermo, raising some controversy over his true birthdate. He was the only child of middle-aged parents, his father, Gioacchino, being forty-eight and his mother, Giuseppina, thirty-six, when they married in 1911. Renato was brought up and went to school in Bagheria, which was both an agricultural centre and the location for country palaces of the aristocracy. The contrast between the lives of the poor agricultural workers and the rich aristocrats was plain for all to see.

The young Guttuso spent a happy but frugal boyhood in Bagheria. Gioacchino worked as a land surveyor, a job which provided a steady, if low, income. While there was enough food on the table, the family could only afford to eat meat occasionally. They were better off than many, for poverty was widespread in the town, with the lucrative lemon trade controlled by the mafia.

Gioacchino was an amateur painter who dabbled in watercolours. He encouraged his son, who showed an interest in painting from an early age. By the time he was thirteen, Renato was signing his own paintings, which included portraits of his father and urban scenes of Bagheria. His first teachers were friends of his father's, Domenico Quattrociocchi, a post-Impressionist, and Emilio Murdolo, a painter of scenes on wooden carts, a traditional art form in Sicily. Among the early influences on Renato, which fired his imagination, were the grotesque statues that decorated the grounds of the Villa Palagonia in Bagheria, commented on by visitors since Goethe. In 1924, a visit to Rome with Gioacchino, and his first sight of the city's exceptional art and architecture, made a lasting impression.

Guttuso continued his education in Palermo, commuting daily from Bagheria. Later he recalled his life as a penniless student, saving money to buy canvasses and eating street food in Palermo's markets. He was trained in this period by Pippo Rizzo, a Futurist painter who encouraged the young artist, and whose connections in the art world proved useful. In 1929, Renato participated in his first exhibition, which took place in the foyer of the Teatro Massimo, Palermo's opera house, from which he received favourable comment.

Two years later, two of his paintings were accepted by an important new exhibition in Rome, the first Quadriennale d'Arte Nazionale (four-yearly national art exhibition). This prompted Guttuso to abandon his academic studies. A young man on the make, he left for Milan with three other Sicilian artists to devote himself full-time to his vocation as a painter. In Milan, he became influenced by Expressionism, which opposed the restraints imposed by the Fascist regime, and looked instead to the work of Picasso, Cézanne and Van Gogh. He joined the *Corrente* movement, which promoted moral commitment in art and the view that it should reflect real life. The symbol of progressive art, favoured by *Corrente,* was Picasso's painting *Guernica,* representing the Basque town obliterated by bombs in the Spanish Civil War.

After completing his military service, Guttuso settled in Rome. Here, in November 1937, he met Mimise Dotti, from a good family in Lombardy, who became his life-long companion. In a portrait from that year, Mimise appears as an elegant northern Italian, fair-haired and fine-featured.

RECOGNITION
Guttuso established his reputation during the period from 1938 to 1941, at the end of which he was thirty years old. Recognition from the Italian art world came with the creation of three paintings, all large, colourful canvasses, depicting violent scenes with realism and strong appeal to the emotions.

The first, *Fucilazione in campagna* (Execution in the country), was conceived as a memorial to the poet Federico García Lorca, who was shot by Franco's soldiers in Spain in 1936. It recalled Goya's painting of a similar subject.

Fuga dall'Etna (Flight from Etna) depicted an all-too-familiar scene in Sicilian history of people fleeing an eruption of Mount Etna. This painting won Italy's top art prize at the state exhibition, the Premio Bergamo, in 1940.

The most complex painting, *Crocifissione* (Crucifixion), was Guttoso's masterpiece and his most famous work. Bold figures and strong colours tell the story of the crucifixion in a modern context. The protagonists are shown in the nude, including a woman, presumably Mary Magdalene, who is holding a shroud over the body of Christ on the cross. Instead of being the centre of attention, Christ's face and figure are partly obscured. In the background, a town is being bombed. According to Guttuso, the nudity was not done to shock but to make the figures timeless. As he commented: 'This is wartime ... I want to paint this torment of Christ as a contemporary scene ... a symbol for all those who suffer abuse, prison and torture for their ideas'.[2] The painting was highly controversial, denounced by the Vatican as unsuitable to be seen by Catholics, and criticised by the Fascist regime for its political implications. Despite the opposition, the painting came second in the Premio Bergamo of 1942.

After the fall of Mussolini in 1943, Guttuso fled Rome, returning a year later to join the partisans fighting the German occupation. He was already a member of the Communist Party. When in hiding, he produced a series of drawings of Nazi atrocities, which after the war were collected in a book entitled *Gott mit uns* (God with Us), a motto of the German army.

THE POST-WAR YEARS

The years following the Second World War saw rapid and profound change in Italy, as the country transformed itself from a predominantly agricultural into an industrial economy. Industry, which was concentrated in the north of the country, attracted mass immigration from the south, including from Sicily. Major expansion of the industrial centres took place in the 1950s and '60s, as people flocked to fill the new jobs on offer. Italy re-emerged onto the international stage as a country of dynamic growth, a close ally of the United States and a founding member of the European Economic Community. For Italians, it was a time of national resurgence and rising confidence.[3]

In this environment, Italy's creative genius reasserted itself. A new wave of writers appeared tackling themes of social realism, from the effects of war to the poverty of the south and the hardship of life in the big cities. Among them were Carlo Levi, Alberto Moravia, Elio Vittorini and Leonardo Sciascia. In the cinema, similar themes were explored by a talented group of film directors that included Luchino Visconti, Vittorio De Sica, Pier Paolo Pasolini and Roberto Rossellini. This was the era of films such as Pasolini's *Mamma Roma* and Visconti's *Rocco e i suoi fratelli* (Rocco and his brothers), which told the stories of ordinary Italians in dramatic style.

In 1946, Guttuso went to Paris to meet Picasso, whose genius he acknowledged. The two men became friends and met regularly thereafter. Picasso remained a major influence on Guttuso throughout his career.

The post-war period was productive for Guttuso who re-established himself in Rome. His social commitment matched the mood of the country and the wave of social realism being portrayed in the arts. He cultivated relationships with his fellow artists, including Mario Mafai, Corrado Cagli and Antonello Trombadori, with whom he liked to exchange ideas. His studio became a meeting place for artists arriving in Rome, who received a glass of wine and words of encouragement from the maestro.

He also built relationships with writers, several of whom, including Vittorini and Sciascia, were Sicilians. Like Guttuso, the Sicilian writers maintained close links to their native island which were reflected in their work. Some of these writers, such as Levi, Moravia and Vittorini, became the subjects of Guttuso's portraits.

The relationships with the writers led to commissions for book illustrations. Guttuso supplied designs for the covers of Sciascia's novels, and drawings to illustrate Vittorini's work. For the publisher Mondadori, he provided illustrations for their new edition of Dante. This work included the Italian editions of foreign authors, such as Hemingway. He did the illustrations for Elizabeth David's *Italian Food*, published in 1954, thus reaching an international audience. Guttuso's interests extended to the theatre and opera, for which he produced costume and set designs.

The artist's commitment to Sicily was demonstrated in three paintings from this period. In *Occupazione delle terre incolte in Sicilia* (Occupation of uncultivated land in Sicily), a group of peasants is marching in the hope of finding land. It is a political subject, with the communist red flag prominent, highlighting the perennial problem of land reform in Sicily, where estates of the aristocracy lay uncultivated. His *Portella della Ginestra* recorded the shooting of eleven people at a workers' festival in the countryside outside Palermo. Guttuso, who remembered the plight of the peasants from his youth, went to Sicily to support the campaign for land redistribution. There followed *Zolfara* (Sulphur mine), a painting showing the inhumane conditions endured by men and young boys in the sulphur mines of Sicily.

These paintings show a distinct change in Guttuso's style. In contrast to his earlier work, which was characterised by well-integrated compositions, they reflect both his illustrations and the crude art of social realism practised in the Soviet Union. They are first and foremost political statements, and while effective as such, lack the appeal of his earlier work.

In 1950, Renato and Mimise were married, following the annulment of Mimise's previous marriage. One of the witnesses was the Chilean poet Pablo Neruda. In the same year, Guttuso made his first trip to Moscow where, as a loyal communist, he received a warm welcome. He made regular visits to Russia for many years.

Guttuso was a dedicated artist, steeped in the works of the Old Masters from Giotto to Raphael and Titian. From Sicily, he recalled a painting entitled *Il trionfo della morte* (The Triumph of Death) which he had copied as a student, and the work of Antonello da Messina. He was passionate about his art, usually completing an eight-hour day in his studio. As the journalist, Giorgio Bocca, noted, 'Guttuso has to be working. As he talks, reminisces, smokes and hands me another cup of coffee, all the while he is doing an ink drawing, passing the pen from one hand to the other'.[4] True to his southern temperament, sensuality filled his life and his paintings, infusing all his canvasses and his drawings, especially his nudes. A charismatic character who made friends easily, Guttuso was also reserved, and had a touch of melancholy which he normally concealed.

THE ESTABLISHED ARTIST

By the 1960s, Guttuso was the most celebrated painter in Rome. The Venice Biennale exhibition of 1960 honoured him with his own room. His contemporary subjects hit a chord with the Italian public. They reminded people of their roots in the countryside at a time of social alienation, as Italy became increasingly industrialised. Photographed alongside well-known figures such as the film-stars Anna Magnani and Vittorio Gassman, Guttuso became a symbol of modern Italian culture. His lithographs and drawings sold in large numbers to the public while his paintings fetched sky high prices at auction.

Increased prosperity led Guttuso to buy a property on two floors in central Rome, near the Colisseum, in the Palazzo del Grillo. The first floor became his studio, while the second floor, with its view of the gardens below, became a private apartment. The studio was where he worked and entertained his guests. The apartment, where he and Mimise lived, was decorated with her portrait, his *Crocifissione*, and works by Picasso and De Chirico. The Guttusos already owned a property in Velate, in Lombardy, an inheritance of Mimise's, where Renato had built another studio. He liked the calm of the Lombard countryside and did some of his best work there.

In 1966, Guttuso produced a pictorial autobiography, a cycle of paintings of the people and places from his past. They included portraits of his father and of Mimise, together with images of Sicily, such as landscapes, traditional painted carts and statues from the Villa Palagonia.

Around this time, Guttuso began a passionate love affair with Marta Marzotto, the wife of a leading industrialist. Marta was a well-known hostess with connections in high society. She became his model and featured in a series of portraits and erotic drawings. Their affair lasted until Renato fell ill towards the end of his life. Under her influence, his studio lost its bohemian lifestyle and became a salon for Rome's rich and powerful elite. Renato never left Mimise, continuing to live with her in the apartment in Palazzo del Grillo, while meeting Marta in his studio.

Guttuso maintained a high work rate in his sixties. In *I funerali di Togliatti* (Togliatti's funeral), he paid homage to the leader of the Italian Communist Party, which he had long supported. It contained portraits of Togliatti and other party leaders surrounded by a sea of red flags. In 1972, he was awarded the Lenin Prize during an exhibition of his work in Moscow.

La Vucciria depicts Palermo's well-known street market, which he remembered from his youth. A large canvas, measuring three metres square, is filled with the produce of Sicily, fruit, vegetables, cheese, fish and meat laid out in neat groups. Enigmatic figures at the sides of the painting create a slightly sinister atmosphere. In a return to his earlier style, the result is a still life recalling the masters such as Caravaggio that captures the essence of the market. It is one of the artist's best-known paintings, copies of which are to be seen all over Palermo.

Autoritratto, a self-portrait, presents the artist with a strong, lined face and swept-back grey hair. Below the head, a disembodied hand holds a paint brush. Above, another hand holds a lighted cigarette pointing accusingly at the head. It was an eerie portent of the future and of the lung cancer that would claim the artist's life.

Guttuso's later work included *Caffè Greco,* a favourite haunt of artists in Rome, and an autobiographical piece, entitled *Spes contra spem* (Hope against hope), in which the artist appears to be saying goodbye to elements of his life while putting his hope in the future.

In 1974, Guttuso bought an apartment in Palermo, in Via Ruggero Settimo near the Teatro Massimo, where he set up another studio. Here he liked to spend New Year and Easter, renewing old acquaintances. In the summer and for Christmas, he preferred his property at Velate, in Lombardy.

His loyalty and generous donations to the Italian Communist Party were rewarded in 1976 by his being made a candidate for the Senate, the Italian parliament's upper house, to which he was duly elected. As a senator, he mixed with the political elite. Visitors to his studio now included not only senior figures from the Communist Party but also Giulio Andreotti, the Christian Democrat grandee, who served as prime minister.

Mimise, whose health had begun to fail in the 1970s, died in 1986. By this time, Renato had been diagnosed with lung cancer. During his last few months he ended his relationship with Marta and received visits from old friends, art historians and politicians. At Christmas 1986, Mass was celebrated in his apartment, attended by over fifty guests, with Guttuso taking Holy Communion. He died on 18 January 1987. His estate was inherited by his adopted son, Fabio Carapezza.

WHERE TO SEE HIS PAINTINGS
There is a museum dedicated to Guttuso's work in the Villa Cattolica, in Bagheria, just outside Palermo. The villa is a fine example of an early eighteenth-century country estate of the aristocracy. It holds

a collection of the artist's paintings from 1924 to 1930 and from the 1960s and '70s, all donated during his lifetime. While it demonstrates his range and versatility, it does not include his best work. In the grounds of the villa lies Guttuso's tomb, an unusual construction in blue marble. The villa also holds work by other twentieth-century Sicilian artists. In a visit to Bagheria, the museum can be combined with the Villa Palagonia and its bizarre statues which intrigued Guttuso.

Guttuso's *Vucciria* can be seen in the Palazzo Chiaramonte, in Piazza Marina, in the historic centre of Palermo, displayed alongside paintings of historic importance.

In Rome, the Galleria Nazionale d'Arte Moderna (National Gallery of Modern Art) holds several of the artist's important works, including his *Fucilazione in campagna* (Execution in the country), and his *Crocifissione* (Crucifixion).

Tate Modern in London has a version of his *Zolfara* (Sulphur Mine).

Reproductions of most of Guttuso's important works can be found in the catalogue from an exhibition in Turin in 2005, entitled *Guttuso, Capolavori dai musei* (Guttuso, Masterpieces from the Museums).[5]

EPILOGUE

The *Associazione Archivi Guttuso* was founded by the artist's adopted son, Fabio Carapezza Guttuso to promote his father's work. It is based in Rome, in the former studio in the Palazzo del Grillo. The Association, which holds a collection of Guttuso's work, maintains documentation on his output and arranges exhibitions. Their website (www.guttuso.com) is an important source of information.

Guttuso's life and art generated a large body of literature, mostly in Italian. The artist left a commentary on his own work and on the role of art in society in a book entitled *Mestiere di pittore* (Profession of Painting), published in 1972. Several of his friends recorded their assessments of him including Sciascia, Moravia, Pasolini, Vittorini and Neruda.[6]

There are two outstanding biographies, one by Costanzo Costantini, *Ritratto di Renato Guttuso*, based on interviews with the artist, and the other by Paolo Parlavecchia, *Renato Guttuso, un ritratto del XX secolo*.

Guttuso remains a popular painter whose exhibitions, held in Rome, Turin, Moscow, St Petersburg, New York and London, attract large audiences. One, held in 2015 at the Estorick Collection in Islington, London, and entitled 'Renato Guttuso: Painter of Modern Life', considered him one of Italy's most widely respected modern painters who played a key role in forging a style that went on to dominate Italian art in the mid-twentieth century.[7]

NOTES

PART I: HISTORY

CHAPTER I INTRODUCTION

1   Fernand Braudel, *La Méditerranée, l'espace et l'histoire* (Paris: Flammarion, 1985), p. 8.

2   For Trinacria and the subsequent names for the island, see Thucydides, *History of the Peloponnesian War*, trans. Rex Warner (London: Penguin Classics, 1972), pp. 462–72. How the island was given a Greek name well before the arrival of the Greeks remains a mystery. The *Triskelion* symbol, also known as *Trisceles*, has ancient origins dating back at least to the seventh century BC. A three-legged design was used on coins around 317 BC by Agathocles, Greek ruler of Syracuse, to demonstrate his dominion over the whole island. The Romans also used it on their coins. A modern version of the *Triskelion* appears on the Sicilian flag.

3   Thucydides, *History of the Peloponnesian War* (1972), pp. 409–537. Livy, *Hannibal's War*, trans. J. C. Yardley (Oxford: Oxford University Press, 2006), pp. 227–31, 285–95. Diodorus Siculus, *Library of History* (Cambridge, MA: Loeb Classical Library, Harvard University Press, 1950). Plutarch, *Rise and Fall of Athens, Lives of Nicias* and *Alcibiades; Age of Alexander, Lives of Dion, Timoleon* and *Pyrrhus; Makers of Rome, Life of Marcellus* (London: Penguin Classics, 1960).

4   Tommaso Fazello, *Della storia di Sicilia* (Palermo: Tipografia Giuseppe Assenzio, 1817, trans. P.M. Remigio; original written in Latin, 1558).

5   Michele Amari, *Storia dei Musulmani di Sicilia* (Catania: Romeo Prampolini Editore, 1933, first published in 1854); Francesco Saverio Cavallari & Adolfo Holm, *Topografia Archeologica di Siracusa* (Palermo: Tipografia del Giornale Lo Statuo, 1883); Isidoro La Lumia, *Storie Siciliane* (Palermo: Virzi, 1883) and *Storia della Sicilia sotto Guglielmo il Buono* (Firenze: Le Monnier, 1867).

6   Edward Freeman, *Historical Essays* (London: Macmillan & Co, 1879), Chapter X, 'Sicilian Cycles', p. 428.

7   For the other books mentioned, see Bibliography, under History.

8   Giuseppe Tomasi di Lampedusa, *The Leopard*, trans. Archibald Colquhoun (London: Collins and Harvill Press, 1961, first published as *Il Gattopardo*, Milan: Feltrinelli Editore, 1958), pp. 29, 147, 148.

9   Vincenzo Consolo, *The Smile of the Unknown Mariner*, trans. Joseph Farrell
    (Manchester: Carcanet Press, 1994, originally published in Italian as *Il sorriso
    dell'ignoto marinaio*: Turin, Einaudi editore, 1976).
10 Leonardo Sciascia, *La Corda Pazza* (Milan: Adelphi Edizioni, 1991), pp. 11–18.
11 Francesco Renda, *Sicilia e Mediterraneo, la nuova geopolitica* (Palermo: Sellerio
    Editore, 2000), pp. 53–80.

CHAPTER 2   THE CASTLE OF DIONYSIUS

1   For Dionysius's rise to power, see Diodorus Siculus, *Library of History*, trans. C.
    H. Oldfather, (Cambridge, MA: Loeb Classical Library, Harvard University
    Press, 1957), Book XIII, pp. 433–47. For the castle, see Book XIV, p. 25.
2   Brian Caven, *Dionysius I: War Lord of Sicily* (New Haven & London: Yale
    University Press, 1990), pp. 78–79, and Teresa Carpinteri, *Siracusa – Città
    Fortificata* (Palermo: Flaccovio Editore, 1983), p. 23.
3   Plutarch, *Age of Alexander*, trans. Ian Scott-Kilvert, (London: Penguin Classics,
    1973), *Timoleon*, p. 171.
4   Cicero, *Verrine Orations* (Cambridge, MA: Loeb Classical Library, Harvard
    University Press, 1935), p. 427.
5   Tommaso Fazello, *Della storia di Sicilia*, trans. P. M. Remigio (Palermo:
    Tipografia Giuseppe Assenzio, 1817), pp. 294–96, (author's English
    translation).
6   Vincenzo Mirabella, *Dichiarazioni della Pianta dell'Antiche Siracuse* (Naples:
    Lazzaro Scoriggio, 1613), pp. 35–37.
7   See Teresa Carpinteri, *Siracusa – Città Fortificata* (Palermo: Flaccovio Editore,
    1983) for photographs and maps of the Spanish fortifications.
8   Francesco Saverio Cavallari & Adolfo Holm, *Topografia Archeologica di Siracusa*
    (Palermo: Tipografia del Giornale Lo Statuo, 1883), pp. 245–48, map facing
    p. 82.
9   Edward Freeman, *History of Sicily* (Oxford: Clarendon Press, 1894, four
    vols, reprinted by Elibron Classics), vol 4, pp. 10–13.

CHAPTER 3   SICILY UNDER THE ROMAN REPUBLIC

1   Polybius, *Rise of the Roman Empire*, trans. Ian Scott-Kilvert (London: Penguin
    Books, 1979), pp. 62, 63, 109. The remains of a Punic warship, possibly sunk
    in this battle, can be seen in Marsala's archaeological museum.
2   M.I. Finley, *Ancient Sicily* (London: Chatto and Windus, 1979), p. 133.

CHAPTER 4   THE ARABS IN SICILY

1   Al-Edrisi, *L'Italia descritta nel Libro del Re Ruggero*, edited by M. Amari and C.
    Schiaparelli (Roma: Salviucci, 1883), p. 29, (author's English translation).
2   Michele Amari, *Storia dei Musulmani di Sicilia* (Florence: Felice Le Monnier,
    1854) 3 vols. As well as his history, Amari made available the writings of

Arab travellers, poets and members of the Norman court, through his translations.
3 Vincenzo Consolo, *Reading and Writing the Mediterranean* (Toronto: University of Toronto Press, 2006), p. 228.

CHAPTER 5 THE CATHEDRAL AT MONREALE

1 John Julius Norwich, *The Kingdom in the Sun, 1130–1194* (London: Faber, 1970), p. 362.
2 Falcandus, *History of the Tyrants of Sicily*, trans. Graham A. Loud and Thomas Wiedemann (Manchester and N.Y: Manchester University Press, 1998), p. 97.
3 Otto Demus, *The Mosaics of Norman Sicily* (London: Routledge & Kegan Paul, 1949), pp. 95–96. This is the definitive work on the mosaics of Sicily. It was based on research which discovered original documents concerning the foundation and creation of the monuments.
4 Ibid., p. 148.
5 Falcandus, p. 259.

CHAPTER 6 FREDERICK II AND THE SICILIAN POETS

1 Michele Amari, *Storia dei Musulmani di Sicilia* (Florence: Felice Le Monnier, 1854), vol 3, pp. 889–90, (author's English translation).
2 For examples of the poetry, see Karla Mallette, *The Kingdom of Sicily, 1100–1250. A Literary History* (Philadelphia: University of Pennsylvania Press, 2005). An imaginative and well-researched account of the Sicilian School.
3 Dante Alighieri, *De vulgari eloquentia* (I, xii, 4), Mallett, *The Kingdom of Sicily,* p. 116.

CHAPTER 7 DOMENICO CARACCIOLO

1 Francesco Renda, *La Grande Impresa* (Palermo: Sellerio Editore, 2010), p. 9, (author's English translation).
2 Angus Campbell, *Sicily and the Enlightenment, the world of Domenico Caracciolo, Thinker and Reformer* (London: I.B. Tauris, 2016). A detailed account of Caracciolo's work, the first in English, it includes extracts from his large correspondence.
3 Ibid., p. 71. Letter to Abbé Galiani, dated 21 December 1781.

CHAPTER 8 THE BRITISH WINE MERCHANTS

1 Raleigh Trevelyan, *Princes Under the Volcano* (New York: William Morrow & Company, Inc., 1973).
2 Nelson, 20 March 1800, quoted in Trevelyan, p. 17.
3 Trevelyan, p. 135.
4 Joseph Whitaker, *The Birds of Tunisia* (London: R.H. Porter, 1905).

5   Joseph Whitaker, *Motya, A Phoenician Colony in Sicily* (London: G. Bell & Sons Ltd., 1921). For Pip's career, see Gaia Servadio, *Motya, Unearthing a Lost Civilisation* (London: Phoenix, Orion Books Ltd, 2000), pp. 123–42.
6   Tina Whitaker, *Sicily and England* (Memphis, USA: General Books, 2018, originally published in 1907).

CHAPTER 9 THE REVOLUTION OF 1848

1   Tina Whitaker, *Sicily and England* (Memphis, USA: General Books, 2018, originally published in 1907), p. 10.
2   Ibid., p. 11.
3   *Sbirri*, a pejorative term for police, is still widely used in Sicily. Historically, policemen who acted as spies for foreign governments were considered traitors. The term derives from the Latin *birrum*, meaning red, due to red uniforms being worn by the police force in the Middle Ages.
4   Denis Mack Smith, *A History of Sicily, Modern Sicily after 1715* (London: Chatto & Windus, 1968), p. 418.
5   Leonardo Sciascia, *Sicilian Uncles*, trans. N.S. Thompson (Manchester: Carcanet Press Limited, 1986, originally published as *Gli Zii di Sicilia*, in 1958), Chapter 3, pp. 85–146.
6   Mack Smith, p. 424.
7   Whitaker, p. 21.

PART II: CITIES

CHAPTER 10 INTRODUCTION

1   Michele Amari, *Storia dei Musulmani di Sicilia* (Romeo Prampolini Editore, Catania, 1933), vol. 2, p. 433, (author's English translation).
2   Statistics from www.tuttitalia/sicilia at 1/1/2016.
3   Leonardo Sciascia, *Occhio di Capra* (Milan: Adelphi Edizioni SpA, 1990), p. 11 (author's English translation). Published by arrangement with The Italian Literary Agency.
4   For statistics on the numbers of visitors from the Regional Government's office, Beni Culturali (Cultural Heritage), see www.siciliapreziosa.it.
5   Cicero, *Verrine Orations*, trans. L.H.G. Greenwood, (Cambridge MA: Loeb Classical Library, Harvard University Press, 1935), p. 209.
6   Al-Edrisi, *L'Italia descritta nel Libro del Re Ruggero*, edited by M. Amari and C. Schiapelli (Roma: Salviucci, 1883), p. 32. (Author's English translation).
7   Johann Wolfgang Goethe, *Italian Journey*, trans. W. H. Auden and Elizabeth Mayer (London: Collins, 1962, first published as *Italienische Reise*, 1816–17), pp. 212, 240. For the other books mentioned, see Bibliography under Cities.
8   Vincenzo Consolo, *L'olivo e l'olivastro* (Milano: Arnoldo Editore, 1994), p. 124.

CHAPTER 11 CATANIA

1   For the origins of Catania, including the name, see Tino Giuffrida, *Catania, dalle origini alla dominazione Normanna* (Catania, Libreria C. Bonaccorso Editrice, 1979) pp 14–22. Plutarch was aware of the 'grater' connection, for in his life of Dion, he quotes Callippus as saying that after he was thrown out of Syracuse but captured Katane, he had lost a city and gained a cheese-grater, Plutarch, *Age of Alexander, Dion*, trans. Ian Scott-Kilvert (London: Penguin Books, 1973), p. 149.

2   Thucydides, *History of the Peloponnesian War*, trans. Rex Warner (London: Penguin Books, 1954), p. 410.

3   Anthony Blunt, *Sicilian Baroque* (London: Weidenfeld & Nicolson, 1968), pp. 18–23.
    Blunt (1907–83) was an art historian, a professor at London University, a director of the Courtauld Institute and Surveyor of the Queen's pictures. He was also a spy who betrayed British secrets to the Soviet Union from the mid-1930s to the early 1950s, a member of the Cambridge spy ring which included Kim Philby, Guy Burgess and Donald Maclean.

4   Patrick Brydone, *A Tour through Sicily and Malta* (London: H.D. Symonds, 1773, reprinted by General Books, Memphis, USA, 2012), p. 7.

5   Edward Hutton, *Cities of Sicily* (London: Methuen & Co Ltd, 1926), pp. 32–33.

6   BBC http://www.bbc.co.uk/newsround/39290481

7   Brydone, p. 22.

CHAPTER 12 TAORMINA

1   Douglas Sladen, *Sicily, the New Winter Resort* (New York, NY: E.P. Hutton, 1907), p. 547.

2   Edward Hutton, *Cities of Sicily* (London: Methuen & Co. Ltd, 1926), p. 20. Title no longer on Methuen list.

3   D. H. Lawrence, *Sea and Sardinia* (London: Penguin Classics, 2007, first published in 1921), p. 141.

4   Lawrence Durrell, *Sicilian Carousel* (London: Faber and Faber, 1977), p. 208.

5   Roger Wilson, *Sicily under the Roman Empire* (Oxford: Aris & Phillips Ltd, 1990), pp. 70–78.

CHAPTER 13 MESSINA

1   Homer, *Odyssey*, trans. E.V. Rieu (London: Penguin Books, 1946), pp. 195–96.

2   Vincenzo Consolo, *Reading and Writing the Mediterranean* (Toronto: University of Toronto Press, 2006), pp. 191–92.

3   Thucydides, *History of the Peloponnesian War*, trans. Rex Warner (London: Penguin Group, 1954), Book 6, p. 411.

4   Al-Edrisi, *L'Italia descritta nel Libro del Re Ruggero*, edited by M. Amari and C. Schiapelli (Roma: Salviucci, 1883), pp. 30–31 (author's English translation and paraphrase).
5   www.comune.messina.it
6   Carlo D'Este, *Bitter Victory, The Battle for Sicily, 1943* (London: Collins, 1988), pp. 519–20.

CHAPTER 14 CEFALÙ

1   Al-Edrisi, *L'Italia descritta nel Libro del Re Ruggero*, edited by M. Amari and C. Schiapelli (Roma: Salviucci, 1883), p. 29. (Author's English translation).
2   Vincenzo Consolo, *La mia isola è Las Vegas* (Milano: Arnoldo Mondadori Editore, 2012), p. 102.
3   Otto Demus, *The Mosaics of Norman Sicily* (London: Routledge & Kegan Paul, 1949), p. 3.
4   Dirk Booms & Peter Higgs, *Sicily, culture & conquest* (London: The British Museum Press, 2016), p. 268.

CHAPTER 15 NOTO

1   Al-Edrisi, *L'Italia descritta nel Libro del Re Ruggero*, edited by M. Amari and C. Schiapelli (Roma: Salviucci, 1883), p. 34. (Author's English translation).
2   Liliane Dufour, *Storia d'Italia* (Turin: Einaudi Editore, 1985), p. 476.
3   Anthony Blunt, *Sicilian Baroque* (London: Weidenfeld & Nicolson, 1968), p. 9.
4   Stephen Tobriner, *The Genesis of Noto* (London: A. Zwemmer Ltd, 1982), pp. 60–65.
    Tobriner is Professor of Architectural History at the University of California.
5   Giuseppe Iacono, *Noto, Città d'Arte* (Messina: Società Editrice Affinità Elettive, 2004), pp. 21–33.

CHAPTER 16 RAGUSA & MODICA

1   Anthony Blunt, *Sicilian Baroque* (London: Weidenfeld and Nicolson, 1968), p. 9.
2   Martina Gatti, *Provincia di Ragusa, l'Isola Felice* (Ragusa: Mora Arti Grafiche, 2005), p. 59.
3   Ibid. p. 47. See also Leonardo Sciascia, *Fatti diversi di storia letteraria e civile, la contea di Modica* (Palermo: Sellerio, 1989), pp. 17–38.
4   Maurizio Clausi, *I luoghi di Montalbano. Una guida.* (Palermo: Sellerio, 2006), pp. 264–71.
5   For the first novel in the series, see Andrea Camilleri, *The Shape of Water*, trans. Stephen Sartarelli (London: Pan Macmillan, 2004, first published

as *La Forma dell'Acqua*: Palermo, Sellerio editore, 1994). Camilleri died in 2019.

CHAPTER 17 PALAZZOLO ACREIDE

1 Thucydides, *History of the Peloponnesian War* (London: Penguin Classics, 1954) Book Six, p. 412.
2 Salvatore Maiorca, *Guida di Akrai* (Comune di Palazzolo Acreide: Tipografia Geny, 2005), p. 3.
3 Ibid., p. 29.

CHAPTER 18 MARSALA

1 Cicero, *Verrine Orations,* trans. L.H.G. Greenwood (Cambridge, MA: Loeb Classical Library, Harvard University Press, 1935), p. 479.
2 Al-Edrisi, *L'Italia descritta nel Libro del Re Ruggero*, edited by M. Amari and C. Schiapelli (Roma: Salviucci, 1883), p. 38. (Author's English translation).
3 Robert Camuto, *Palmento, A Sicilian Wine Odyssey* (Lincoln: University of Nebraska Press, 2010), p. 89.
4 Rossana De Simone, *Marsala* (Marsala: La Medusa Editrice, 2010), pp. 140–43.
5 Edward Lear, *A Book of Nonsense* (London: Routledge, Warne & Routledge, 1846), pp. 420–21.

PART III: ANCIENT SITES

CHAPTER 19 INTRODUCTION

1 For a comprehensive list of sites see Raleigh Trevelyan, *The Companion Guide to Sicily* (Woodbridge: Boydell & Brewer Ltd, 1996), pp. 384–87, and for a map of the most important, see Dirk Booms and Peter Higgs, *Sicily, Culture and Conquest* (London: The British Museum, 2016), p. 42.
2 Booms and Higgs, p. 84.
3 Thucydides, *History of the Peloponnesian War*, trans. Rex Warner (London: Penguin Books, 1954), Book Six, pp. 409–12.
4 Ibid., Introduction by M.I. Finley, pp. 18–19. Herodotus writes of Gelon capturing Megara Hyblaea at a date reckoned to be 483 BC, see Herodotus, *The Histories*, trans. Aubrey de Sélincourt (London: Penguin Books, 1954), pp. 469–70. According to Thucydides, the city flourished for 245 years prior to this event, putting its foundation at 728. The date of Syracuse's foundation in 733 is confirmed as nearly as possible by archaeology, see Paul Cartledge, *Ancient Greece* (Oxford: Oxford University Press, 2009), p. 115.

CHAPTER 20 PANTÀLICA

1   See Luigi Bernabò Brea, *Sicily before the Greeks* (London:Thames & Hudson, 1957)
    and Robert Leighton, *Sicily before History* (London: Duckworth, 1999). Robert
    Leighton is senior lecturer in archaeology at the University of Edinburgh.
2   Homer, *Odyssey*, trans. E.V. Rieu (London: Penguin Books, 1946), p. 359.
3   Brea, pp. 151–62.
4   Thucydides, *History of the Peloponnesian War*, trans. Rex Warner (London:
    Penguin Books, 1954), p. 410.
5   Ibid., p. 411.
6   Ibid., p. 412.
7   Leighton, p. 155.

CHAPTER 21 SEGESTA

1   Guy de Maupassant, *La Vie Errante* (Paris: Paul Ollendorff, 1890), p. 43.
    (Author's translation).
2   Thucydides, *History of the Peloponnesian War*, trans. Rex Warner (London:
    Penguin Books, 1954), pp. 412, 413. Thucydides's claim that the Elymians
    were survivors from Troy is now discounted. It is possible, however, that
    their arrival in Sicily came shortly after the fall of the city. They may have
    come from Asia Minor or from the Italian mainland.
3   Ibid., pp. 414–537, for the full story of the Athenian Expedition.
4   Dirk Booms and Peter Higgs, *Sicily, Culture and Conquest* (London: British
    Museum, 2016), p. 115.
5   Ibid., p. 119.

CHAPTER 22 SELINUNTE

1   *Independent*, 'Selinunte, site of an ancient massacre yields the secrets of a lost
    city' (www.independent.co.uk David Keys, November 2015).
2   Thucydides, *History of the Peloponnesian War* (London: Penguin Books, 1954)
    Book 6, p. 411 and Margaret Guido, *Sicily, An Archaeological Guide* (London:
    Faber & Faber, 1967), p. 87.
3   The ancients distinguished between 'marsh selinon', which we call celery,
    and 'mountain selinon', which we call parsley. These plants belong to the
    same family. Opinions vary as to which plant grew in ancient Selinus and
    gave its name to the city. Given the marshy conditions, it was probably celery.
    See   https://aggiehorticulture.tamu.edu/archives/parsons/publications/
    vegetabletravelers/celery.html
4   Dora P. Crouch, *Geology & Settlement: Greco-Roman Patterns* (Wooton-under
    Edge, Glos: Clarendon Press, 2003), p. 73.
5   Diodorus Siculus, *Library of History*, Book XIII (Cambridge, MA: Loeb
    Classical Library, Harvard University Press, 1950), pp. 273–89.
6   *Independent*, article quoted above.

CHAPTER 23 AGRIGENTO

1   Thucydides, *History of the Peloponnesian War*, trans. Rex Warner, (London: Penguin Classics, 1972), p. 411.
2   Diodorus Siculus, *Library of History*, trans. C. H. Oldfather, (Cambridge, MA: Loeb Classical Library, Harvard University Press, 1957), Book XIII, 81, p. 351.
3   For the reference to Phalaris, see *Odes of Pindar*, trans. C.M. Bowra (London: Penguin Classics, 1969), Pythian I, 95, p. 136. For Cicero see, *Verrine Orations*, trans. L.H.G. Greenwood (Cambridge, MA: Loeb Classical Library, Harvard University Press, 1935), vol II, iv, 74, p. 373.
4   Pindar, p. 80.
5   For Empledocles, see Bertrand Russell, *History of Western Philosophy* (London: George Allen & Unwin, 1946), pp. 72–76.
6   Diodorus Siculus, Book XIII, 82, p. 355.
7   Ibid., 81, p. 351.
8   Tommaso Fazello, *Della Storia di Sicilia* (Palermo: Tipografia Giuseppe Assenzio, 1817, trans. P.M. Remigio; original written in Latin, 1558), p. 360, (author's English translation and paraphrase).
9   For the comparison with the Parthenon, see Dirk Booms & Peter Higgs, *Sicily, culture & conquest* (London: British Museum, 2016), pp. 107–08. The Olympieion measured 110 x 53 metres compared to the Parthenon in Athens 69 x 30 metres. For the decorations, see Diodorus Siculus, Book XIII, 81, pp. 351–53. A *telamon* was the name given to a male statue used to support architecture on the back of its neck or with bent arms. The name comes from the father of Ajax, who was among the first of the Greek heroes to break through the walls of Troy.
10 *Il Giornale di Sicilia*, 23 December 2017.
11 See website, *The Ancient Coins of Sicily*, http://snible.org/coins/hn/sicily.html.

CHAPTER 24 MOZIA

1   Dirk Booms and Peter Higgs, *Sicily, culture and conquest* (London: British Museum, 2016), p. 80.
2   Thucydides, *History of the Peloponnesian War* (Penguin Classics, London, 1972), Book 6, p. 410.
3   Joseph Whitaker, *Motya, A Phoenician Colony in Sicily* (London: G. Bell & Sons Ltd, 1921), p. 54 and Gaia Servadio, *Motya, Unearthing a Lost Civilisation* (London: Victor Gollancz, 1988), p. 26.
4   Servadio, pp. 95–109.
5   Diodorus Siculus, *Library of History*, trans. C.H. Oldfather (Cambridge, MA: Loeb Classical Library, Harvard University Press, 1957), Book XIV, p. 147.

6   Ibid., for the full campaign see pp. 143–61.
7   Ibid., pp. 153–59.
8   Whitaker, p. vii.
9   Servadio, pp. 190–201.
10   Booms & Higgs, pp 80–81.
11   Andrew Graham-Dixon, *Daily Telegraph,* 9 August 2012, *Motya Charioteer Comes to London,* https://www.telegraph.co.uk/culture/art/9461513/The-Motya-Charioteer-comes-to-London-the-most-tantalising-marble-sculpture-in-the-world.html

CHAPTER 25 ROMAN VILLA DEL CASALE

1   Roger Wilson, *Piazza Armerina* (London: Granada Publishing Ltd, 1983).
2   Ibid., p. 37. The date is corroborated by R. Ross Holloway, *The Archaeology of Ancient Sicily* London: Routledge, 1991), p. 169.
3   The obelisk at one end of the Circus has been recognised by some archaeologists as the one brought over to Rome from Egypt by the Emperor Constantine in 357. This is later than the date usually attributed to the villa's construction. This claim remains unproven.
4   Wilson, pp. 98–99.

PART IV: ARTISTS

CHAPTER 26 INTRODUCTION

1   Gioacchino Di Marzo, *Delle Belle Arti in Sicilia* (Palermo: Salvatore Di Marzo Editore, 1858–64) 4 vols.
2   Anthony Blunt, *Sicilian Baroque* (London: Weidenfeld & Nicolson,1968); Stephen Tobriner, *The Genesis of Noto: An Eighteenth-century Sicilian city* (London: A. Zwemmer Ltd, 1982); Donald Garstang, *Giacomo Serpotta and the Stuccatori of Palermo 1560–1790* (London: A. Zwemmer Ltd, 1984).
3   Raleigh Trevelyan, *The Companion Guide to Sicily* (Woodbridge: Boydell & Brewer Ltd, 1996), pp. 392–400.

CHAPTER 27 ANTONELLO DA MESSINA

1   Salvatore Tramontana, *Antonello e la sua città* (Palermo: Sellerio editore, 1981), pp. 32–49.
2   Luke Syson, *Renaissance Faces, from Van Eyck to Titian, Witnessing Faces, Remembering Souls,* (London: National Gallery, 2009, published to coincide with an exhibition at the National Gallery from 15 October 2008 to 18 January 2009), p. 23.

3 Keith Christiansen, *Antonello da Messina, Sicily's Renaissance Master, The Exalted Art of Antonello da Messina* (London & New Haven: Yale University Press, 2005, published to coincide with an exhibition at the Metropolitan Museum of Art, New York, from 13 December 2005 to 5 March 2006), p. 15.

4 Gioacchino Barbera, *Antonello da Messina, Sicily's Renaissance Master, The Life and Work of Antonello da Messina* (London & New Haven: Yale University Press, 2005), p. 29.

5 Ibid., p. 29.

6 Giorgio Vigni, *All the paintings of Antonello da Messina*, trans. Anthony Firmin O'Sullivan (London: Oldbourne Press, 1963. Milan: Rizzoli editore, 1963), pp. 23–36.

7 Giorgio Vasari, *Lives of the Artists*, trans. E.L. Seeley (New York: The Noonday Press, 1957, original in Italian, Florence, 1550), pp. 88–90.

CHAPTER 28 ANTONELLO GAGINI

1 Leonardo Sciascia, *La Corda Pazza* (Milano: Adelphi Edizioni, 1991), p. 252 (author's English translation and paraphrase). Published by arrangement with The Italian Literary Agency.

2 Gioacchino Di Marzo, *I Gagini. La Scultura in Sicilia nei secoli XV e XVI* (Palermo: Tipografia del Giornale di Sicilia, 1883), 2 vols. Vol 1, p. 24.

3 For the tribune see Benedetto Patera, *Il Rinascimento in Sicilia. Da Antonello da Messina ad Antonello Gagini* (Palermo: Gruppo Editoriale Kalòs, 2008), pp. 119–120 and p. 124 for the reconstruction by Salvatore Rizzuti.

4 Di Marzo, Vol II, pp. 497–507.

5 Douglas Sladen, *Sicily, the new winter resort* (New York: EP Dutton and Company, 1907), p. 181.

CHAPTER 29 CARAVAGGIO

1 Walter Friedlaender, *Caravaggio Studies* (New York: Schocken Books, 1955), pp. 119, 130–3, 269–87.

2 A. Spadaro, in a document from the eighteenth century, quoted in Andrew Graham-Dixon, *Caravaggio* (London: Allen Lane 2010), pp. 393, 474.

3 Vincenzo Mirabella, *Dichiarazioni della pianta delle Antiche Siracuse* (Napoli: Lazzaro Scoriggio, 1613), Tavola 5, p. 89, author's paraphrase and translation.

4 Francesco Susinno, *Le vite dei pittori messinesi* (1724) quoted in Howard Hibbard, *Caravaggio* (London: Thames & Hudson, 1983), pp. 380–87.

5 Pietro Bellori, *Michelangelo da Caravaggio* (1672), quoted in Hibbard, p. 251.

6 Michele Cuppone, *La Natività di Palermo: un quadro del 1600 o 1609?* (www.news-art.it, 2015) and Giovanni Mendola, *Il Caravaggio di Palermo e l'Oratorio di San Lorenzo* (Palermo: Kalòs, 2012), p. 111.

7 *Guardian* (16 June 2010).

CHAPTER 30 PIETRO NOVELLI

1   Eliana Calandra, *Il seicento e il primo festino di Santa Rosalia* (Palermo: Città di
    Palermo Assessorato alla Cultura, 1996), p. 84.
2   Guido Di Stefano, *Pietro Novelli* (Palermo: Flaccovio Editore, 1989, originally
    published in 1939), p. 275.
3   Ibid., p. 30.
4   Ibid., pp. 175–275.
5   Maurizio Calvesi, *Pietro Novelli e il suo ambiente* (Palermo: Flaccovio Editore,
    1990, p. 134.

CHAPTER 31 GIACOMO SERPOTTA

1   Anthony Blunt, *Sicilian Baroque* (London: Weidenfeld & Nicolson, 1968), p.
    34.
2   The traditional account, quoted above, is based upon Giovanni Pietro Bellori's
    biography of Caravaggio, published in 1672. A new version of events has
    recently been put forward claiming that Caravaggio painted this *Nativity* in
    Rome in 1600. This theory is based upon documentary evidence and on an
    examination of the painting's style, which is much closer to the artist's work in
    Rome than in Sicily. See Giovanni Mendola, *Il Caravaggio di Palermo e l'Oratorio di
    San Lorenzo* (Palermo: Gruppo Editoriale Kalos, 2012) and Michele Cuppone,
    Caravaggio. La Natività di Palermo: un quadro del 1600 o 1609? (www.news-art.
    it).
3   Blunt, p. 34.
4   Donald Garstang, *Giacomo Serpotta and the Stuccatori of Palermo 1560–1790*
    (London: A. Zwemmer Ltd, 1984), p. 60.
    Garstang was an American scholar who in the 1970s became fascinated by
    the work of Serpotta. His book is the definitive work on the subject.
5   Idem., p. 79.
6   Maria Luisa Monteperto, *Oratorio di San Lorenzo* (Palermo: Amici dei Musei
    Siciliani, 2013), pp. 13–17. An excellent concise guide to the oratory.

CHAPTER 32 ROSARIO GAGLIARDI

1   Liliane Dufour quoted by Vincenzo Consolo, *The Rebirth of the Val di Noto*
    in *Reading & Writing the Mediterranean* (Toronto: Toronto University Press,
    2006), pp. 214–15.
2   Gagliardi's date of birth is uncertain. According to Stephen Tobriner, *The
    Genesis of Noto: An Eighteenth-century Sicilian City* (London: A. Zwemmer,
    1982), p. 43, a tax document showed the date as 1698, which has been
    quoted by several historians. Other documents, quoted by Marco Rosario
    Nobile and Maria Mercedes Bares in *Rosario Gagliardi (c.1690–1762)*
    (Palermo: Edizioni Caracol, 2013), a catalogue for an exhibition in Noto, 22
    March – 21 June 2013, p. 14, showed Gagliardi in 1708 carrying out work as

an executor for a noble family for which he must have been mature. Nobile's version has been followed in this book.

3   Anthony Blunt, *Sicilian Baroque* (London: Weidenfeld & Nicolson, 1968), p. 9.

4   Tobriner, p. 152.

5   Ibid., p. 219, note 19.

6   Donatella Germano, *Rosario Gagliardi, Architetto Siciliano del '700* (Rome: Ellemme Editrice, 1985), p. 9, note 6.

7   Tobriner, p. 231.

8   Tobriner, p. 170.

9   See UNESCO site: http://whc.unesco.org/en/list/1024
The eight cities are Caltagirone, Militello Val di Catania, Catania, Modica, Noto, Palazzolo Acreide, Ragusa and Scicli

CHAPTER 33   ERNESTO BASILE

1   For Palermo in the Belle Époque, see Orazio Cancila, *Palermo* (Bari: Editori Laterza, 1988), pp. 165–86.

2   Edmondo De Amicis, *Ricordi d'un viaggio in Sicilia* (Catania, Niccolò Giannotta, 1908), pp. 41–42 (author's English translation).

3   For the Massimo, see Luigi Maniscalco Basile, *Storia del Teatro Massimo di Palermo* (Firenze: Olschki Editore, 1984).

4   Ettore Sessa, *Ernesto Basile* (Palermo: Flaccovio Editore, 2010), pp. 97–106.

CHAPTER 34   RENATO GUTTUSO

1   Leonardo Sciascia, *La Sicilia come metafora* (Milano: Arnoldo Mondadori Editore, 1991), p. 7 (author's English translation). Copyright Leonardo Sciascia Estate. Published by arrangement with The Italian Literary Agency.

2   Paolo Parlavecchia, *Renato Guttuso, un ritratto del XX secolo* (Turin: UTET Libreria, 2007), p. 86.

3   Modern Italy has experienced two major periods of economic expansion and optimism in the future. The first came after unification in the late nineteenth century, the next after the Second World War in the twentieth. The first ended with Mussolini, the second with Berlusconi.

4   Parlavecchia, p. 190.

5   Fabio Carapezza Guttuso, *Guttuso, Capolavori dei Musei* (Milano: Electra Mondadori, 2005).

6   Renato Guttuso, *Mestiere di pittore, scritti sull'arte e la società* (Bari: De Donato, 1972). For a bibliography on the artist, see Fabio Guttuso, p. 219.

7   Estorick Collection exhibition, 14 January to 4 April 2015.

BIBLIOGRAPHY

PART I: HISTORY

Amari, Michele, *Storia dei Musulmani di Sicilia* (Catania: Romeo Prampolini Editore, 1933, originally published in 1854, three vols).

Braudel, Fernand, *La Méditerranée, l'espace et l'histoire* (Paris: Flammarion, 1985).

Camilleri, Andrea, *Come la penso* (Milano: Chiarelettere Editore, 2013).

Carpinteri, Teresa, *Siracusa – Città Fortificata* (Palermo: Flaccovio Editore, 1983).

Cavallari, Francesco Saverio, & Holm, Adolfo, *Topografia Archeologica di Siracusa* (Palermo: Tipografia del Giornale Lo Statuo, 1883).

Caven, Brian, *Dionysius I, War Lord of Sicily* (New Haven & London: Yale University Press, 1990).

Cicero, *Verrine Orations*, trans. L.H.G. Greenwood (Cambridge, MA: Loeb Classical Library, Harvard University Press, 1935).

Consolo, Vincenzo, *The Smile of the Unknown Mariner*, trans. Joseph Farrell (Manchester: Carcanet Press, 1994, first published as *Il sorriso dell'ignoto marinaio*, Turin: Einaudi Editore, 1976).

Diodorus Siculus, *Library of History*, trans. C. H. Oldfather, (Cambridge, MA: Loeb Classical Library, Harvard University Press, 1957), Books XIII and XIV.

Falcandus, Hugo, *The History of the Tyrants of Sicily* (Manchester and New York: Manchester University Press, 1998, trans. Graham A. Loud and Thomas Wiedemann).

Fazello, Tommaso, *Della Storia di Sicilia* (Palermo: Tipografia Giuseppe Assenzio, 1817, trans. P.M. Remigio; original written in Latin, 1558).

Finley, M.I., *Ancient Sicily* (London: Chatto & Windus, 1968).

Finley, M.I., Mack Smith D., C.J.H. Duggan, *A History of Sicily* (London: Chatto & Windus, 1986).

Freeman, Edward, *Historical Essays* (London: Macmillan & Co, 1879) third series.

Freeman, Edward, *History of Sicily* (Oxford: Clarendon Press, 1894, four vols, reprinted by Elibron Classics).

La Lumia, Isidoro, *Storia della Sicilia sotto Guglielmo il Buono* (Firenze: Le Monnier, 1867).

La Lumia, Isidoro, *Storie Siciliane* (Palermo: Virzi, 1883).

Lampedusa, Giuseppe Tomasi di, *The Leopard*, trans. Archibald Colquhoun (London: Collins and Harvill Press, 1961, first published as *Il Gattopardo*, Milan: Feltrinelli Editore, 1958).

Livy, *Hannibal's War*, trans. J.C. Yardley (Oxford: Oxford University Press, 2006).

Mack Smith, Denis, *A History of Sicily, Medieval Sicily, 800–1713* (London: Chatto & Windus, 1968).

Mack Smith, Denis, *A History of Sicily, Modern Sicily after 1715* (London: Chatto & Windus, 1968).

Mallette, Karla, *The Kingdom of Sicily, 1100–1250, A Literary History* (Philadelphia: University of Pennsylvania Press, 2005).

Norwich, John Julius, *Sicily, A Short History from the Ancient Greeks to Cosa Nostra* (London: John Murray, 2015).

Norwich, John Julius, *The Normans in the South, 1016–1130* (London: Faber & Faber, 1967).

Norwich, John Julius, *The Kingdom in the Sun, 1130–1194* (London: Faber & Faber, 1970).

Pindar, *The Odes of Pindar*, trans. C.M. Bowra (London: Penguin Classics, 1969).

Plutarch, *The Age of Alexander, Lives of Dion, Timoleon and Pyrrhus*, trans. Ian Scott-Kilvert, (London: Penguin Classics, 1973).

Plutarch, *The Rise and Fall of Athens, Lives of Nicias and Alcibiades*, trans. Ian Scott-Kilvert (London: Penguin Classics, 1973).

Plutarch, *Makers of Rome, Life of Marcellus*, trans. Ian Scott-Kilvert (London: Penguin Books, 1965).

Polybius, *The Rise of the Roman Empire*, trans. Ian Scott-Kilvert (London: Penguin Books, 1979).

Renda, Francesco, *La Grande Impresa* (Palermo: Sellerio Editore, 2010).

Renda, Francesco, *La storia della Sicilia dal 1860 al 1970* (Palermo: Sellerio Editore, 1999).

Renda, Francesco, *La storia della Sicilia dale origini ai giorni nostri* (Palermo: Sellerio Editore, 2003).

Renda, Francesco, *Sicilia e Mediterraneo, la nuova geopolitica* (Palermo: Sellerio Editore, 2000).

Runciman, Steven, *The Sicilian Vespers* (New York, NY: Cambridge
  University Press, 1958).
Sciascia, Leonardo, *Sicilian Uncles*, trans. N.S. Thompson (Manchester:
  Carcanet Press Limited, 1986). Originally published as *Gli Zii di
  Sicilia* (Torino: Giulio Einaudi Editori, 1958).
Sciascia, Leonardo, *Sicily as Metaphor, Conversations presented by Marcelle
  Padovani,* trans. James Marcus (Vermont: Marlboro Press, 1994).
Thucydides, *History of the Peloponnesian War* trans. Rex Warner (London:
  Penguin Classics, 1972).
Trevelyn, Raleigh, *Princes Under the Volcano* (New York: William Morrow
  & Company, Inc., 1973).
Whitaker, Joseph, *Motya, A Phoenician Colony in Sicily* (London: G. Bell &
  Sons Ltd, 1921).
Whitaker, Tina, *Sicily and England* (Memphis, USA: General Books,
  2018, originally published in 1907).
Wilson, R. J. A., *Sicily under the Roman Empire* Oxford: Aris & Phillips
  Ltd, 1990).

PART II: CITIES

Blunt, Anthony, *Sicilian Baroque* (London: Weidenfeld & Nicolson,
  1968).
Brydone, Patrick, *A Tour through Sicily and Malta* (London: H.D.
  Symonds, 1773; reprinted Memphis, General Books, 2012).
Camilleri, Andrea, *The Shape of Water,* trans. Stephen Sartarelli (London:
  Pan Macmillan, 2004, first published as *La forma dell'acqua*: Palermo,
  Sellerio editore, 1994).
Camuto, Robert V, *Palmento, A Sicilian Wine Odyssey* (Lincoln: University
  of Nebraska Press, 2010).
Clausi, Maurizio, *I luoghi di Montalbano. Una guida.* (Palermo: Sellerio,
  2006).
Consolo, Vincenzo, *La mia isola è Las Vegas* (Milano: Arnoldo Mondadori
  Editore, 2012).
Consolo, Vincenzo, *Le pietre di Pantàlica* (Milano: Arnoldo Mondadori
  Editore, 1988).
Consolo, Vincenzo, *L'olivo e l'olivastro* (Milano: Arnoldo Mondadori
  Editore, 1994).
Consolo, Vincenzo, *Reading and Writing the Mediterranean* (Toronto:
  University of Toronto Press, 2006).

Consolo, Vinzenzo, *Lo spasimo di Palermo* (Milano: Arnoldo Mondadori Editore, 1998).

Cronin, Vincent, *The Golden Honeycomb* (London: Rupert Hart-Davis, 1954).

D'Este, Carlo, *Bitter Victory* (London: Collins, 1988).

De Amicis, Edmondo, *Ricordi d'un viaggio in Sicilia* (Catania, Niccolò Giannotta, 1908).

De Simone, Rossana, *Marsala* (Marsala: La Medusa Editrice, 2010).

Dufour, Liliane, *Storia d'Italia* (Turin: Einaudi Editore, 1985),

Dummett, Jeremy, *Palermo, City of Kings: The Heart of Sicily* (London: I. B. Tauris, 2015).

Dummett, Jeremy, *Syracuse, City of Legends: A Glory of Sicily* (London: I. B. Tauris, 2010).

Durrell, Lawrence, *Sicilian Carousel* (London: Faber and Faber, 1977).

Edrisi, -al, *L'Italia descritta nel Libro del Re Ruggero*, edited by M. Amari and C. Schiapelli (Roma: Salviucci, 1883).

Farrell, Joseph, *Sicily, A Cultural History* (Oxford: Signal Books, 2012).

Gatti, Martina, *Provincia di Ragusa, l'isola felice* (Ragusa: Mora Arti Grafiche, 2005).

Giuffrida, Tino, *Catania, dale origini alla dominazione Normanna* (Catania: Libreria C. Bonaccorso Editrice, 1979).

Goethe, Johann Wolfgang, *Italian Journey*, trans. W. H. Auden and Elizabeth Mayer (London: Collins, 1962; first published as *Italienische Reise*, 1816–17).

Houel, Jean Pierre Laurent, *Voyage pittoresque des isles de Sicile, de Malte et de Lipari* (Paris: Imprimerie de Monsieur, 1787).

Hutton, Edward, *Cities of Sicily* (London: Methuen, 1926).

Iacono, Giuseppe, *Noto, città d'arte* (Messina: Edizioni Affinità Elettive, 2004).

Jubayr, Ibn, *The Travels of ibn Jubayr*, trans. R.J.C. Broadhurst, (London: Jonathan Cape, 1952).

Keahey, John, *Seeking Sicily* (New York: Thomas Dunne, 2011).

Keahey, John, *Sicilian Splendours* (New York: Thomas Dunne, 2018).

Lawrence, D. H, *Sea and Sardinia* (London: Penguin Classics, 2007, first published 1921).

Levi, Carlo, *Words Are Stones: Impressions of Sicily*, trans. Antony Shugaar (London: Hesperus Press, 2005, first published in 1955 in Italian, *Le parole sono pietre*).

Lewis, Norman, *In Sicily* (London: Jonathan Cape, 2000).

Lowe, Alfonso, *The Barrier and the Bridge* (New York: WW Norton & Co Inc, 1972).

Maiorca, Salvatore, *Guida di Akrai* (Comune di Palazzolo Acreide: Tipografia Geny, 2005).

Maupassant, Guy de, *Sicily* (Palermo: Sellerio Editore, 1990) originally published in *La Vie Errante*, Paris: Paul Ollendorff, 1890).

Mirabella, Vincenzo, *Dichiarazioni della pianta delle Antiche Siracuse* (Napoli: Lazzaro Scoriggio, 1613).

Quennell, Peter, *Spring in Sicily* (London: George Weidenfeld and Nicolson, 1952).

Sciascia, Leonardo, *Fatti diversi di storia letteraria e civile, la contea di Modica* (Palermo: Sellerio,1989),

Sciascia, Leonardo, *Il consiglio d'Egitto* (Torino: Giulio Einaudi Editore, 1963).

Sciascia, Leonardo, *La corda pazza* (Milano: Adelphi Edizioni, 1991).

Sciascia, Leonardo, *La palma va a nord* (Milano: Edizioni Quaderni Radicali, 1982).

Sciascia, Leonardo, *Occhio di capra* (Milano: Adelphi Edizioni, 1990).

Sladen, Douglas, *In Sicily* (London: Sands & Co, 1901).

Sladen, Douglas, *Sicily, the New Winter Resort* (New York: E.P. Dutton, 1907).

Swinburne, Henry, *Travels in the Two Sicilies* (Dublin: Luke White, 1786).

Tobriner, Stephen, *The Genesis of Noto: An Eighteenth-century Sicilian City* (London: A. Zwemmer, 1982).

Trevelyan, Raleigh, *The Companion Guide to Sicily* (Woodbridge: Boydell & Brewer Ltd, 1996).

Virgil, *The Aeneid* (London: Collector's Library, 2004).

PART III: ANCIENT SITES

Aubet, Maria Eugenia, *The Phoenicians and the West* (Cambridge: Cambridge University Press, 1993).

Bernabò Brea, Luigi, *Sicily before the Greeks* (London: Thames and Hudson, 1957).

Booms, Dirk and Higgs, Peter, *Sicily, Culture and Conquest* (London: The British Museum, 2016).

Cartledge, Paul, *Ancient Greece* (Oxford: Oxford University Press, 2009).

Ciurca, Salvatore, *I mosaici della villa 'Erculia' di Piazza Armerina* (Bologna: Officina Grafica Bolognese, 2000).

Crouch, Dora, *Geology & Settlement: Greco-Roman Patterns* (Oxford: Oxford University Press, 2004).

Fiordalisco, Francesco, *Selinunte, Città di Pace* (Marsala: Casa Editrice La Siciliana, 1996).

Guido, Margaret, *Sicily: An Archaeological Guide* (London: Faber & Faber, 1967).

Holloway, R. Ross, *The Archaeology of Ancient Sicily* (London: Routledge, 1991).

Homer, *The Odyssey*, trans. E.V. Rieu (London: Penguin Books, 1946).

Jenkins, Kenneth, *Coins of Greek Sicily* (London: British Museum Publications Ltd, 1966).

Leighton, Robert, *Sicily before History* (London: Duckworth, 1999).

Maiorca, Salvatore, *Guida di Akrai* (Comune di Palazzolo Acreide: Tipografia Geny, 2005).

Richardson, Alexandra, *Passionate Patron: The Life of Alexander Hardcastle and the Greek Temples of Agrigento* (Oxford: Archaeopress, 2009).

Servadio, Gaia, *Motya, Unearthing a Lost Civilisation* (London: Phoenix, 2000).

Tusa, Vincenzo, *La scultura di pietra di Selinunte* (Palermo: Sellerio Editore, 1983).

Volpi, Aldo, *Motya: In the World of the Phoenicians* (Marsala: La Medusa Editrice, 2007).

Von Gunten, Ruth, *Segesta* (Marsala: La Medusa Editrice, 2005).

Whitaker, Joseph, *Motya, A Phoenician Colony in Sicily* (London: G. Bell & Sons, 1921).

Wilson, R. J. A., *Piazza Armerina* (London: Granada, 1983).

Woodhead, A.G., *The Greeks in the West* (London: Thames & Hudson, 1962).

PART IV: ARTISTS

Barbera, Gioacchino, *Antonello da Messina, Sicily's Renaissance Master* (London & New Haven: Yale University Press, 2005).

Basile, Luigi Maniscalco, *Storia del Teatro Massimo di Palermo* (Firenze: Leo Olschki Editore, 1984).

Bologna, Ferdinando, *Caravaggio, the Final Years* (Naples: Elector Napoli, 2005).

Braun, Emily, ed., *Italian Art in the Twentieth Century, Painting and Sculpture, 1900–88* (Munich: Prestel-Verlag, 1989).

Bussagli, Marco, *Antonello da Messina* (Firenze: Giunti Editore, 2006).

Calandra, Eliana, *Il seicento e il primo festino di Santa Rosalia* (Palermo: Città di Palermo Assessorato alla Cultura, 1996).

Calvesi, Maurizio, *Pietro Novelli e il suo ambiente* (Palermo: Flaccovio Editore, 1990).

Camilleri, Andrea, Renato Guttuso, *La Vucciria* (Milano: Skira Editore, 2008).

Christiansen, Keith, *Antonello da Messina, Sicily's Renaissance Master* (London & New Haven: Yale University Press, 2006).

Costantini, Costanzo, *Ritratto di Renato Guttuso* (Brescia: Comunia Editrice, 1985).

Costanzo, Cristina, *Pietro Novelli, maestro del seicento in Sicilia* (Palermo: Casa Editrice Contesti, 1982).

Demus, Otto, *The Mosaics of Norman Sicily* (London: Routledge & Kegan Paul: 1949).

Di Marzo, Gioacchino, *Antonello Gaggini e la sua scuola* (Palermo: Ristampe Anastatiche Siciliane, 2001).

Di Marzo, Gioacchino, *Delle belle arti in Sicilia*, 4 vols. (Palermo: Salvatore Di Marzo Editore, 1858–64).

Di Marzo, Gioacchino, *La scultura in Sicilia nei secoli XV e XVI* (Palermo: Tipografia del Giornale di Sicilia, 1883).

Di Natale, Maria Concetta, *Il museo diocesano* (Palermo: Flaccovio Editore, 2010).

Di Stefano, Guido, *Pietro Novelli* (Palermo: Flaccovio Editore, 1989).

Ferguson, George, *Signs & Symbols in Christian Art* (New York: Oxford University Press, 1954).

Friedlaender, Walter, *Caravaggio Studies* (New York: Schocken Books, 1955).

Garstang, Donald, *Giacomo Serpotta and the Stuccatori of Palermo 1560–1790* (London: A. Zwemmer, 1984).

Germano, Donatella, *Rosario Gagliardi, architetto Siciliano del '700* (Rome: Ellemme Editrice, 1985).

Graham-Dixon, Andrew, *Caravaggio* (London: Allen Lane 2010).

Guttuso, Fabio Carapezza, *Capolavori dei musei* (Milano: Electra Mondadori, 2005).

Guttuso, Renato, *Mestiere di pittore, scritti sull'arte e la società* (Bari: De Donato, 1972).

Hibbard, Howard, *Caravaggio* (London: Thames & Hudson, 1983).

Meeks, Carroll, L.V, *Italian Architecture, 1750–1914* (New Haven & London: Yale University Press, 1966).

Meli, Filippo, *L'Arte in Sicilia* (Palermo: Editrice Reprint, 1994).

Mendola, Giovanni, *Il Caravaggio di Palermo e l'Oratorio di San Lorenzo* (Palermo: Gruppo Editoriale Kalòs, 2012).

Montaperto, Maria Luisa, *Oratorio di San Lorenzo* (Palermo: Amici dei Musei Siciliani, 2013).

Nobile, Marco Rosario, *Antonello Gagini, architetto* (Palermo: Flaccovio Editore, 2010).

Nobile, Marco Rosario and Bares, Maria Mercedes, *Rosario Gagliardi (c.1690–1762)* (Palermo: Edizioni Caracol, 2013).

Nobile, Marco Rosario, and Piazza, Stefano, *L'Architettura del settecento in Sicilia* (Palermo: Gruppo Editoriale Kalòs, 2009).

Parlavecchia, Paolo, *Renato Guttuso* (Pescara: UTET Libreria, 2007).

Patera, Benedetto, *Il rinascimento in Sicilia, da Antonello da Messina ad Antonello Gagini* (Palermo: Gruppo Editoriale Kalòs, 2008).

Pirajno, Rosanna, *Giuseppe Damiani Almeyda* (Palermo: Edizioni Salvare Palermo, 2008).

Salomon, Xavier, F., *Van Dyck in Sicily* (Milan: Silvana Editoriale, 2012).

Sessa, Ettore, *Ernesto Basile* (Palermo: Flaccovio Editore, 2010).

Seymour Jr, Charles, *Sculpture in Italy, 1400–1500* (Harmondsworth: Penguin Books, 1966).

Sitwell, Sacheverell, *Southern Baroque Revisited* (London: Weidenfeld & Nicolson, 1967).

Syson, Luke, *Renaissance Faces, from Van Eyck to Titian, Witnessing Faces, Remembering Souls*, (London: National Gallery, 2009).

Tobriner, Stephen, *The Genesis of Noto: An Eighteenth-century Sicilian City* (London: A. Zwemmer, 1982).

Tramontana, Salvatore, *Antonello e la sua città* (Palermo: Sellerio Editore, 1981).

Vasari, Giorgio, *Lives of the Artists* (New York: The Noonday Press, 1957).

Vigni, Giorgio, *All the Paintings of Antonello da Messina*, trans. Anthony O'Sullivan (Milan: Rizzoli Editore, 1963).

ACKNOWLEDGEMENTS

My thanks go firstly to Joanna Godfrey, my editor at I.B. Tauris, for encouraging me to write this book, and secondly to Claire Browne, my editor at Bloomsbury, for her work in seeing it through to publication. Their support was essential to this project.

For the research, the British Library supplied its usual first-class service.

Input on different subjects was provided by the following people, to whom I am most grateful: Dolores Le Fanu, Maria Carla Martino, Sergio Morabito, Thomas Lemann, Luisa Montaperto and Michele Cuppone.

For my website (www.jeremydummett.com), which features my three books on Sicily, I have to thank Georgina Kirk and Iain Moran.

MAPS

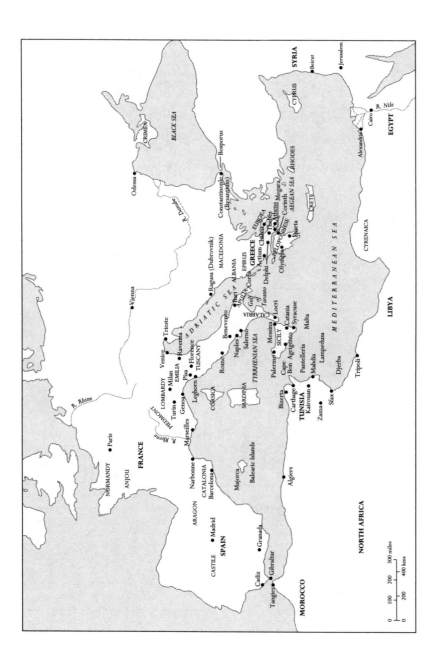

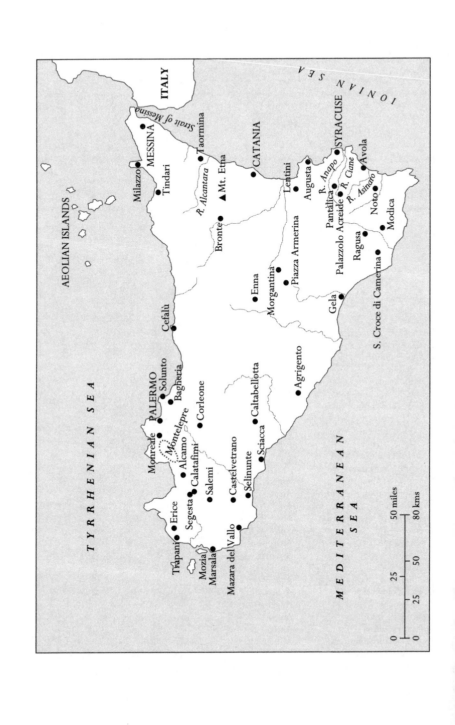

INDEX